# Uncommon
# Sense
# About
# Organizations

# Uncommon
# Sense
# About
# Organizations
### Cases, Studies,
### and Field
### Observations

## Geert Hofstede

**SAGE** Publications
*International Educational and Professional Publisher*
Thousand Oaks   London   New Delhi

*For information address*:

SAGE Publications, Inc.
2455 Teller Road
Thousand Oaks, California 91320

SAGE Publications Ltd.
6 Bonhill Street
London EC2A 4PU
United Kingdom

SAGE Publications India Pvt. Ltd.
M-32 Market
Greater Kailash I
New Delhi 110 048 India

Printed in the United States of America

**Library of Congress Cataloging-in-Publication Data**

Hofstede, Geert
    Uncommon sense about organizations: cases, studies, and field
observations / author, Geert Hofstede.
        p.  cm.
    Includes bibliographical references and index.
    ISBN 0-8039-5366-6 (cl). — ISBN 0-8039-5367-4 (pb)
    1. Organizational behavior—Case studies. 2. Work—Case studies.
3. Personnel management—Case studies. I. Title.
    HD58.7.H64  1994
    302.3′5—dc20                                                                 93-46435
                                                                                    CIP

94  95  96  97  98  10  9  8  7  6  5  4  3  2  1

Sage Production Editor: Yvonne Könneker

# Contents

# Preface

To quite a few practitioners, behavioral science research rarely reveals more than the obvious. Behavioral scientists, in this view, only express in sophisticated words what experienced practitioners already knew. This, if it were true, would not necessarily condemn behavioral science. Even common sense deserves to be written down for the benefit of the less experienced or less well informed.[1]

The present volume groups a number of studies in and about organizations that, I believe, produced nonobvious insights. To me the possibility of finding such unexpected results is the fun of behavioral science research. In this book I try to share some of my excitement with readers.

The target group for the book includes my fellow researchers, interested practitioners, and students. For the latter group (and for the convenience of their teachers) I have formulated some questions to test understanding and for discussion after each chapter. All chapters appeared earlier, as journal articles, chapters in readers, or teaching cases, in the period between 1972 and 1980. Two were coauthored; for the remainder I am the sole author. There are several justifications for reissuing these previously published studies. Behavioral science research tends to have a short memory, which leads to frequent reinventions of the wheel. All the issues covered are still relevant today. Nevertheless the studies do show a historical trend at three levels. The broadest level is the development of Western societies in the past decades. For example, issues of power sharing and codetermination were very topical around 1968 but have since lost some of their luster. At a more specific level this is reflected in shifting interest areas for behavioral science research in organizations. Participative management and job design were favorite subjects in the 1970s, but less so in the 1980s; they may return to focus in the 1990s. Finally, at the most specific level, I experienced the trend in my own research interests. As researchers we are children of our times to a larger extent than we realize at any moment. An additional reason for the republication is that these studies, some of which may be difficult to locate elsewhere, when grouped produce a synergy effect not evident before.

All studies reproduced here are about people in organizations. In some, I focus on individuals or small groups. These can be considered as belonging to organizational psychology. In others, I compare larger social entities. These can be classified as contributions to organizational sociology. A number are in-depth case studies of single, complex organizational events. They belong to what has more recently been labeled organizational anthropology. The three disciplinary domains are inseparable. When the object of our research is organizations, disciplinary boundaries between different behavioral sciences are obstacles best avoided.

The three parts of the book correspond with three interest areas. Since the appearance of *Culture's Consequences* in 1980, my work has mostly focused on "culture" in the anthropological sense, around and within organizations. But this interest obviously had its history. In the 1970s I studied the phenomena of stress and of differences in values among organizational members (mainly psychological issues). The comparative study of values led me into studying cultures. Ever since the late 1960s, I have been interested in the domains of control and of power in and around organizations (mainly sociological and anthropological issues). These proved to contain profound cultural connotations. Finally, also since the late 1960s, I have used classroom situations in which I play a trainer role for experimenting with relatively simple research tools. Some of these produced outcomes that were quite revealing, as much to the multicultural participant population as to me.

The original articles and case studies on which the 17 chapters in the book are based have been edited to avoid duplications and inconsistencies in terminology. I thank my coauthors Louis A. de Bettignies and László I. Rajkay for their approval to reprint our joint papers, and the various journal and reader publishers and case copyright owners for their permissions. Special thanks are due to Ingrid Regout for her help in transferring publications from before the computer age onto diskettes, and to friends who read and criticized the manuscript or parts of it: Bart Hofstede, Gert-Jan Hofstede, Rokus Hofstede, Rachel Kats, Sjo Soeters, Ad van Iterson, Bob Wilkinson, and Cass Williamson.

GEERT HOFSTEDE

# Note

1. In U.S. history, a political pamphlet dated 1776 by Thomas Paine called *Common Sense* enumerated the arguments for independence from the British crown and played a major role in mobilizing colonists for the Revolution.

# PART I

# The Impact of Jobs on People

The six chapters of Part I all deal with what Kuylaars (1951) called the *internal* productivity of labor, that is, the extent to which people are affected by the work they do. Of course talents and education play a role in the distribution of jobs among people, and their effect is often difficult to separate from the impact of the structure and organization of the job proper. This will become evident in these chapters.

Here are three cases and three statistical studies. All three cases are from the Netherlands, and all three statistical studies are based on the massive international survey data the author had access to when working as a personnel researcher for the multinational IBM.

The first case (Chapter 1), translated into English for this book, is a very special one: It is composed from the author's own diary notes during a participant observation as a semi-skilled fitter in a small engineering factory in Amsterdam as far back as 1955. The role of this first chapter in this book is to show that the situation of people at work is a function of both the people and the work. The actors in the case are real personalities with whole lives, in which work assumes only one place next to other interests.

Chapter 2 is a survey study about factors that motivate employees. It illustrates the wide differences in work goal priorities between less educated employees, more educated employees, and managers, and it warns against oversimplified assumptions about employee motivation.

Chapter 3 deals with attempts to render the work of the less skilled employees in factory and office jobs more intrinsically rewarding. Since the 1970s such attempts have been known as "humanization of work." This chapter expands on the findings of differences in work goals shown in Chapter 2 by introducing another measure of the importance of different work aspects: the extent to which these aspects contribute to the overall satisfaction of workers of a certain category. The differences among more and less educated people all but disappear in this case, and earnings and challenging tasks are shown to be major contributors to overall satisfaction for everybody. This justifies attempts at humanization of work, but it poses a strategic problem: how to humanize the work of less skilled workers whose conscious priorities lie elsewhere.

Chapter 4 introduces yet another important aspect of the impact of work on people: job stress and mental health. On the basis of a literature survey the chapter shows that job stress is only harmful for a person's health if it cannot be released into activity; the extent of this release is measured by the person's job satisfaction. A diagram maps the stress/satisfaction balance of 38 job categories within the same corporation (IBM in France, Germany, and Great Britain). The risky jobs from a mental health point of view are those with high stress and low satisfaction, and these are again the less skilled factory and office tasks. This is one more powerful argument for promoting the humanization of work described in the previous chapter.

Chapters 5 and 6 are case studies, both covering humanization of work developments over a span of several years. Both show the strength of the resistances to be overcome, from the organization as well as from the people. Both picture humanization "heroes," and in both cases these are middle-level managers with an engineering background who enthusiastically grasped the idea of social innovation along with technological innovation. As humanization of work means an intervention in the sociotechnical system of the organization, it calls for a combination of technical and social science insights.

# 1

# All in the Factory

## A Participant Observation

This chapter reports on my participant observation when I was employed as a semiskilled fitter in an Amsterdam engineering plant, back in 1955. It provides a view of the organization and its people from below: the men in the crew, the job, the payment system, informal group norms, and what we talked about—marriage and family, hobbies, politics, religion. It contains very little about higher management levels, because these were both irrelevant and invisible. It is mainly about the people who actually do the work, and who in spite of their working-class status come through as remarkably bourgeois.

## Experiencing Life
## on the Shop Floor in 1955

In the Netherlands in the 1970s, the study of social systems through participant observation received renewed attention in the context of an "anthropology of industrial society" (Bovenkerk & Brunt, 1976). This, the oldest of all social research methods, provides insights into reality as a "whole" lacking in more analytical techniques. Participant observation was popular in the Netherlands at the time of the Amsterdam socio-

This chapter was originally published in Dutch under the title "Amsterdamse arbeiders in 1955: Een participerende waarnemig" in *Amsterdams Sociologisch Tijdschrift*, 5(3), December 1978, pp. 516-539. Reprinted with permission.

graphic school, around 1930.[1] The present report, though inspired by a study from this older school, dates from 1955, when the public interest in participant observation had temporarily waned; my experience at that time was unusual.

For 4 months, from March to July 1955, I worked as a semiskilled fitter for the Mercedes Fast Printing Press Manufacturing Company in the industrial northern borough of Amsterdam; then for another month, I was an unskilled laborer at the British-American Tobacco Company's cigarette factory on the "Prinsen" island in central Amsterdam. My participant observation did not serve any scientific purpose. I had earlier attended a technical college (H.T.S.) and graduated with an Ir. (M.Sc.) degree from Delft Technical University. Within the curricula of these schools I completed 14 months of internships in various industries, but as a student trainee I never really shared the life of the ordinary worker. As I wrote in the diary I kept in 1955, "I want to experience company life from below, without the status advantage of the student trainee, and try to understand what is important and unimportant from a worker's point of view." I had been introduced to a distinguished sociology professor at Leiden University, Fré Van Heek, himself a product of the Amsterdam sociographic school, who encouraged my plans and gave me some important advice and literature for inspiration.[2]

The following chapter is almost identical to an abstract made for Professor Van Heek from my 1955 diary. I did not expect at that time that anyone would want to publish it. Like Molière's Monsieur Jourdain, who did not know that he spoke prose, I was not aware that I was contributing to the anthropology of industrial society. It was not until 12 years later that I completed my Ph.D. in social science, and 23 years later that these diary notes were finally published as a result of the new wave of interest in participant observation research.

## Getting a Job

I had explained my intentions to the Amsterdam employment service, and they found me a suitable company, fairly small (about 150 employees), with a mediocre reputation as an employer and a lot of labor turnover, so that my entry as an atypical worker would not cause the least surprise. There was full employment in the Netherlands in those years, and even more than that, a very tight labor market in which almost anybody could get several job offers. The owner/manager and the plant superintendent had been informed by the employment service about my unusual qualifications, but the information stayed at that level, and I did not maintain any special communication with them. During the entire period I worked there, I spoke to the superintendent only twice, by telephone, about administrative details related to my employment; I never met him—quite surprisingly, in a plant of that small size. One Monday morning at 7:30 I reported at the factory gate, blue coverall and lunch box under my arm. The benevolent-looking door-keeper handed me over to a foreman who in turn transferred me to Jaap, my charge hand.[3] I was introduced as a former clerk from Hengelo in the east of the country who had learned some metalworking skills during military service and moved to Amsterdam because of his girlfriend. Jaap gave me a ticket for the necessary personal tools, and at 9:00 I was at work. Nobody had told me what the factory's products were; I still don't know how those printing presses worked.

## The Factory

Before World War II, Mercedes was a small shop; by 1955, with 150 employees, it counted as medium sized. Fast growth and technological change had created numerous social problems, which management did not cope with very successfully. Except for a very small core of old-timers, employees did not stay long. People did not identify with this employer and left easily for more attractive jobs elsewhere. Conflicts between management and workers, but also between higher and first-line management, were frequent. Just before I came there had been a strike organized by the Communist labor union EVC.

In spite of this inharmonious climate, the working pace was high. Workers were paid a performance bonus, based on rather shaky standards. People worked harder here than I had experienced during my internships. Little time was lost at the beginning or end of the day; we worked from buzzer to buzzer. Colleagues with whom I talked about this said that Amsterdam people always worked harder, but an Amster-dammer who had come from one of the larger local firms also complained that he had never had to work so hard. The fast pace could partly be explained by close supervision—talking, sitting on your bench, or eating during working time led to immediate reprimands—but another contributing factor could have been that the frequent personnel turnover prevented the growth of a strong informal organization, so that there was no social norm of "goldbricking" (Whyte, 1955) or taking it easy and avoiding excessive zeal.

Higher management could be characterized as commercially rather than industrially oriented. Wages were comparatively high, but in my scarce contacts with the higher-ups I noticed surprise, even indignation, that people's loyalty to the company could not be bought with money. This lack of understanding among higher management of what makes people tick undoubtedly reinforced the common negative attitude about the company among workers. Their link with their work was strongly financial: everybody tried to get as much as possible for himself, and the company interest was considered the bosses' worry. Consequently the ties among workers were equally weak; although during my stay there was some improvement on this score: a personnel club was founded through an initiative of some of the workers.

From now on I will continue in the present tense, following closely my diary notes.

## The People

My crew consists first of all of Jaap, the charge hand, a somewhat stocky man between 30 and 40, but looking older. The only old-timer among us, he joined the company before the war. He is a fairly strict disciplinarian, although he excuses himself regularly by saying that he has to behave in this way because otherwise he'll be in trouble with the foreman. They say he was "wrong" (sympathized with the Nazis) during wartime. Still, he is not so bad. Colleagues claim that he could have been promoted ("wear a dust coat"), but that he prefers to wear a coverall and to work along with us, from a kind of comradeship ideal that could fit with his political past. His wife has left him, and he now lives with another woman.

Facing me at the bench are Willem and Frits. Willem is a "farmer"—he comes from Hoogeveen in the northern province of Drente where he worked as a farmhand; he entered the metalworking profession via a garage and moved to Amsterdam. He lives in Tuindorp Oostzaan, one of the better working-class suburbs, and has a wife and two boys. He is 39, a skinny fellow, sometimes cantankerous—he has stomach complaints—but also a source of juicy stories, at least to those who understand his dialect. One of my better friends. Frits is 20, an inconspicuous fellow, refused for military service because of weak eyes. His glasses make him look like a clerk.

A special personality is Uncle Ko, an authentic "Jordaner" (inhabitant of the Jordaan, Amsterdam's oldest and most typical working-class quarter), but now living in the northern suburb. Now aged 65, he is a retired worker from the municipality and he works for some extra money for the education of his granddaughter, who lives with him and his wife. A short, sturdily built, jovial man, he can swear like a trooper.

Bep and Karel usually work together. Bep is in his early 30s and he has been married for 10 years. He has three nice children, 7, 8, and 9 years old, who often come to meet him at the factory gate; he lives very close by. A decent, somewhat nervous face. He grew up in an old-fashioned SDAP (Social Democrat) family, has been a member of the Socialist Youth Movement (AJC), and reads the socialist newspaper *Het Vrije Volk*, even if he is no longer active in the party; he has a rather sober view of politics. Bep is my closest friend here. I am undoubtedly one of the more respectable-looking guys, and so is Bep—we attract one another. Via Bep I get closer to Karel, a person who at first looked rather unfriendly. Karel is almost 50, and he has just had all his teeth pulled. His new false teeth either haven't arrived yet or they bother him too much to wear; his toothless mouth makes his face look old and shabby. During the prewar economic crisis years he worked in the German war industry, not uncommon in those years. Karel's wife is often ill, another worry. Karel is the crew's informal authority on issues related to the productivity bonus, for example what percent bonus one can afford to make before the industrial engineers would become suspicious and cut the rate.

Koos arrived shortly before me. He came from a large local company where he did not stay very long, and he seems to have had numerous employers before; this has a lot to do with his obstinate character. He was fired by his previous employer because, having reported ill, he was found at home by the visiting doctor doing household work for his wife. Koos is 36 but looks 10 years younger. After 6 years of marriage he now hopes to become a father soon; he considers himself terribly important for this reason. Both his wife and he take evening courses in general education; his wife has worked in an office. In the crew, Koos is not much appreciated. Especially Willem, a rather obstinate person himself, dislikes Koos and misses no opportunity to show his antipathy.

Ap and Kees are the ones I know least well. They are close friends, in their mid-20s; both were in the military in Indonesia (where the Dutch sent conscripts in the 1946-1949 period) and both are married. Kees has recently been on disability benefits for half a year due to pleurisy; he still works only half days. He has a baby daughter and lives in Slotermeer, a new suburb in western Amsterdam. Ap is a younger brother of Jaap, our charge hand, but he doesn't resemble Jaap at all. Ap and Kees sing a lot, the latest U.S. hits in quite acceptable English, although they do not seem to understand the words.

As far as I know, with the exception of Willem, all members of the crew completed a vocational school education.

## Attitudes About Work

"It's a humdrum kind of fitting job over here," is the way Jaap introduces me to the type of work. The fitting shop's task is to hand finish batches of parts that have been machined elsewhere in the plant: trimming 100 edges here, tapping 60 holes there. It doesn't demand high skills, and the crew members are no great craftsmen. Every now and then, more interesting jobs come through, and "when we have seen that you're a bit of a fitter," I could expect to get some of it.

Willem is one of those who gets the better jobs. He has been on the same task for months, filing a complex part that cannot be machined here, respecting quite narrow tolerances. He loves his work and confesses it spontaneously: "the finest fitting job in the whole plant." The subjectivity of such an opinion becomes clear when a newcomer is assigned to the same job and quits after a day, claiming to have got "the lousiest job in the whole plant." This man is a chronic complainer, a character who will never find satisfaction anywhere. "Why didn't you stay in office work? You won't get tired there!" he advises me. As far as Willem is concerned, I have noticed before that skilled workers who were promoted from unskilled jobs show more satisfaction than those with a vocational school education. Or is it because he is an agrarian, with a different mind from the Amsterdam grumblers? In any case, he is the only one who talks positively about his work, without even being asked.

Jaap, the charge hand, also likes his work. He helped develop the machines that are now batch produced, and the only personal remark I ever hear him make is when we pass a fully assembled machine, and he tells me proudly that he would be able to take it apart and put it together again even in his sleep. And of course, he has now got his responsibility as a charge hand.

Bep is satisfied with his work as well, but for a different reason. He did complete the vocational school, but before he came here he worked for 8 years as a doorman in a movie theater downtown, which meant he had to commute twice a day by ferry across the harbor, and he never got home before midnight. Now he works close to home, and he has a much more regular life. He makes more or less the same amount of money as before, even though—like me—he only gets the rate for semiskilled work; he does voluntary overtime 3 evenings a week, the legal maximum, to feed his family. So Bep basically doesn't appreciate the work for itself as much as for the source of income. But he never grumbles; he manages the lousy jobs as they come along, and he is happy if he gets one of the better ones.

The rest of the crew don't talk positively about the work, although I wonder whether their real feelings are as negative as their words; it is a common ritual to scold the work. Karel, after having asked about my job history, and after I have told him my fictitious story, comments: "Okay, I understand, if you didn't have to, you wouldn't be here, a guy has got to live, all of us are here by necessity." If one has money, one doesn't work, and the fact that reality contradicts this opinion is not recognized; what, for example, the plant owner and the other higher managers do is not working: "Those guys have no cares in the world" (it must be said the managers do look well fed), "but by the time our kind of people is 40, you can tell by looking at us that we had to work."

For a rather annoying job that keeps coming back, I invent a gadget that helps to finish the job faster, easier, and better. I show it to Bep, who is technically interested, thinks it is a good idea, and calls in Karel for his practical advice. Karel's comment is about as follows: "If it is a new job, you should wait until the rate has been fixed for it. When it has got a rate, you can use a gadget to work faster, but keep it to yourself and make sure the industrial engineers don't discover it, because otherwise they'll come and cut the rate." When I answer that the rate for this kind of job is so bad that I suppose they must have already assumed the use of some gadget, Karel warns me, "Never say that in the office, because they'll check it and if they cannot find it in their books, you may be fired for lying." Then he adds a morale to the story, which is that I shouldn't worry too much about improving working methods; that's not the job for me, but for "all those bosses who make a 150 guilders a week" (he says that twice). Karel thus looks at the matter only from a point of view of income. Bep likes the technical fun of inventing something; he is a tinkerer. Nobody I meet in this factory ever refers to the company interest or the quality of the product. There is a suggestion box, but it doesn't seem to function; people have stuffed it with old newspapers.

During a casual conversation with a fitter from another crew whom I know only by his last name, Morsink, I ask him how he likes his job. He is not very satisfied, but not because of the work itself (although he also gets rather boring jobs), but because of the poor quality of his tools (I know by personal experience that having to work with inadequate tools is very irritating), the lack of friendship (he is rather a loner), the insufficient "benefits" (I don't know what exactly he means by this), and the fact that people talk to the boss behind other people's backs and try to buy the boss's favor by offering cigarettes. Morsink would like to quit, but he stays for the high wages. I think that in the case of this man specific personal grudges spoil his job satisfaction.

Whether one likes the job does interest others, and in the beginning I am asked several times "And, how do you like it here?" (to which I respond with a noncommittal answer). Personally I find even the stupid

jobs not unpleasant, and they supply an outlet for my energy. Only when
the time allowed is too short, the quality controller difficult, or the tools
(and my skills) inadequate, do I feel an aversion.

## The Payment System

The incentive payment system in this factory is a straight piece rate
with a guaranteed minimum. This means that everybody gets at least the
base rate, and on top of that one normally earns an individual performance bonus based on the standard time for the jobs completed divided
by actual time spent. Standard times are supposed to be set at a level
such that a normal worker can earn a 33% bonus; weekly pay is based
on this assumption. Bonuses over the normal 33% are paid once every 4
weeks.

The factory uses so-called experience standards, that is, standard job
times are not determined by time-and-motion studies, but estimated by
the foreman or the industrial engineer. At best they may be based on a
single sample measured with a stopwatch, usually unrepresentative. The
charge hand knows approximately what the well-paid and the bad jobs
are, and tries to share them fairly among his men. An underpaid job is
not always a disadvantage, because if you need so much time that your
pay for this job would sink below your base rate the job may get exempt
from the bonus system. That means you get your "P.A." (Personal
Average bonus), so you're okay again. At least this applies if normally
you're someone who performs reasonably. In that case the industrial
engineers will assume that the rate is really wrong or that the conditions
were exceptional. Even the engineers do not trust the standards.

Managing the proper bonus level takes quite a lot of ingenuity from
the worker. If you haven't done so well on one job, you are often able to
balance it with surplus time from a previous job that was overpaid; most
of us have a "kitty" of job tickets for this purpose (Argyris, 1952). It is a
matter of having your job tickets stamped at the right time. A widely
used stratagem is to extend the time of jobs exempt from the bonus
system so that you gain spare time for your bonus jobs. Of course all
these things are forbidden: they say you can be fired on the spot for them,
but in these days of full employment that is not a credible threat.

A conflict of conscience may arise when you get a bad job, for which
everybody knows the standard time is too short, and you fix the ticket
with time from another job. In the office they keep cards showing how
much time a job takes each time; if these show that the "bad" job has once
been completed within the allowed time, you spoil the chances for a

revision of the rate, and your comrade who gets the job next time may not be in a position to "fix" it. Everybody in the crew knows this problem, but the issue is so delicate and complex (you also don't want to be known as a person who always complains and can't make his rates) that there are no clear informal rules on how to handle it.

There does exist an informal norm for the maximum bonus one should make on a job that is overpaid. In our crew that is 50%, and the newcomer is immediately told about this. Even the charge hand Jaap, when in the beginning he encourages you to speed up, also warns you not to overdo it, "for then you spoil the job for someone else." The assumption is that in this case the industrial engineers will be alarmed and revise the rate downward.[4] Jaap's opinion carries weight with the industrial engineers, and one can negotiate with him. Sometimes he will give you extra time for technical trouble; sometimes, but this is more difficult, he will arrange a permanent improvement of the rate. I score a few victories of this kind, with Jaap trying to read from the big clock in the factory hall whether I spent 2 or 3 minutes on a job; then we haggle for a while and finally settle for 2½. After having discovered the tactics, I can improve the outcome by raising my initial demand.

One may wonder whether an awkward system like this one offers any real incentive to work. By itself, it probably doesn't. However, independent of the system, the working pace in this factory is quite high, as mentioned earlier. The "incentive" system has at least partly another function: in those years in the Netherlands, the government exercised strict controls on the levels of wages paid, to combat inflation. Companies that could demonstrate they had an incentive system got permission to pay more, which enabled them to attract more and better personnel in a tight labor market.

Nevertheless, for the ordinary man in the factory, this ramshackle bonus system does affect his working climate to a considerable extent. In another company with a similar system, someone once told me "I like the system, because you can determine yourself how much money you are going to make!" Even if this is not completely true, all of us who share in the system have our personal notebooks, and we calculate job by job how much time we should use and how much we will then earn. This does give us the illusion of working for ourselves, and most of us like that. So the system does motivate us, but in a way not foreseen by its designers: through its defaults rather than through its merits.

Working for oneself can be a source of conflict with the interests of the group. "Rate busting" (Whyte, 1955) means breaking the unofficial norm for the maximum allowable bonus—the 50% mentioned above. Karel, as mentioned earlier, is the crew's authority on bonus issues; when I have achieved a rate increase, I go to see him first to find out how much I am now allowed to make on the job. After some reflection, Karel says, for example, 44%: not too much, in order to avoid suspicion. So 44% is what I will make. On one occasion we receive the weekly bonus calculations and Bep shows me his with a reproachful look. For a job which we did together and for which I calculated the time, the ticket indicates a bonus of 69%: "that means the rate has already gone to hell." I feel quite upset and start checking the mathematics, and thank God the error must be in the office, they will have a look at it. After a few days they send a correction: we get a decent 45%, and I feel rehabilitated.

Yet there are rate busters. I discover three categories of them: first, the sneaky ones, who will do it every now and then and try to hide it from their mates; these people will actually have higher P.A.s (Personal Averages, see earlier) than they dare confess. Second, the antisocial ones, who defy ostracism; we will meet one of them, Torenstra, later on. The third category are the unusually talented, or at least those with this reputation—usually old-timers who have gained an exceptional position vis-à-vis the boss as well as the group.

## Use of Money

During a lunch break Willem explains in great detail and with obvious pleasure his financial situation. He normally takes home 68 guilders a week, of which a fixed amount of 62 guilders is handed to his wife. The remainder, about 6 guilders, is his allowance, from which he buys cigarettes (four 75-cent packs) and a cup of coffee on the weekend and gives the boys their pocket money. From whatever is left after that, the cafeteria coffee has still got to be paid. Once every 4 weeks the company pays the extra bonus earned above the standard rate. If that is, for example, 20 guilders, his wife gets 15 and he gets 5, for extras—he smokes an occasional cigar. Most of this is saved. His wife has some side earnings too: cleaning at the grocery shop, 2 half days and 1 full day a week; at times she also acts as a shop assistant. Whatever she earns that way is also saved. In this way they accumulated 700 guilders for their two mopeds, and there still is a little money left for a bad day. I think Willem is unusually conscientious in financial matters, probably because of his agrarian background. He and his wife never buy on credit. Willem has a lot of natural wit. He speaks sneeringly about acquaintances who didn't have a cent but all the same were married in white with coaches and everything. When he and his wife married in Groningen they took the streetcar, and he had had 3,000 guilders in his piggy bank. One could better use the money for purchases!

Morsink plans to get married, and he mentions an amount of 5,000 guilders as needed for that purpose. He is 31 now, and he prefers to wait for another year rather than suffer poverty; but when he does get married, he will have his 4,000 or 5,000 guilders of savings.

Bep, who married during the war years at the age of 21, will probably be of a different opinion. He won't have had much, nor will his wife. Yet they, too, are conscientious; their little home contains no expensive pieces of equipment bought on credit, and they don't own a radio, they are just connected to the "distributie" (the communal radio system). With his semiskilled worker wage of 1.48 guilders an hour and the maximum number of overtime hours, plus once every 4 weeks a bonus of 20 to 30 guilders if he has worked well, he can feed his family of five and save something for the education of his 8-year-old son. He is lucky, because his rent is only 3.95 guilders a week; for new apartments in the western suburbs rents are three times that amount. This is also the reason Bep stays where he is. With his three children he would be entitled to allocation of a larger house; his present house is really too small. The two older children, a girl, 9, and a boy, 8, share a side room, and the youngest girl, 7, sleeps in her parents' bedroom, and that is not ideal either. Nevertheless, in their street there are similar houses where families of the same size even keep boarders: these are put on the floor in the living room after the family has gone to bed.

An opinion that I heard several times is "Working doesn't make one rich." The crew are rather cryptic about the things that do make one rich; these must be suspect. Their conception of "working" is often rather narrow (as I mentioned earlier in the case of the management); I over-hear a long tirade against small shop owners who spend their day with "a pound of sugar, madam?" and "therefore" don't really work.

Of course, people play the national lottery. Some people in the crew, Karel and Jaap for example, share in a lottery club for which they put some money aside every week. At the last draw they got a "breakeven" (their money back), and this money, of course, is immediately reinvested in a new lot. The new draw takes place during the time I am there, and 2 days before the final deadline both the main prize (100,000 guilders) and their number are still in the game. Then, on the last day but one, the blow falls: the main prize goes to someone else, with another breakeven for the club. There is also an unofficial soccer "pool" for the factory, in which you can participate for 25 cents, and that is managed by the industrial engineers. Every week the first- and second-prize winners divide the pool, some 20 guilders. At lunchtime there is one table where people always play cards for money, but the amounts are small. I think the game is more important than the cents, in view of the large number of passive but faithful onlookers. For some time I participate in a group that plays canasta at lunchtime (introduced by Bep who got it from *Panorama*, a popular weekly), and we don't even count points, just estimate them. But someone always figures how much it would have been if we had played for money.

## Mutual Solidarity

The weak ties among workers, referred to earlier, do not mean that there is no mutual solidarity, especially within our small crew. We do provide one another with support and advice, lend our tools, help fish a broken tap end from a hole, and so forth. During overtime, when I can't complete a job within the time allowed, Bep comes to help me, although this is strictly forbidden and could get him into great trouble. Respecting the rules of solidarity is enforced by social control. When the coffee trolley passes while a member of the crew is not at the bench we always go to look for him. When I forget, this gets me a serious reprimand from Willem: "Are you that kind of guy?" The last half hour on Saturday morning is reserved for cleaning the shop and the machines and not included in the bonus time; thus, if you are short on your bonus, it is attractive to continue at your own job for a bit, letting others do the cleaning. But as soon as the clock shows it's cleaning time, everybody stops, and when I don't, Bep intervenes: "That's not the way we do it here."

Birthdays within the crew are celebrated with extra coffee at the bench, not from our own mugs, but in real cups from the canteen lady; one colleague who wins the internal soccer pool treats the entire crew to coffee and cakes, which must cost him a substantial part of the prize.

Charge hand Jaap takes a special position in the crew: he represents formal authority, divides the work, and has a substantial say in bonus issues, but in other respects is still felt to be "one of us"; he eats his lunch in the cafeteria with the crew members and shares in the treats. We know he won't do us in, and if a bonus rate has been fixed at too high a level, and we have an easy time for a job, he will pretend not to notice it. A young boy who joined after me calls him Uncle Jaap.

Karel is a kind of informal leader. I referred to his authority in bonus issues. He also provides educative advice: it happens one day that I am quite unjustly rebuffed by the chief quality controller, when I only wanted to ask him something. Back at the bench I pour out my troubles to Karel, who comforts me: "Let me explain that to you. Yesterday or the day before that man was rebuked upstairs in the office, because some controller made a mistake, and now the mood within the quality control department is low for a few days, but it will pass!"

Solidarity with other crews is not so strong. It happens more than once that members of other crews use one of our machines and take to their heels when it breaks down, although according to the rules of the plant the last user has got to repair it. They know that one of us will have to fix it on his bonus time; there is no provision of extra time for small breakdowns. On one occasion I get into a big row with such a parasite, and members of the crew come to my support.

The work itself in our crew is mostly done individually; only exceptionally are jobs (and bonuses) shared among two or three men. Bep and Karel work together when they can and seem to like it. Van Harten, an old man from another crew who is temporarily assigned to ours, shows himself quite unhappy that he has to share a ticket with two others. Seeing me busy on an individual job, he sighs, saying that it is "much nicer to tinker on your own like that!," and explains that he prefers to set his own pace rather than having to adapt to others. The funny thing is that he has been transferred to our crew at his own request, to have company; before, he worked alone.

## Marriage and Family

The fact that I get married during the time I am with Mercedes leads to many discussions about marrying and being married. "Why do you marry?" Karel asks me. "Why did you?" I retort. "Well, I had to! A fellow has to remain decent, after all!" My impression is that forced marriages are frequent in this social environment, although I am sure of only a few cases. Being forced to marry is considered quite normal, one of the most common reasons for an early marriage. Uncle Ko, "at the request of Kees who didn't dare to ask himself," came to ask whether it was the same in my case. Sex before marriage is very general, but some are more careful than others. Koos belongs to the careful category. After 6 years of marriage he will now soon be a father, and he explains that they have waited on purpose. His wife had a job and they wanted to go on vacation in the summers. They have among other things been to Austria with a group. They will probably be members of the Planned Parenthood Association (NVSH), at that time the main distributor of contraceptives in the Netherlands. How the others practice birth control I don't know. Willem, as stated, has two sons; he says, "If I could know that the third would be a daughter, I would have let go once more" (sons cost more than daughters), but they hadn't taken the risk. The discussion moves to large families: Frits tells about someone in his neighborhood with 24 children. "That man has no morals," says Willem. The standard for the people I have spoken to is two children, maybe three.

The good advice I get for my marriage is very amusing. The fitting foreman says "be wiser, man." Willem asks considerately, "shouldn't you have a tryout?" Koos suggests we should wait until December, which is advantageous for tax purposes, and Bep, when I tell him how long we have known each other, says "we only knew each other 2 months, but I haven't regretted it for a second!" His marriage is very good, as I have been able to observe myself; Bep is the only crew member whom I visited at his home. Except Jaap's, all marriages in the crew seem to be good. The men like talking about their wives, sometimes also about their children. Willem even describes bathroom scenes, not to be scabrous, but utterly unembarrassed. Another time he lights a cigar during work, and confides to me "I have a good wife; some wives take all the money and let their man roll his own cigarettes, but she doesn't begrudge me my cigars!" One day is his ninth wedding anniversary: "She didn't remember it this morning, but I'll bring a bunch of flowers tonight!" Karel has his worries because his wife is in hospital, and many colleagues sympathize with him.

One evening when we have planned to do overtime together, Bep with a somewhat shy smile shows me a note that the doorkeeper has brought him, a sheet from a scribbling block, written in an unskilled hand: "Bep, I would like to go to the movies. Do you work overtime or not?" Of course he doesn't that night. His children are already waiting for him at the gate. And Uncle Ko one evening treats everybody to cigarettes. "Is this your birthday, Uncle Ko?" "Not mine: my girl's!"; and when someone else doesn't understand it either, he explains again "my other half is having her birthday!"

When I come back after my 2 days of official wedding leave, I find a big bunch of flowers at my place at the bench, plus, on a piece of sheet metal, my portrait drawn in chalk, with a cloud coming from the mouth "hi fellows I'm married" and around it, nicely calligraphed, "many congratulations on your wedding." All from the crew. I shake dozens of hands and I hear as many times "hope you won't regret it." I treat the crew to coffee and cakes and a cigarette. At lunchtime the chairman of the works committee gives a little speech and hands me an envelope with a money gift from the personnel fund, a pool to which employer and employees contribute equally. The next day everything is back to normal. Nobody even makes any jokes about being just married, but Willem gets the inspiration to tell about his own honeymoon: "Those were the best days of my life, nice and early to bed with my wife." A young fellow from another department with whom I stand waiting at the toolroom window asks me "and how do you feel now?" And before I can answer he continues "do you feel very wicked?"—evidently a dysfunctional relic from a "Christian" education.

There is one more wedding in this same period: Uncle Hein, an old transport hand with a funny, silly face. He has been living with this woman for 12 years, but getting married before he retires will improve his pension claims, so he does it—and happily takes his 2 days' wedding leave and his envelope from the pool.

## Leisure: Hobbies

The older members of the crew, starting with Bep, all have hobbies they like to talk about. Next to their families, these seem to be what occupies them most. From the younger guys I don't hear about any hobbies, although I notice younger people elsewhere in the factory talking about radios or photography. Karel is a gardener. He talks about it before the morning buzzer goes at 7:30 a.m., when there is always a group of early birds around the bench (some regularly arrive 15 minutes early!) and an animated social conversation. In a discussion with a friend Karel demonstrates an impressive know-how about fruit trees. He had to sell his allotment garden, but he now wants to start anew. It's an incurable disease, he says. Bep's interest includes vegetables: for lack of anything but a minuscule front garden he grows potted plants, in particular cactuses, a subject on which he has studied five books. He knows all Latin names faultlessly by heart. He is also a handyman, having himself made some of his furniture. Presently he spends a lot of time on the recently founded Personnel Club, of which he is a committee member.

Willem is an angling fanatic. He is also an amateur carpenter at home, and on weekends he and his wife with their two little sons make trips on the mopeds bought with their savings. Willem tells me a lot about his home life, because at lunchtime he usually sits with me, and then it is no trouble to get him speaking: one encouraging word and he talks for another 5 minutes. He obviously appreciates my attentive listening. Unfortunately quite a bit of what he says is lost to me by the unintelligibility of his Drente dialect, which I only gradually start to master. He demonstrates how Robbie, his younger boy, who is almost 7, handles the fishing gear, and he explains that they have the rule at home that whoever says a "bad word" owes a cent to whoever catches him at it. The boys seem to have a nice side income that way.

Jaap owns a very old but skillfully reconditioned car, in which he drives to work, and into which besides his money he also invests his free time. He is not the only one with this hobby: at the factory gate one regularly sees three cars belonging to workers. To say nothing about the often brand-new motorbikes.

Fitter Morsink's hobbies are drawing and "visiting museums," but he is a unique case. He prefers pen-and-ink drawings: a dead hare hanging from a nail, horses' heads. He says he always gives his work away: he is never satisfied with it himself.

When the Personnel Club is founded, all kinds of subactivities are started, most of which die an early death, but which do offer an impressive inventory of the various interest areas: soccer, card playing, cabaret, radio, photography, volleyball, and walking. There is also a "flower club," but this is something else: one pays 85 cents a month and for this money one gets a plant or a bunch of flowers from a nursery, accompanied by directions for use. There are quite a few participants: the people like flowers (flower peddlers and shops thrive in the Amsterdam working-class neighborhoods!).

General subjects for discussion are soccer matches, movies, and personal adventures or adventures of friends, rather than facts or abstract issues. Koos occasionally demonstrates knowledge acquired from books, to the extreme irritation of, among others, Willem. Bep is also a reader; at home he has some 30 novels, mostly from some series, and he also borrows from the public library, but he rarely talks about it. Karel sometimes mentions his gramophone.

## Attitudes Toward Politics

Amsterdam in the 1950s was a stronghold of the Dutch Communist party, and sometime before my arrival there had been Communist-inspired labor unrest at Mercedes. Consequently the company presently hires only personnel of nonsuspect political color. During the time I work there I do not notice any agitation. In the crew there are no overt Communists. Most are members of the socialist labor union NVV; many read the socialist newspaper *Het Vrije Volk* or the local Amsterdam paper *De Courant—Het Nieuws van de Dag*. Most are lukewarm about parties and unions; union membership is useful—"it can come in very handy at times"—but all leaders, whether from the Communist union EVC or from the socialist NVV, are regarded with distrust. In the eyes of the common man, these leaders too belong to the authorities, and as such they are suspect.

On Labor Day, May 1, pamphlets are handed out in the street, early in the morning, inviting us to join the Labor Day procession organized by the Communist party. Everybody takes one out of curiosity, but many throw it away instantly; a trail of paper leads to the various factory gates. Inside the plant I hear mostly negative reactions: "Just looking for trouble where there is none," says Koos. Two young guys in the changing room poke fun at the pamphlet. At the bench, Uncle Ko, sitting on a cask, reads the pamphlet carefully. "Will you participate?" I ask him. "Not me!" he answers, "but in the old days I often participated—and then there were more people around than there will be today."

Of course, this is a more or less politically selected population. Only among the more senior Mercedes workers some overt Communists survive, whose opinion may be quite different. During a lunch break I overhear a heated discussion about class distinctions, clearly initiated by one particular man. Another time I bike to the ferryboat with a mechanic who asks where I come from. When I mention Hengelo, he asks "whether they have class struggle there too?" But this is the only time I hear this term used.

One day there is a strike of the ferryboat personnel, inspired by the Communist union EVC and condemned by the socialist NVV. The men to whom I talk about it all sympathize with the strikers, who are people they know, or with whom they feel a community of interests, and whose social status they can judge; this has more appeal than some directive from above, even if issued by their own union. At the ferry, signatures are collected to protest against victimization of strikers, and everybody signs. People scold the NVV leaders who leave the strikers out in the cold.

The older crew members fear above all a return of the Depression of the 1930s. After 20 years, the Depression is still referred to at least once a week. "The Depression to us was worse than the war." And if people tell about their life: "father unemployed for years, poverty at home, you don't know how it feels taking your girl out on a Saturday and not even having 10 cents to buy her an ice cream." The Depression threatened their human dignity, the war their safety; the former to some was harder to bear than the latter.

As far as the war is concerned there is a difference in perspective between the younger people who served in the army after the war and after the Indonesian expedition, who don't know too much about what a war means and like to talk about their military experiences, and the older ones, most of whom strongly despise war and all that goes with it. Bep belongs to the latter category, and he has forbidden his kids to play with military toys.

## Attitudes Toward Religion

My crew has no church members. The only people in the plant whom I know to profess a religion are Morsink, a member of the Roman Catholic Labor Union, and a man called Torenstra, who belongs to the Protestant Christian Labor Union, and who for some time, for lack of other company, uninvitedly sits with Willem and me during lunch. Torenstra is not an ideal specimen of his faith, because he is the biggest rate buster of the plant, reported to make regularly more than 100% bonus. He is at loggerheads with everybody, and his sour face scares people away. "I know more about fitting shafts than about soccer" is one of his statements during lunchtime. "Wouldn't you kick a guy like that in the ass?" is the crew's comment on his bonuses. "That Christian should first learn to get along with his mates better," Bep says grimly.

Bep and Koos sometimes tune in to the VPRO radio station (at that time, of a liberal Christian tone). During overtime the three of us get involved in a fairly confused discussion about religious persecution. Bep criticizes the Roman Catholics and cites a popular VPRO radio preacher, the Reverend Spelberg. Koos protests that this preacher shouldn't say such things, because he is there for the good of the people, and that means he shouldn't attack another faith. Then Catholicism, Communism, National Socialism, and "Christianism" (what is meant is the Dutch style of Calvinism) are all mentioned in the same breath, with examples of the fanaticism to which these "faiths" may lead. My colleagues obviously associate "faith" primarily with "intolerance."

My attempts to talk about religious matters with Willem remain unsuccessful. He only enumerates how many Catholics and fundamentalist Calvinists lived in his village in Drente. Then in one breath he mentions the people who idolize the Royal Family as another incomprehensible group. He isn't like that—why should everything the Royal Family did be written in the newspaper? I suggest that this may be the journalists' choice, but that is an argument he rejects. The Royal Family worries him; he comes back to the issue another time.

In the morning, before the buzzer, I overhear a curious conversation at the bench. It is about death; one man says he reckons he will go to hell anyway, but a moment later he states, "For me, everything ends at the Northern Cemetery." One very old fellow with a Brabant accent (which means he is probably a Catholic) warns him that he will still be frightened when the day comes!

It is difficult to fathom to what extent the men recognize other aspects of religion besides persecution and (life after?) death. The only person I meet who shows a broader perspective is Bep's wife. During a conversation at their home she condemns sensational movies based on biblical themes: that is not what these stories are meant for, she judges. Women do tend to be more religiously sensitive than men.

## Final Remarks

Two remarkable conclusions stand out from these notes. One is the virtually complete lack of any reference to higher management, which at least in this company was both irrelevant and invisible at our level. Jaap the charge hand was our only source of authority; even the next higher man, the fitting shop foreman, interfered rarely. Organizations do look very different from below than from above, and those who aspire to higher positions should be aware of this fact—if they ever want to understand how jobs really get done.

The second conclusion is about the bourgeois life pattern of these Dutch working-class persons in 1955. They did not suffer from the "alienation" described by classical sociology as a combination of powerlessness, meaninglessness, and normlessness.[5] Their lives were well organized and purposeful, and there was a recognizable set of norms, even if not everybody respected these. But of course these were mostly skilled workers, with some semiskilled associates like myself.[6] After leaving Mercedes I worked for another month as an unskilled laborer at the British-American Tobacco Company's cigarette factory, where I found a very different situation: there my colleagues were an alienated, marginal, virtually antisocial bunch.[7] Which also means one should be careful about generalizing about "the Amsterdam worker"—or any group like that—before really knowing it.

The impact of jobs on people, as this chapter has illustrated, depends both on the jobs and on the people. And for these people, their jobs were only one aspect of their lives—an indispensable but not necessarily the most important aspect. Work behavior cannot be fully understood if work is not put in perspective with other life interests of the workers.

## Discussion Questions

1. To what causes does the chapter attribute the high employee turnover at Mercedes? If this analysis is correct, what kind of changes would be needed for creating greater employee loyalty to the company?

2. What is meant by a "bourgeois life pattern" among the employees of Mercedes? Give some examples from the chapter.

3. The incentive payment system at Mercedes does not work as formally intended. Nevertheless the chapter suggests that if informal processes are taken into account, the system may not be so bad at all. Explain how this is possible.

4. How were leadership roles in the crew divided among (a) the fitting shop foreman, (b) Jaap, and (c) Karel? Do you see any problems here?

## Notes

1. In a Dutch reader, *De rafelrand van Amsterdam,* Bovenkerk and Brunt (1977) republished a number of classic papers from this period, including two—by Dijkhuis and Huberts—that are based on participant observation.

2. Van Heek drew my attention to Henk Dijkhuis's "Vijftig dagen in een Jordaans kosthuis" (Fifty Days in a Boarding House in the Jordaan [Amsterdam's most typical old neighborhood]), dating from the early 1930s and republished in Bovenkerk and Brunt (1977).

3. A *charge hand* is an appointed crew leader, that is, a worker who spends part of his or her time assisting the foreman in simple management tasks.

4. Voluntary limitation of one's performance on overpaid jobs is extensively described in the British (Marriott, 1971) and in U.S. literature (Whyte, 1955).

5. Seeman (1959) in a conceptual article identified these three aspects plus isolation and self-estrangement.

6. Goldthorpe, Lockwood, Bechhofer, and Platt (1968) described the British "affluent worker" of the 1960s as having little proletarian class consciousness, without for that reason becoming bourgeois.

7. Blauner (1964), on the basis a series of field research projects in the United States, also indicates the influence of the kind of work on whether or not the workers are alienated.

# 2

# The Colors of Collars

## Occupational Differences in Work Goals

Over 18,000 employees in 16 subsidiaries of a large multinational corporation answered survey questions about the importance to them of 19 work goals. Their answers are compared across seven occupational categories: research professionals, systems analysts, service technicians, plant technicians, clerical workers, unskilled workers, and managers. The comparison reveals considerable differences among occupations in the order of importance of the various work goals, leading in some cases to an almost complete reversal. The differences are explained by the job content and the expectations of the job occupants based on comparison with their social environment. The consequences for management, in terms of what is supposed to motivate employees, are discussed.

## The Impact of the Nature of
## the Job on People's Motivation

What motivates people to work? The answer is that it all depends on the people and on the work. In the management literature, general recipes for employee motivation are as popular as recipes for making gold were in the Middle Ages, but unfortunately both are equally ineffective. What is true for assembly line operators is not necessarily true

This chapter was originally published in *Columbia Journal of World Business*, 7(5), September/October 1972, pp. 72-80. Copyright © 1972 *Columbia Journal of World Business*. Reprinted with the permission of the journal.

for clerks, salespersons, research scientists, janitors, or secretaries, and it may also depend on the person's age, gender, education, or even nationality.

The impact of the nature of the job on the motivation, and therefore on the behavior, of employees is increasingly relevant as the distribution of people among jobs is changing drastically in modern society. Certain tasks are transferred to computers or robots, altering the remaining jobs beyond recognition and affecting education requirements and status hierarchies. Ideas about people in jobs date from situations that do not exist any more, like the terms "blue collar" and "white collar," curiously archaic but still in occasional use.

## Data on Work Goals
## From a Large Multinational

Data highlighting the impact of the nature of jobs on people's motivation were collected in overseas subsidiaries of a large U.S.-based multinational corporation manufacturing and selling electronic equipment. This corporation over a number of years has surveyed the attitudes of its employees in all kinds of jobs, all around the world. The part of the surveys relevant to the present chapter deals with people's *work goals*: what employees want from a job.

Although data were collected in many different countries, this chapter will not deal with between-country differences; these have been reported elsewhere.[1]

The "work goals" questions were introduced by the following general instruction: "Try to think of those factors which would be important to you in an ideal job. Disregard the extent to which they are contained in your present job." Each goal was scored on a 5-point scale, from 1 = "of utmost importance" to 5 = "of very little or no importance." Mean scores on this scale were calculated for each goal for each category of employees. Table 2.1 shows the rank order of these mean scores for 19 work goals obtained for one of the first job categories, studied in 1968: 2,500 systems analysts. The rank orders are assigned according to average importance scores, starting with the goal assigned the highest average importance (i.e., the lowest mean score).

Systems analysts, who are professionals with a college level education, according to Table 2.1 rate as their most important goals (1-5 on the list) those concerned with the content of their jobs (training, challenge, freedom, up-to-dateness, use of skills), next (6-8 on the list) those dealing

**TABLE 2.1** Work Goal Ranking for Systems Analysts

| Rank | Goal | Questionnaire Wording |
|------|------|----------------------|
| 1 | Training | Have training opportunities (to improve your skills or learn new skills). |
| 2 | Challenge | Have challenging work to do—work from which you can get a personal sense of accomplishment. |
| 3 | Freedom | Have considerable freedom to adopt your own approach to the job. |
| 4 | Up-to-dateness | Keep up-to-date with the technical developments relating to your job. |
| 5 | Use of skills | Fully use your skills and abilities on the job. |
| 6 | Advancement | Have an opportunity for advancement to higher level jobs. |
| 7 | Recognition | Get the recognition you deserve when you do a good job. |
| 8 | Earnings | Have an opportunity for high earnings. |
| 9 | Cooperation | Work with people who will cooperate well with one another. |
| 10 | Manager | Have a good working relationship with your manager. |
| 11 | Personal time | Have a job that leaves you sufficient time for your personal or family life. |
| 12 | Friendly department | Work in a congenial and friendly atmosphere. |
| 13 | Company contribution | Have a job that allows you to make a real contribution to the success of your company. |
| 14 | Efficient department | Work in a department that is run efficiently. |
| 15 | Security | Have the security that you will be able to work for your company as long as you want to. |
| 16 | Desirable area | Live in an area desirable to you and your family. |
| 17 | Benefits | Have good fringe benefits. |
| 18 | Physical conditions | Have good physical working conditions (good ventilation and lighting, adequate work space, etc.). |
| 19 | Successful company | Work in a company that is regarded in your country as successful. |

with their rewards (advancement, recognition, earnings). Further down the list (9-12), we find the social goals (cooperation, manager, family, department). Finally (13-19) we find goals related to the company and the living and working environment (contributing to the company, efficient department, security, living area, benefits, working conditions, successful company).

The importance attached to various work goals by these systems analysts corresponds very much to prevailing U.S. theories about motivation to work (e.g., Herzberg, Mausner, & Snyderman, 1959; Maslow, 1970). The job content comes first, then the recognition, then the interpersonal relationships, then the environmental factors. In the company in which the research was carried out, the data were considered evidence that motivating employees was no problem. In an early analysis, Sirota and Greenwood (1971) stated:

> These employees do not have to be motivated. They are eager and ambitious, interested both in having their skills utilized on present jobs and in moving ahead to more responsible and better paying jobs. The task of management—in the United States as well as multinationally—is to create organizational and job conditions that harness, rather than stifle, the considerable energy employees bring to their work. (p. 58)

## Seven Occupational Categories

This optimistic point of view had to be modified when in the next round of surveys (1969), the work goals of employees in occupations requiring less education became available: first, of employees in relatively simple administrative jobs, and subsequently, of employees in production jobs in manufacturing plants (the traditional blue-collar workers).

Table 2.2 shows the work goal rankings for seven different occupational categories surveyed in 1968 and 1969, selected to represent the full scale of occupations within this company in 16, mainly European, country subsidiaries (Austria, Belgium, Denmark, Finland, France, Great Britain, Germany, Ireland, Israel, Italy, Netherlands, Norway, South Africa, Spain, Sweden, and Switzerland). The approximate numbers of employees surveyed within the different occupations are:

1. 40 research professionals, all university educated (mostly Ph.D.s), working in a research laboratory
2. 2500 systems analysts, predominantly college educated, working in branch offices spread over the countries (the group covered by Table 2.1)
3. 5000 service technicians, mostly with vocational school training until the age of 17 or 18, working out of branch offices
4. 2500 plant technicians, mostly with a vocational school training similar to the service technicians, or slightly less, working in various manufacturing plants as maintenance technicians, toolmakers, or draftsmen

**TABLE 2.2** Goal Ranking for Seven Occupational Categories in 16 Countries

| | Professionals | | Technicians | | Clerical Workers | Unskilled Workers | |
| | | | Nonmanagers | | | | |
| Goal | Research Laboratory | Branch Offices | Branch Offices | Manufacturing Plants | Branch Offices | Manufacturing Plants | Managers |
|---|---|---|---|---|---|---|---|
| Training | 13 | 1 | 1 | 14 | 12 | 14 | 5/6 |
| Challenge | 1 | 2 | 3 | 3 | 5/6 | 13 | 1 |
| Freedom | 3 | 3 | 11 | 9/10 | 5/6 | 16 | 2 |
| Up-to-dateness | 2 | 4 | 4 | 7/8 | 17 | 17 | 9 |
| Use of skills | 4 | 5 | 6/7 | 7/8 | 7 | 12 | 8 |
| Advancement | 12 | 6 | 5 | 5 | 10/11 | 11 | 7 |
| Recognition | 6 | 7 | 13 | 9/10 | 8/9 | 6 | 13 |
| Earnings | 9 | 8 | 8 | 2 | 10/11 | 3 | 10 |
| Cooperation | 5 | 9 | 6/7 | 6 | 1 | 8 | 3/4 |
| Manager | 7 | 10 | 10 | 4 | 2 | 7 | 3/4 |
| Personal time | 16 | 11 | 9 | 12/13 | 14 | 9 | 15 |
| Friendly department | 8 | 12 | 12 | 12/13 | 3 | 5 | 14 |
| Company contribution | 11 | 13 | 15 | 17 | 15 | 18 | 5/6 |
| Efficient department | 10 | 14 | 14 | 16 | 4 | 15 | 11/12 |
| Security | 17/18 | 15 | 2 | 1 | 13 | 2 | 11/12 |
| Desirable area | 14 | 16 | 16 | 18 | 16 | 10 | 16 |
| Benefits | 15 | 17 | 17 | 15 | 18 | 4 | 18 |
| Physical conditions | 19 | 18 | 18 | 11 | 8/9 | 1 | 17 |
| Successful company | 17/18 | 19 | 19 | 19 | 19 | 19 | 19 |

5. 1600 clerical workers in nonprofessional administrative jobs, mostly with high school education until the age of 16 or 17, working in branch offices

6. 3200 unskilled workers in manufacturing jobs, mostly with elementary school education only, or some years of high school

7. 4000 first- and second-line managers from all parts of the company

Categories 1, 2, 3, 4, and 7 are predominantly male (less than 10% women). Category 5 is 70% female, and Category 6, 30% female.

Table 2.2 shows that there are virtually no goals on the list for which the ranking does not differ widely among some of the occupational categories. The only exception is "working in a successful company," which comes last or near the bottom in all cases.

The goal that shows the widest variation in rank across these occupations is "physical working conditions": from a score of 19 out of 19 for the research workers down to 1 out of 19 for the unskilled. Relatively equal in rank for all occupational categories (less than 10 places difference between the highest and the lowest) are:

- "Rewards" goals: advancement, recognition, and earnings
- "Family" goals: personal time and living in a desirable area
- "Social" goals: working relationship with manager and cooperation
- "Job content" goals: full use of skills

The nonmanagers consist of two categories of professionals (laboratory researchers and systems analysts in branch offices), two categories of technicians (in branch offices and in plants), one group of clerks and one group of unskilled workers.

The two categories of professionals show roughly the same work goal ranking. Advancement and training appeal less to the researchers than to the systems analysts, and the social goals of cooperation and a friendly department are relatively more important to them. These differences must be due to the nature of the jobs that these people perform and to which they feel attracted. The researchers look for rewards other than making a career in the company, and they put higher value on the social context within which they work (cooperation and friendly department).

The two categories of technicians also show about the same work goal ranking. Compared to the professionals, both technician categories are much more concerned with job security. The primary reason is probably the fact that they have a lower professional education level and therefore are more vulnerable to labor market conditions. Another reason, reinforcing the previous one, may be that in most European societies there is a traditional pattern of stable employment and a high premium on security. The higher educated have emancipated themselves more from this pattern than those with an intermediate education like these technicians. Both technician categories score fairly low in the importance attached to freedom. Their jobs offer less freedom than the professional jobs, and people at intermediate technical levels know this already when they start their studies.

The two technician categories differ in the importance of training and—to a somewhat lesser extent—of up-to-dateness; both are more important for the service technicians. This reflects the specific situation in this company, where those working in the branch offices depend on continuous updating to master the rapidly developing technology. In the plants developments on the whole are more gradual and generally do not have such severe implications for the kind of work the technicians do. In contrast, plant technicians attach more importance to earnings, to the relationship with their manager, and to physical working conditions. In this respect they are more similar to the unskilled plant workers. It seems that the plant environment with its traditional "blue-collar" image supports the concern for earnings. And obviously plant technicians are more dependent on the relationship with their manager and their physical conditions than the service technicians in the branch offices, who spend most of their time on their own, out with the customers.

The clerks (30% men, 70% women) are different from all other occupational categories in that their most important work goals are all social: cooperation, relationship with their manager, and a friendly department. Then follows the goal of working in an efficient department, which is more important to the clerical workers than to any other group. Other goals are ranked similar to the professionals, except that for the clerks, training and up-to-dateness score lower.

The goal ranking for unskilled workers is almost a reversal of that for professional technical personnel. The unskilled workers rate as their most important goals physical working conditions, security, earnings, and benefits. Then follow the social goals. The typical job content goals—challenge, use of skills, and freedom—rank relatively low.

The goal ranking for the managers resembles the rankings for the professionals, but they attach relatively more importance to the social goals of cooperation and the relationship with their own boss. They are more oriented toward the social aspects of their work situation, which is a logical consequence of their role as managers. They are relatively less concerned about training and up-to-dateness. They also attach less importance to recognition; maybe as managers they take a certain recognition for granted. The most remarkable difference between the managers and all nonmanager categories is that the former attach a much greater importance to making a real contribution to the success of the company. Managers, obviously, identify more with their company than do non-managers.

## A Maslowian Interpretation of the Findings

Most readers will be familiar with the concepts of human motivation as they were first described by the late A. H. Maslow (1970).[2] According to Maslow, we are all motivated by a number of basic needs. Some of these are more fundamental than others, so that our needs can be ordered in a hierarchy, from more to less fundamental. At the base of the hierarchy are physiological needs (food, shelter, sex) and needs for security. About in the middle are social needs (to have rewarding human contacts), and on the higher levels the needs for self-esteem, esteem from others, and the need for self-actualization (to realize as fully as possible the potential that is in us). The hierarchy implies that needs at lower levels are active motivators *only until they are reasonably satisfied;* then the next higher level need takes over. A satisfied need is not an active motivator any longer. But humans are wanting animals—there will always be a higher need to take the place of a satisfied one.

Table 2.3 groups goals into the need categories of Maslow: high (self-actualization and esteem) includes challenge, training, freedom, up-to-dateness, use of skills; medium (social) includes cooperation, good relationship with manager, friendly department, efficient department; low (security and psychological) includes security, benefits, and physical conditions. For the less educated employees, earnings also belong to this category. In Table 2.3 only the top (most important) four goals in the work goal ranking for each job category are listed.

It can be seen that

- Professionals ranked all four top goals corresponding to "high" Maslow needs.
- Clerks ranked all four top goals corresponding to "medium" Maslow needs.
- Unskilled workers ranked all four top goals corresponding to "low" Maslow needs.
- Managers and technicians present a mixed picture, but with at least one goal in the "high" Maslow category.

People will attach "importance" to the fulfillment of a need by comparison to relevant others in the society and class to which they belong.

**TABLE 2.3** The Four Most Important Goals by Occupational Category

| Goals ranked in "Needs Hierarchy" | Professionals (research laboratories) | Professionals (branch offices) | Managers | Technicians (branch offices) | Technicians (manufacturing plants) | Clerical Workers (branch offices) | Unskilled Workers (manufacturing plants) |
|---|---|---|---|---|---|---|---|
| *High* | | | | | | | |
| Self-actualization and esteem needs: | | | | | | | |
| Challenge | 1 | 2 | 1 | 3 | 3 | | |
| Training | 3 | 1 | | 1 | | | |
| Freedom | 2 | 3 | 2 | | | | |
| Up-to-dateness | | 4 | | 4 | | | |
| Use of skills | 4 | 4 | | | | | |
| *Middle* | | | | | | | |
| Social needs: | | | | | | | |
| Cooperation | | | 3/4 | | | 1 | |
| Manager | | | 3/4 | | 4 | 2 | |
| Friendly department | | | | | | 3 | |
| Efficient department | | | | | | 4 | |
| *Low* | | | | | | | |
| Security and physiological needs: | | | | | | | |
| Security | | | | 2 | 1 | | 2 |
| Earnings | | | | | 2 | | 3 |
| Benefits | | | | | | | 4 |
| Physical conditions | | | | | | | 1 |

A work goal will be rated important if its attainment is possible, but not self-evident: It cannot be taken for granted. A work goal will be rated less important if it is beyond reach or if its fulfillment is taken for granted in any job a person might consider.

Based on this assumption, an explanation of the above results might run as follows:

- Professionals in present-day society across the countries surveyed take the fulfillment of their "lower" Maslow needs for granted and therefore rate the corresponding work goal less important. This is less true for clerks and least true for unskilled workers.
- Unskilled workers in present-day society in the countries surveyed are not likely to attain work goals like job challenge and job freedom. Therefore, their aspirations for the fulfillment of the corresponding "higher" Maslow needs will be lower, and they will also rate their importance lower. The likelihood of the attainment of these goals is higher for clerks and highest for professionals. Of the occupational categories studied, professionals' jobs offer the highest opportunities for self-actualization and gaining esteem. They can therefore aspire to fulfilling their higher level needs and attach importance to the corresponding work goals.

A consequence of this interpretation of our findings is that changes in the society in which people live will affect the importance they attach to the fulfillment of different work goals. For example, a society in which job security increases would see the importance attached to the security goal diminish and "higher" goals take its place; the opposite would happen in a period of decreased security.

Differences in job category often stand for differences in education level and gender as well. The education a person has received will certainly affect his/her work goals (and vice versa). However, a comparison between the two categories of professionals in our data (with similar education levels) and the two categories of technicians indicates that the job has an influence beyond the education level. Gender may have an impact on work goals, too. The two categories in our research whose most important goals come lowest in the Maslow hierarchy (clerical workers and unskilled workers) were also the categories with the highest percentages of women, but the answer patterns obtained from these occupational categories are not caused by the gender distribution. When comparing the answers by men and women in the same jobs, we find considerable similarity that outranks the sex difference.

One objection to the results obtained in this research should be mentioned. The employees questioned gave conscious answers on the importance they attached to various job aspects. But do people really know themselves? Do their scores on these questions really correspond to what moves them unconsciously? Have not the answers been given in terms of how they feel they ought to be motivated, rather than in accordance with their real motives? We will come back to this question in Chapter 3, which will show evidence that the differences shown in the present chapter do reflect real employee motivation.

## Implications for Management

This chapter has shown a dramatic influence of people's occupation on the kind of issues they rate important in a job, and the job itself—its opportunities for self-actualization and gaining esteem—seems to be the determining factor. The consequences for management are far reaching. There may be no problem of how to motivate professionals; the job itself takes care of that. For clerical workers the situation is more difficult, and for unskilled workers even more so. Technicians are somewhere in between, especially in manufacturing plants. Motivating managers, finally, is also a different thing from motivating nonmanagerial employees.

Unlike professionals, clerical workers attach the highest importance to work goals whose attainment the manager can directly influence: cooperation, their relationship with him or her, a friendly and efficient department. Unskilled workers, on the other hand, attach the highest importance to goals whose attainment is not so much in the hands of the individual manager, but depends on the company as a whole: its personnel policies, benefits, working conditions, and the like.

These are the issues that can be dealt with by collective action on the part of the workers. Security, earnings, benefits, and better working conditions are goals that a union can successfully fight for. To employees to whom these issues are of primary importance, it makes sense to engage in union activity if their needs are not otherwise satisfied. This is partly true, too, for technicians, less so for clerical workers, and least for professionals. It is difficult to fight collectively for better worker-manager relationships and more efficiency. And how much success is to be expected in collective action for an individualistic goal like job challenge? Maybe least likely of all to succeed is a collective fight for more job freedom. Collective action itself means a sacrifice of freedom. The most probable outcome, if the action is successful, is a shift of some control from management to workers' representatives—not an increase of the freedom of any individual worker.

Some management authors—like Herzberg (1966)—consider the kind of data as revealed by this research as an indication that something is wrong: They want to change employees' orientation to the importance of various work goals. This has led to "job enrichment" projects for clerical and unskilled workers. If these attempts are successful, the workers should shift their goal rankings more in the direction of those of the professionals.

The research findings reported in this chapter show that there is no blanket answer to the question: "What motivates employees?" A lot depends on the occupational category the employees are in, and it is not sufficient to classify them by the supposed color of their collars. As motivation theorists have stated, the job itself is a powerful potential motivator, but large categories of the working population seem neither to have nor to expect the kind of jobs in which this motivation potential is realized. They are primarily motivated by the more traditional factors of supervision, earnings, security, and working conditions.

## Discussion Questions

1. This chapter shows that Maslow's hierarchy of human needs corresponds with the status hierarchy (inside and outside organizations) of occupations (Table 2.3). One could say that Maslow's need hierarchy reflects a social class hierarchy. How do you explain this?

2. What changes in a person's motivation pattern can be predicted when a professional is promoted to manager? A technician? A clerk?

3. Calculate the range (highest minus lowest rank) for each of the 19 goals in Table 2.2 and put the goals in order of range. Goals with a wide range are occupation dependent; goals with a narrow range occupation independent. Argue why the order of range and occupation dependence is as it is.

4. What differences do you expect, on the basis of this chapter, between the problems of a personnel manager in a research laboratory and in a manufacturing plant?

## Notes

1. I originally referred to Sirota and Greenwood (1971) for a first analysis of between-country differences. The between-country analysis later on led to much more fundamental conclusions (Hofstede, 1980, 1991).

2. In Hofstede (1980, pp. 375-376) I question the universal applicability of Maslow's hierarchy of human needs across national cultures. But this does not refute the usefulness of a Maslowian interpretation of differences among *occupations*, at least in industrial societies.

# 3

# Humanization of Work

## *A Matter of Values*

This chapter interprets the movement toward humanization of work as an attempted third Industrial Revolution; it places it in a historical context. This revolution has been started by other people than the supposed beneficiaries. Chapter 2 showed a wide gap between the values of the professionals (who tend to supply the humanizers) and the workers in simple clerical and production tasks. Additional data show that when we take as our criterion the work aspects that correlate most with overall job satisfaction there remains hardly any difference between professionals and unskilled workers: Earnings and challenge are major contributors to overall satisfaction for everybody. This is a justification of efforts at humanization, but it still poses the strategic problem to what extent the workers with their different set of conscious values can be mobilized for humanization.

## Three Industrial Revolutions

The large-scale replacement of human and animal muscle power by machines in the 19th century has been called the (first) Industrial Revo-

This chapter was originally published under the title "Humanization of Work: The Role of Values in a Third Industrial Revolution" in C. L. Cooper and E. Mumford (Eds.), *The Quality of Working Life in Eastern and Western Europe*, London: Associated Business Press, 1979, pp. 18-37. It was reprinted in D. Ondrack and S. Timperley (Eds.), *The Humanisation of Work: A European Perspective*, London: Armstrong Publishing, 1982, pp. 215-239. The version published here has been abridged but supplemented with data from Hofstede (1976b).

lution. The father of cybernetics, Norbert Wiener, labeled the explosive development of information technology after World War II the second Industrial Revolution (Wiener, 1954, pp. 136ff). It led to the replacement of programmable human mental processes by computers and similar devices. These societal changes have been called revolutions because they fundamentally changed the relationship between people and work. Therefore they have affected the economic system and the structure of society as a whole, at least in the developed part of the world. The movement in several Western countries toward "humanization of work," which started in the 1960s, aims at changes of the same scope and therefore merits to be identified as a potential third Industrial Revolution, leading us into a "postindustrial" era (e.g., Yankelovich, 1981).

The overall trend across all three Industrial Revolutions is one of an increasing appreciation of work as a meaningful activity per se and a decreased appreciation of work as a necessity. Up to the first Industrial Revolution, leisure was the privilege of the upper strata in society. Work was a necessary evil for those who could not afford leisure.

Christian teaching, and especially Protestantism, dignified work, but leisure remained the unwritten ideal for the upper classes in most countries. The first Industrial Revolution affected the attitude toward work of both the upper strata and the masses. The upper strata in the industrializing countries, mostly through an influx of new members, adopted what Max Weber labeled the Protestant ethic (Gerth & Mills, 1948). Working became the ideal, and having no productive activity, disreputable (Van Biemen, 1950, p. 147). The masses were at first thrown into a work slavery worse than before, but in the longer run the technological and economic development led to an improvement of wages and a reduction of working hours. Work remained a necessity, but it became tolerable, and part of the middle and lower classes even adopted the upper strata work ethic. The Great Depression of the 1930s with its massive unemployment made work a privilege, and in 1948, the "right to work" became Article 23 of the Universal Declaration of Human Rights (United Nations, 1963).

The second Industrial Revolution, like the first, has taken a long time to realize its potential for replacing human effort by machine effort. As this happened progressively, it has led into a new wave of unemployment, and the right to work has become a more crucial issue than ever before. In the meantime there is also a new phenomenon: a loss of work ethic and a revaluation of leisure, this time not among the upper strata of society but among its lower and middle strata. This is a break with both the capitalist and the Marxist tradition, which are unanimous in their glorification of work. It has been called an "allergy to work"

(Rousselet, 1974). Its forerunner was Marx's son-in-law, Paul Lafargue (1880/1975), whose book *Le Droit à la Paresse* (The Right to Laziness), written in 1880, gained new popularity in the 1970s. In the advanced industrialized countries of this world, the economic system cannot escape from having to enable all citizens to survive, whether they work or not. We seem to be moving to a society opposite to the ancient one in which the upper strata enjoy the privilege of working hard and the lower suffer from imposed leisure.

The two previous Industrial Revolutions, although triggered by technological innovations, were fed by economic developments: toward mass production in the first, and mass consumption in the second revolution. In both, "things" had priority over "people"; at work, a person is mainly a means of producing things. It is this priority that the third Industrial Revolution, humanization of work, seeks to change. It tries to respond to a crisis of legitimacy and motivation (Habermas, 1973) by establishing a new kind of legitimacy for industrial activity: a legitimacy rooted in the meaningfulness of productive activity per se, which therefore should be designed to be meaningful.

The challenge of the third Industrial Revolution is so formidable and the resistances are so strong that it may remain a dream; anyway, it has a chance only in affluent societies. In different industrialized countries there have been different approaches to stimulate it (Organization for Economic Co-operation and Development [OECD], 1975): spontaneous experimentation in Sweden (Swedish Employers' Confederation [SAF], 1975), government-sponsored experimentation in Germany (Bartölke & Gohl, 1976), government-sponsored expert reports in the United States (*Work in America*, 1973) and in France (Sudreau, 1975). This chapter will trace the history of the third Industrial Revolution and the role of the value systems of the various parties involved. Research in various national subsidiaries of a multinational corporation will be described, demonstrating occupational differences among these value systems together with their consequences for the strategy of the revolution.

## The History of the Humanization Revolution

Like every revolution, this third Industrial Revolution had its forerunners. As early as 1847, Karl Marx and Friedrich Engels in the *Communist Manifesto* made the prophetic statement:

> Owing to the extensive use of machinery and to division of labor, the work of the proletarians has lost all individual character and, consequently, all

charm for the workman. He becomes an appendage of the machine, and it is only the simplest, most monotonous, and most easily acquired knack that is required of him. (trans. from Thompson & Tunstall, 1971, p. 241)

There is more about this in Marx's (1844/1966) early Parisian manuscripts. In their later work, Marx and Engels did not follow up on this aspect of the first Industrial Revolution. They probably assumed that it would be corrected with a change of ownership of the means of production. In the meantime we have seen that in countries with state ownership the dehumanization of work has been worse than in those with private ownership (e.g., Vilmar, 1973, pp. 115ff).

Frederick W. Taylor's "scientific management" in the first two decades of the 20th century became the leading ideology of the first Industrial Revolution. Taylor saw it as being in the interests of the workers themselves, and to the extent that the workers shared in the increased wealth that scientific management made possible, he was undoubtedly right. But even in Taylor's days in the United States there were academic critics who pointed to the dangers of Taylorism for the workers' real interests and life situation. In 1915 two books against Taylorism appeared, by Horace B. Drury and Robert F. Hoxie (George, 1972, pp. 123-124).[1] The Hoxie-Taylor dispute coincided with the struggle toward unionization of U.S. labor. Taylor was against unionism, Hoxie in favor of it. Hoxie and unionism lost at the time; the post-World War I economic boom gave Taylorism its chance. Many of the disastrous effects on workers against which Hoxie had warned surfaced in the subsequent economic depression of the 1930s and they led to the New Deal legislation in the United States that reinforced unionization. But U.S. unions maintained a Tayloristic interest in the economic rewards of work rather than its impact on the worker. The latter issue was much more salient to U.S. academics and enlightened business leaders after the research of Elton Mayo and the birth of the human relations ideology in the 1920s and 1930s (Bartell, 1976). The human relations ideology can be seen as a forerunner of the third Industrial Revolution, but until 1945 it tinkered mainly with the symptoms of worker alienation rather than with the problem itself. The most eloquent pre-World War II criticism of Taylorism came not from the academics but from an artist, Charles Chaplin, in his 1936 film *Modern Times*.

After 1945 there were some signs of a break with Taylorism in the United States; for example, in 1948 the results of the wartime "job enlargement" experiments at IBM in Endicott were published (Richardson & Walker, 1948). This countercurrent was quickly swept away by the postwar economic boom and the advent of the second Industrial Revolution, which led to an even more powerful neo-Taylorism (Kirsch, 1973). The critics of the system this time were found in Europe rather than in the United States. In France, the leading anti-Taylorist from this period is Georges Friedmann (1946/1954, 1950/1963, 1956/1964); in Great Britain, after 1951 the Tavistock Institute started to develop its sociotechnical concepts (E. J. Miller, 1976). A pioneer of the third Industrial Revolution who, unfortunately, remained virtually unknown outside the borders of his own small country, is the Dutch Jesuit Father A. M. Kuylaars,[2] who published a book on intrinsic job satisfaction in 1951. In its English summary he stated:

> Labor is an activity exercised by man as an economic being. As an *economic* activity it is a means of the economic system, it is a factor of production and as such it produces, together with other factors of production, goods and services which are the conditions of the life worthy of human beings. In this respect labor is *externally* productive. As a *human* activity labor is one of the ends of the economic system, because man needs to work. Man needs labor as an occupation which in more than one sense gives meaning and content to his life. Besides, man needs the guidance and social compulsion which are conditioned by labor. Especially owing to this latter circumstance labor has a unique function which practically cannot be replaced by anything else. As a human activity labor is also *internally* productive, that is to say it is directly a personal enrichment for the worker. Therefore the economic system has to provide work which is both internally and externally productive. As to the former, certain necessary conditions will be required with regard to the quantity and quality of the work. (Kuylaars, 1951, pp. 217-218)

Kuylaars's conclusions (which were supported by participant observation and interview data) contain a distinction between external and internal productivity of labor at the level of society. A parallel distinction at the level of the individual (extrinsic versus intrinsic satisfaction and motivation) was developed in the United States about 10 years later, following the formulation of a two-factor theory of motivation by Herzberg et al. (1959). The U.S. approaches to the humanization of work have ever since been geared to individual jobs rather than to social systems (job enrichment, participative management). In Europe, on the contrary, humanization has been seen more as a problem affecting social systems or even society as a whole (sociotechnical system development, work restructuring). In the 1970s, the term "quality of working life" became current on both sides of the Atlantic, and sociotechnical reform concepts received some attention in the United States.

## The Dynamics
## of the Humanization Revolution

In the dynamics of political revolutions one usually finds four interest groups: a ruling elite (the "top dogs"); a revolutionary elite; an oppressed mass (the "underdogs"); and large numbers of others not directly involved, such as various classes in the middle and minorities. In the revolution toward humanization of work, we can distinguish the same four groups:

1. The ruling elite consists of employers and top management, and sometimes the union leadership. The ruling elite reflects the impact of another revolution, the "managerial revolution" (Burnham, 1941/1962): It consists of a majority of professional managers (technocrats) and a shrinking minority of owners (at least in the most developed countries).
2. The revolutionary elite consists of the "humanizers": academics, management consultants, some politicians, some professionals and junior managers in work organizations, some union leaders, almost without exception people with a higher professional education.
3. The oppressed mass consists of workers performing dehumanizing, alienating tasks.
4. The others are workers with nonalienating tasks (see for example, Blauner, 1964). Of course there is no consensus on which tasks are alienating and which are not. In Chapter 7 I will even label the tasks of certain managers in a large multinational corporation headquarters as alienating. Also, the others include migrant workers brought in to perform tasks felt by the local population as alienating, and these operate at least initially from an entirely different frame of reference.

The humanizing revolution resembles most political revolutions in that the initiative and the dominant values of the movement are on the side of the revolutionary elite and not of the alienated workers, who rarely demand humanization of their jobs (Hespe & Wall, 1976). Humanization efforts are generally the result of a peaceful power struggle between humanizers and the ruling elite. As in the case of other innovations, successful humanization experiments tend to be the outcome of a coalition between a power holder and an expert (see Witte, 1973; the German terms are *Machtpromotor* and *Fachpromotor*). The revolution remains at best a palace revolution. This is because both humanizers and ruling elite hold values quite different from the alienated workers, as I will now illustrate with research data.

# The Work-Related
# Values of the Various Parties

Within subsidiaries of a large multinational corporation, data were collected on work-related values as measured by the importance (in an "ideal" job) that people, when presented with paper-and-pencil questionnaires, attribute to different work goals. In the previous chapter I showed that the ranking of average importance of work goals varies strongly with the respondents' occupation and education level (see Table 2.3).[3] Considerable differences in goal ranking occurred between managers, professionals, skilled workers (including technicians), clerks, and unskilled workers.

In terms of the interest groups in the humanization revolution identified in the previous section, the values of the managers are closest to those of the ruling elite; the values of the professionals are closest to those of the revolutionary elite (the humanizers); the skilled workers and technicians represent the nonalienated part of the work force, whereas clerks and unskilled workers represent the "oppressed," those involved in often alienating tasks. In Table 2.3, there is *no overlap* between the most important goals for the professionals, for the clerks, and for the unskilled workers. There is overlap between the values of professionals, managers, and skilled workers with regard to the importance of job content. There is also overlap between the values of managers, skilled workers, and clerks on the importance of interpersonal relations. There is overlap between skilled and unskilled workers on the importance of security and earnings.

The values explicit in humanization efforts tend to be in the areas of job content and learning: values that a priori are more salient to the humanizers than to those to be humanized. Only in the European, sociotechnical current of humanization do we find stress on interpersonal relations, which according to the above corresponds more to the a priori values of skilled workers and clerks. Humanization efforts do not as a rule stress the goals most salient to the unskilled: physical working conditions, security, earnings, and benefits.

It is evident that the scoring of work goals on paper-and-pencil questionnaires, on which the numbers in Table 2.3 are based, leads to answers that contain a component of social desirability. People respond in terms of what they consider socially desirable in their reference group. Saleh and Singh (1973) have shown that in Canada the answers of low-income employees on work goal importance questions reflect the occupational levels of their father: the higher the skill level of the father's profession, the more the children stressed the importance of job content, learning, recognition, and advancement. Pennings (1970) has shown that in the Netherlands the answers of low-level white-collar workers on such questions reflect the promotion rates in their unit and therefore the group with which they identify: superiors or peers. The values expressed in the scores of Table 2.3 are thus not individual values, but reference group, or social class values. In other publications I have shown that they also differ by country: They contain a national cultural component (Hofstede, 1980, 1991). What the data demonstrate, therefore, is that the values of the humanizers' reference groups are very different from those of the alienated workers' reference groups.

## The Similarity of Human Nature

Another, more indirect way of measuring the relative importance of various work goals is to determine (also through paper-and-pencil questionnaires) the level of respondents' satisfaction with the fulfillment of each work goal and some overall satisfaction with their employment situation. Those work goals for which, across a category of respondents, the satisfaction is most strongly correlated with overall satisfaction can be considered as the most important ones and vice versa.

For different subpopulations of respondents from the multinational business corporation mentioned before (Hofstede, 1976b, section 8), I compared the ranking of the correlation coefficients between goal satisfaction and overall satisfaction to the ranking of the importance respondents consciously attached to the same work goals. Table 3.1 summarizes the results of this study. The subpopulations used are:

1. 4,260 college-educated sales persons from 33 different countries around the world, surveyed in 1972
2. 6,622 college-educated systems analysts from the same 33 countries, surveyed in 1972
3. 2,522 college-educated administrative and technical office professionals from 18 European countries, surveyed in 1969
4. 5,506 clerical and secretarial employees from 18 European countries, surveyed in 1969
5. 698 semiskilled machine operators in small manufacturing plants in 12 European countries, surveyed in 1969
6. 1,561 administrative and technical managers in offices in 18 European countries, surveyed in 1969

**TABLE 3.1**  Goal Ranking for Six Occupational Categories

A.  Based on Self-Rated Importance

| | Nonmanagers | | | | | |
| | Professionals | | | | Semiskilled | |
| Goal | Sales | Systems | Office | Clerks | Operators | Managers |
|---|---|---|---|---|---|---|
| Training | 6 | 2 | 1 | 6 | 14 | 7 |
| Challenge | 1 | 1 | 2 | 4 | 11 | 1 |
| Freedom | 3 | 3 | 6 | 5 | 12 | 4 |
| Use of skills | 5 | 4 | 3 | 3 | 9 | 5 |
| Advancement | 4 | 9 | 5 | 10 | 13 | 6 |
| Recognition | 7 | 7 | 9 | 7 | 7 | 10 |
| Earnings | 2 | 6 | 8 | 11 | 5 | 8 |
| Cooperation | 10 | 8 | 4 | 1 | 4 | 3 |
| Manager | 9 | 10 | 7 | 2 | 3 | 2 |
| Personal time | 8 | 5 | 10 | 12 | 8 | 11 |
| Security | 12 | 12 | 13 | 9 | 1 | 9 |
| Desirable area | 11 | 11 | 11 | 13 | 10 | 12 |
| Benefits | 13 | 14 | 14 | 14 | 6 | 14 |
| Physical conditions | 14 | 13 | 12 | 8 | 2 | 13 |

B.  Based on Correlation Between Goal Satisfaction and Overall Satisfaction

| | Nonmanagers | | | | | |
| | Professionals | | | | Semiskilled | |
| Goal | Sales | Systems | Office | Clerks | Operators | Managers |
|---|---|---|---|---|---|---|
| Training | 8 | 9 | 8 | 9 | 11 | 8 |
| Challenge | 1 | 1 | 4 | 3 | 3 | 6 |
| Freedom | 4 | 7 | 7 | 8 | 12 | 9 |
| Use of skills | 6 | 3 | 2 | 4 | 6 | 3 |
| Advancement | 3 | 5 | 3 | 2 | 1 | 2 |
| Recognition | 5 | 4 | 5 | 5 | 4 | 5 |
| Earnings | 2 | 2 | 1 | 1 | 2 | 1 |
| Cooperation | 10 | 8 | 10 | 12 | 8 | 10 |
| Manager | 7 | 6 | 6 | 7 | 5 | 4 |
| Personal time | 12 | 12 | 12 | 11 | 13 | 12 |
| Security | 9 | 10 | 9 | 6 | 9 | 7 |
| Desirable area | 14 | 13 | 14 | 13 | 14 | 13 |
| Benefits | 11 | 11 | 11 | 10 | 7 | 11 |
| Physical conditions | 13 | 14 | 13 | 14 | 10 | 14 |
| Rank correlation (rho) from A to B | .87 | .59 | .57 | .14 | .07 | .53 |

In the surveys from 1972 on, the number of goals was reduced to 14. Therefore, only these 14 goals are listed in Table 3.1 (as compared with 19 in Table 2.1).

From Table 3.1 it becomes evident that patterns of correlations between work goal satisfaction and overall satisfaction vary much less by occupation[4] than the direct measures of work goal importance from Table 2.1. Regardless of the occupation and educational level of the respondents, earnings, advancement, challenge, use of skills, and recognition are always among the six work goals whose satisfaction is most correlated with overall satisfaction.

The bottom line in Table 3.1 shows rank correlation coefficients (Spearman's rho) between the ranks of the 14 goals in Part A and in Part B. The two rankings are almost identical (rho = .87) for the salespersons, moderately similar (rho = .59, .57, and .53) for the other professionals and for the managers, but entirely different (rho = .14 and .07) for the clerks and semiskilled operators.

In a study of a representative sample of the U.S. working population, Barnowe, Mangione, and Quinn (1973) obtained a similar result: They found that job characteristics associated with overall satisfaction differed only marginally for more and less educated workers. For both categories, job characteristics associated with job challenge contributed most to overall satisfaction.

The two measures of work goal importance (self-rated importance and the correlation of goal satisfaction with overall satisfaction) do not, therefore, cover the same thing. Earlier research on the equivalence of these two measures had led to contradictory results—some studies found the two measures to be equivalent, some not—but the researchers did not establish the relationship between the nature of the jobs studied and the equivalence of the measures (Hofstede, 1976b, p. 23). My data show that the two measures lead to more or less similar results for professionals and managers but to very different results for clerks and unskilled workers (there is also a significant country effect; see Hofstede, 1980).

One way of explaining the difference between goal-overall satisfaction correlations and self-rated goal importance is that when consciously rating the importance of a work goal, we do so in terms of a total *life* self-concept that is not necessarily the same as *job* satisfaction. For clerks and unskilled workers, the two obviously do not correspond at all. For one thing, the feasibility to them of experiencing satisfaction on the job is relatively low (see for example, Shepard, 1973). The high correlation between a work goal and overall job satisfaction not only means that when the goal is satisfied, satisfaction is high, but also that when the goal is dissatisfied, job satisfaction is low. If people believe that the chances of satisfying a work goal such as challenge are poor, they may in their conscious importance ratings be led to deemphasize it: This is a "maximin" strategy (maximize their minimum job satisfaction) that is more logical than a "maximax" strategy that may lead to a "minimin" solution. Arthur Kornhauser, in a study of Detroit automobile workers in the 1950s wrote:

> Our basic explanation emphasizes the common goals, the fact that workers at different occupational levels share fundamentally similar wants but are confronted by decidedly dissimilar opportunities for satisfying these wants. . . . A most important example is seen in the tendency of men to accommodate their aspirations to their appraisal of the opportunities open to them—hence the frequently commented on "wantlessness" of the poor. . . . Industrial workers, like all the rest of us, are caught in the horns of the dilemma: if they want *too much* relative to what they are prepared to strive for with some degree of success, the result is defeat and frustration; if they want *too little*, the consequence is a drab existence devoid of color, exhilaration and self-esteem. (1965, pp. 269-270)

Also, our life space contains more than work alone. A work goal will be evaluated by its effect on our family, our leisure, our status in peer groups or other reference groups, and our self-image as well. The reference group is very important: Personal values are influenced by group norms and they reflect what the group considers desirable. This applies to unskilled workers as well as to managers and professionals. The latter fairly consistently rate "earnings" as less important than it appears to be according to its correlation with overall job satisfaction: For them, strongly stressing "earnings" is evidently socially undesirable.

To summarize, the correlation between goal satisfaction and overall satisfaction is a *psychological* measure related to the narrow issue of an individual's satisfaction on the job, whereas the self-rated importance scores are a *sociological* measure, related to an individual's total life space including nonwork aspects, his/her position in society, and so forth. The psychological measure is largely unconscious and unaffected by social desirability. The sociological measure is strongly affected by social desirability; we can even consider it a measure of the social desirability of items in the respondents' reference groups. Social psychologists try to avoid measures containing social desirability. Likert (1961, p. 195) thus considers importance ratings to be less valid (Hofstede, 1976b, p. 31). However, the two measures simply cover different things. Only for populations for whom the job occupies a central position in their life space, we see that the psychological and sociological measures coincide. This is the case for professionals and managers more than for clerks and unskilled workers.[5] The psychological measure shows the similarity of human nature regardless of occupation or country; the sociological measure shows the dissimilarity of human group and class norms that affect our conscious values.

## The Strategy and Ethics
## of the Humanization Revolution

The distinction between psychological and sociological measures of work values resolves a theoretical confusion and an ethical dilemma. The theoretical confusion is evident in, for example, a literature review by Hulin and Bloom (1968): They claim that worker culture (for instance, an urban versus a rural location) modifies the relationship between job level (job challenge) and satisfaction with work. My findings suggest that worker culture rather affects the job characteristics that workers will aspire for.

The ethical dilemma is whether it is right to engage workers in humanization experiences they have not asked for, and which will give them rewards that are low on their self-rated work goal importance scale. In fact this means that the humanizers and managers impose something that is desirable according to their own values on other people, in this case the workers. On the other hand, the research data presented in this chapter show that if humanization of work leads to increased job chal- lenge, this will increase the overall satisfaction level of the workers involved, even if they did not ask for it. At least, this applies at the col- lective level; it does not necessarily apply to each individual worker as individual reactions will depend on personal characteristics (Hackman & Lawler, 1971) and on the consequences of the increased job challenge for other parts of the worker's life space (Stjernberg, 1977). As, on average, humanization of work will bring the workers more good than harm, it is still defendable from an ethical point of view.

The humanization revolution, in my view, raises more strategic than ethical problems. We can identify both revolutionary and counterrevolu- tionary forces. Forces possibly supporting humanization are:

1. The conviction of the humanizers.
2. The ecological limits to growth—the impossibility for the world to continue according to the logic of earlier industrial revolutions, which becomes

evident to more and more responsible people and forces a restructuring of the economic system in which new values will perhaps have a chance.

3. The increasing rates of structural unemployment that push in the same direction.
4. The increase in educational opportunities in the developed countries, which affects people's values and expectations as to work content, as well as their ability to undertake more challenging tasks. This is reinforced by reduced economic growth rates that increase the intellectual surplus among workers.
5. The higher standard of living in affluent countries, which provides a satisfaction of basic needs to everybody. Workers' needs are becoming more diffuse (Habermas, 1973, p. 116) and less focused on material issues only. For a representative sample of the U.S. working population in 1969-1970, Herrick (1973) showed those under 30 to be less satisfied with their job throughout and putting more emphasis on job content.
6. The increasing research into and concern for mental health will identify some of the alienating jobs as bad health risks (see Chapter 4 of this book).

As counterrevolutionary forces I see:

1. The passivity of the alienated workers themselves, caused by the difference between their values and those of the humanizers.
2. The resistance of ruling elites to a loss of power in whatever area.
3. The inertia of the industrial and administrative establishment, especially in large organizations (such as multinational corporations; see Whitsett, 1976; but also the IBM Typewriter case in Chapter 5 of this book).
4. The uncertainty about what represents feasible new structures.
5. Technological "imperatives" in the development of work processes, which take no account of their impact on the nature of the work needed (see the Philips case in Chapter 6 of this book).

The role of labor unions in the humanization revolution is unclear. If worker education levels increase, unions will experience an influx of more educated members, which will affect the issues they are concerned with (Bairstow, 1974); humanization of work could thus receive more union attention than it has in the past. The question is whether the values of union leaders will be sufficiently adaptable. Some changes in union leadership attitudes with regard to work humanization have been reported from the United States (Foy & Gadon, 1976, p. 82) and from Germany (Gohl, 1976).

Humanizers, in general, tend to be hardly aware of the fact that they are a revolutionary elite, and even less aware of the strategic aspects of their revolution. There is a stress on techniques (Delplanque, 1976). The strategies necessary for humanization of work to advance are very likely different from one country to the next, as they depend on political, institutional, educational, and cultural factors.[6] Only history will show whether and where the third Industrial Revolution really happened.

## Discussion Questions

1. What does the chapter conclude about the difference between *life* satisfaction and *job* satisfaction?

2. The chapter opposes two measures of work goal importance, a "sociological" and a "psychological" one. What kind of survey questions are used by either measure, and what kind of mathematical treatment of the answer scores?

3. Is it ethically correct to humanize the jobs of unskilled workers who did not ask for it?

4. What implications do the findings of this chapter have for the industrial development of poor countries, including those of the former Soviet bloc?

## Notes

1. Extracts from Hoxie's book *Scientific Management and Labor* were republished in Klein (1976).

2. Dr. Kuylaars was later transferred to Indonesia by the Jesuit Order, where he worked as a management teacher; he changed his name to Kadarman.

3. Similar results have been obtained in various studies in the United States (Friedlander, 1965; Quinn, 1973; Shepard, 1971, pp. 101ff).

4. They also vary less by country; see Hofstede (1980, pp. 284-285).

5. In a comparison between countries, the psychological and sociological measures are more equivalent in Japan and Germany than in France and the Netherlands, pointing to a stronger centrality of work in people's life space in the former two countries (Hofstede, 1976b, p. 32; 1980, p. 285).

6. This is why the summit meeting of the European Community countries in Maastricht in December 1991 stumbled over the social paragraphs in the harmonization agreement.

# 4

# The Stress/Satisfaction Balance
# of Occupations

In a series of attitude surveys more than 50,000 employees from subsidiaries of a major multinational corporation in France, Germany, and Great Britain answered questions about their subjective stress level and their overall satisfaction with their work situation. The respondents could be divided into 38 occupations. Respondents in managerial occupations reported relatively high stress combined with high satisfaction; professionals and technicians reported low stress and low satisfaction. Sales representatives, clerks, and unskilled workers appeared to have the worst of both worlds: high stress and low satisfaction. A few exceptional occupations combined relatively low stress with high satisfaction. Studies from occupational medicine have suggested that harmful health effects of work stress are mitigated by high job satisfaction. The survey results reported in this chapter help explain why some occupations present more stress-related health hazards than others. These results have consequences for policies of work (re)structuring.

## Stress in the Work Situation:
## A Review of the Literature

There is probably no human being who does not feel stressed at times. Stress is a state of mind and of the body that is functional for the

This chapter was originally published under the title "Occupational Determinants of Stress and Satisfaction," in B. Wilpert and A. R. Negandhi (Eds.), *Work Organization Research: European and American Perspectives,* Kent, OH: Kent State University Press, 1978, pp. 233-252. Reprinted with permission of Kent State University Press.

preparation for aggression in animals (including *Homo sapiens*). Stress can be released through acts of aggression. When social norms forbid showing aggression, modern humans must cope with their stress in different ways.

A body of research reports show that within the work environment people in lower status jobs (especially unskilled workers) have poorer physical and mental health than those in higher status jobs (professionals or managers).[1] A study from France (Desplanques, 1973) reports the life expectancy of unskilled workers at age 35 to be 7 years less than that of higher managers, self-employed professionals, and elementary school teachers (the latter seem to have the most healthy occupation in the country). That the lower life expectancy of the unskilled in France is not only a matter of poorer hygiene and physical conditions is proven in the same study by an analysis of death causes: Unskilled agricultural and industrial workers show by far the highest suicide rates of any occupation, almost twice the national average. In a classic study in the Netherlands (Vertin, 1954), it was found that the rate of peptic ulcers among workers was negatively correlated with the skill levels in their jobs. In the United States Kornhauser (1965) used data from interviews with Detroit automobile workers in the 1950s to show that the mental health of the interviewees also decreased with the skill levels in their jobs.

In 1962 Kasl and J. R. P. French postulated that low self-esteem was the crucial mediating variable explaining poor mental health for low-status jobs. Ten years later, J. R. P. French and R. D. Caplan (1972), studying the occurrence of heart disease, considered job tension and low job satisfaction as alternative risk factors next to low self-esteem, and they concluded that job dissatisfaction was probably the most powerful risk factor. In a survey of reasons for absenteeism among 2200 Dutch workers, Gadourek (1965) also found a relationship between job satisfaction and health. In short, there is considerable evidence that people in lower status jobs have increased risks of poorer physical and mental health. It is not fully clear how much of this is due to pure stress, how much to low job satisfaction, and how much to other causes.

Another extensive body of research has dealt with stress, satisfaction, and health of those in medium and higher status jobs: clerks, professionals, and managers of various levels. Stress for these groups has been related in U.S. studies to role conflict and role ambiguity (Kahn & Quinn, 1970; Kahn, Wolfe, Quinn, Snoek, & Rosenthal, 1964; Seeman, 1953). J. R. P. French and R. D. Caplan (1972) in a study of a U.S. space flight center found that administrators (managers) experienced more stress than engineers or scientists. R. H. Miles (1976) in a questionnaire survey of U.S. laboratory professionals showed that role conflict was concentrated among those involved in "integration and boundary-spanning activities." These were the managers, group leaders, and appointed "integrators." On the other hand, Kets de Vries, Zaleznik, and Howard (1975), in a large questionnaire survey of a Canadian service organization, found that nonmanagerial professionals and people in staff roles reported more stress related health problems than managers in spite of their assumed lower amount of role conflict. They suggest two possible explanations: Either managers have a stronger tendency to deny health problems (an explanation they reject) or the higher job satisfaction of the manager group, which was shown by the survey, compensated for the greater amount of role conflict.

There is other evidence that within the higher status job categories those at the top levels are both more satisfied and healthier. The fact that people at upper hierarchical levels show greater job satisfaction was found to apply universally in 50 industrial companies in five countries by Tannenbaum, Kavcic, Rosner, Vianello, and Wieser (1974, p. 132). Several medical studies show that health problems are more frequent among the lower than among the higher management categories. Vertin (1954) found more peptic ulcers among Dutch foremen (lower level managers) than among workers, but in the United States at least, not only workers but also executives (higher managers) showed lower frequencies of peptic ulcers than foremen (Dunn & Cobb, 1962). Kasl and J. R. P. French (1962, p. 70) quote research showing that for heart diseases, too, first-line managers and nonmanagerial clerks had higher illness and mortality rates than top-level executives. Also, nonprofessionals had higher rates than professionals. The first-line manager finds him- or herself in a "double bind" situation (Zaleznik, Ondrack, & Silver, 1970, p. 127). Jenkins (1971, p. 308) in an extensive review of psychologic and social precursors of heart disease, concluded that "stress" and "dissatisfaction" in their effects on heart disease should be considered in conjunction. Which positions in the status hierarchy of an organization are most costly in terms of cardiovascular health may also depend on the societal context, and Jenkins warns against generalizations from one society to another (p. 247).

A compensating factor for the adverse health effects of stress for the higher status occupations may also be the self-selection of those who choose such occupations, and who may better than others be able to cope with role conflict (Aldridge, 1970). Top management jobs attract certain personality types, with a frequency of those with "Type A" behavior traits (Friedman & Rosenman, 1975). The typical Type A person tries to do more and more things in less and less time; the opposite "Type B" persons are unhurried and patient. Type A people may like stress, but they are more likely to get coronary heart disease all the same (J. R. P. French & R. D. Caplan, 1972).

In summary, the literature reviewed suggests the following:

1. When examining the effect on people's physical and mental health, one should consider stress and job satisfaction in conjunction.
2. Occupational effects on people's physical and mental health vary for different types of occupations and may also vary within different sociocultural environments.
3. With regard to Point 2, there is some evidence that in developed, Western societies: (a) Unskilled-worker jobs are in an unfavorable position because of low job satisfaction combined with low opportunities for self-esteem, (b) clerical and lower managerial jobs are in an unfavorable position because of high role conflict and ambiguity, (c) higher managerial jobs are in a more favorable position because of higher job satisfaction in spite of the role conflict imposed by boundary-spanning activities, and (d) professional and skilled technical jobs are in a more favorable position because of a relative absence of role conflict and ambiguity. Such jobs provide more opportunities for enhancement of self-esteem.

## Subjective Stress:
## New Research Data

In a series of employee attitude surveys within a large multinational corporation operating in 66 countries (Hofstede, Kraut, & Simonetti, 1976), the following question was asked: "How often do you feel nervous or tense at work?" The precoded answers were:

1. I always feel this way.
2. Usually.
3. Sometimes.
4. Seldom.
5. I never feel this way.

This question is considered as a simple operationalization of subjective stress. It was borrowed from earlier surveys of managers in one large national subsidiary of the corporation's medical department. Researchers and management did not want to include purely medical questions in the regular employee attitude surveys, but the medical surveys had shown that across employee categories, answers to this general question correlated significantly with questions on medical symptoms. Among 13 departments totaling about 1500 respondents, mean scores on the "How often nervous or tense" question differed significantly,[2] and these mean scores correlated with mean scores on "How often are you bothered by having an upset stomach?"[3] but not with "Headaches" or "Trouble getting to sleep or staying asleep." Interestingly, mean scores on the "How often nervous or tense" question were *negatively* correlated with mean scores on "Do you have any particular physical or health problem now?"[4] suggesting that denial of health problems could also be part of the stress syndrome. For reasons of privacy the medical files showing the correlations between answers on the subjective stress question and answers on medical symptoms questions *across individuals within the departments* were not preserved. It was on the basis of these individual correlations that the "subjective stress" question had originally been selected for inclusion in the attitude surveys.

Answers on the "How often nervous or tense" question were available for virtually all employees of the corporation in 66 countries and in all kinds of occupations in research, development, manufacturing, administration, sales, and customer service (Hofstede, 1980, 1991). The surveys, in 18 different language versions, were taken between 1967 and 1973. Some occupations were surveyed twice during this period, others only once. The total number of responses available for analysis was about 116,000, from 88,000 different individuals. The overall distribution of answers is about normal:

| 1 | 2 | 3 | 4 | 5 | | |
|---|---|---|---|---|---|---|
| *Always* | *Usually* | *Sometimes* | *Seldom* | *Never* | | Standard |
| | | | | | Mean | Deviation |
| 4% | 17% | 47% | 26% | 6% | 3.13 | .90 |

An individual's answer on this question reflects the influence of at least four factors: personality, nonwork environment, work environment, and sociocultural environment. The respondent's mood of the moment will certainly play a role as well. The way in which the data were collected— through anonymous employee attitude surveys—prevented the measurement of personality and nonwork environment data, but the age brackets and gender of the respondents were known. Seniority brackets (length of service with the corporation) were also available. Seniority and age were obviously intercorrelated (at about the .60 level). An analysis of partial correlations for three large categories of respondents showed that the relationship of the "nervous or tense" scores was with seniority rather than with age.[5]

There is thus a tendency for more senior employees to score themselves as more nervous (see Table 4.1). The most likely explanation for

**TABLE 4.1** Mean Scores on the Question "How often do you feel nervous or tense at work?" by Sex and Seniority, for Two Large Categories of Respondents

| Mean Scores on "How Often Nervous, Tense" (1 = always, 5 = never) for | 15,000 Office Personnel | 14,000 Factory Personnel |
|---|---|---|
| Total personnel | 3.17 | 3.09 |
| Seniority less than 1 year | 3.43 | 3.30 |
| 1-3 years | 3.22 | 3.14 |
| 3-7 years | 3.10 | 3.07 |
| 7-15 years | 3.04 | 2.92 |
| More than 15 years | 2.98 | 2.99 |
| All men | 3.18 | 3.12 |
| All women | 3.12 | 2.99 |

this tendency is the fast rate of technological and organizational change in the corporation, which forces employees with many years of seniority to undertake tasks very different from those for which they were hired. Table 4.1 also shows that men tend to rate themselves as slightly less nervous than do women. The difference is again significant but small, and it is smaller in the office environment than in the factory environment. This latter difference is probably due to the kind of occupations in the factories in which most women are employed: To wit, the lower skilled production jobs, as will be shown later, are more stressful. In general, gender differences are difficult to separate from occupational differences, as women and men often do different jobs. For one occupation (technical experts) that is carried out by both men and women, the women scored slightly more nervous (3.20) than the men (3.28), but the difference was not statistically significant.

We see that even the apparent demographic differences in "nervous or tense" scores are likely to be due to work-related causes. More obvious work-related variables affecting the scores are departmental pressures of various kinds. For example, in one large office with about 350 persons divided into 23 working groups, group mean scores on the "nervous or tense" question varied between 2.69 and 3.56.[6] Discovering such group differences on this and other questions and feeding them back to the groups was in fact one of the main reasons for the surveys. Group pressures leading to such stress differences are very diverse and do not lend themselves to a macroanalysis.

The main organizational distinctions that do allow a macroanalysis are the *occupation* and the *country* of the respondents. The first reflects the influence of the task, the second the sociocultural environment. The data bank containing the survey data distinguishes 50 different occupations. On the basis of the literature reviewed in the first part of this chapter, significant differences in subjective stress between these occupations can be expected.

To determine the relative strength of the occupational versus the country effect, 10 occupations with widely varying required education levels and 10 countries in very different parts of the world were selected in such a way that all cells in this 10 × 10 matrix contained at least 20 respondents. The 100 mean scores were subjected to a two-way analysis of variance (ANOVA). This showed a strong country effect and a weaker, but still significant occupation effect, but no second-order Country × Occupation interaction effect. Country and occupation together accounted for 91% of the total variance in means. This analysis of variance therefore proved that mean stress scores by category (Country × Occupation) were fairly accurately predictable, in spite of considerable differences in answers among individual respondents. Because of the absence of an interaction effect, the mean scores could simply be predicted from the overall mean for the country (across all occupations) and the overall mean for the occupation (across all countries).

This is a confirmation of findings by Kraut and Ronen (1975, Table 5). They used the same stress measure for five countries and two occupations, and found country to be a strong and occupation a weaker but still significant predictor of stress scores. The strong country effect has been explored in a separate study (Hofstede, 1975-1976, resumed in 1980, 1991). The occupation effect will be analyzed below.

## Mapping Subjective Stress
## for 38 Occupations

Occupation means for the "How often nervous or tense?" question were compared for three large country subsidiaries in which all of these occupations were present: France, Germany, and Great Britain. In these countries, mean scores for 38 occupations represented by at least 15 respondents per country could be computed. The sample was stratified so that each of the three countries carried equal weight. For those occupations surveyed twice (in 1967-1970 and 1971-1973) the scores used were the arithmetical means between the scores for the two surveys. Data were added for one international group of 38 research professionals for which the nationality mix is about equivalent as far as its effect on the stress score level goes.

The resulting mean scores for the occupations are presented in Figure 4.1.[7] In this diagram, the 38 occupations have been divided into five main categories: managers (all people responsible for the work of others), salespersons and clerks (people with nonmanagerial but organizational/ administrative tasks), professionals (college-trained people with complex technical tasks), technicians and skilled workers (vocational school or equivalently trained people with somewhat less complex technical tasks), and unskilled workers.

Figure 4.1 clearly confirms the picture already extracted from the literature. The higher stress jobs are those of the unskilled workers, the managers, and the salespersons and clerks. The professional and technical jobs are relatively less stressful.

The diagram shows a number of interesting details:

1. In the category of unskilled workers there is a highly significant difference of .20 points between Unskilled Plant Workers B (production workers) and Unskilled Auxiliary Plant Workers. These groups had about equal qualifications and worked in the same environment, but the production workers were subject to an imposed work rhythm; the auxiliary workers filled jobs like transport hand, janitor, or storekeeper. The difference in tasks accounts for the difference in stress scores: Production workers report the highest stress (in fact, they are the single most stressed occupation among all 38). The skilled plant workers, who also worked in the same environment and were also involved in production, but in more complex tasks, were *not so highly* stressed; they scored at the same level as their unskilled auxiliary colleagues.

2. Sales representatives, who fulfill a typical boundary spanning role between the company and its customers, report high stress.

3. In the four categories managers, clerks, professionals, and technicians, factories (manufacturing plants) are always perceived as more stressful than laboratories (development and research). The least stress is felt by those laboratory professionals engaged in research rather than in development. In the office environment, the head office is particularly stressful (compare Chapter 7 of this book) and the data processing departments report the lowest stress.

## Relationships of Stress to Job Satisfaction

The results of the international attitude surveys of the particular multinational corporation were extensively factor-analyzed, but the question "How often do you feel nervous or tense at work?" did not

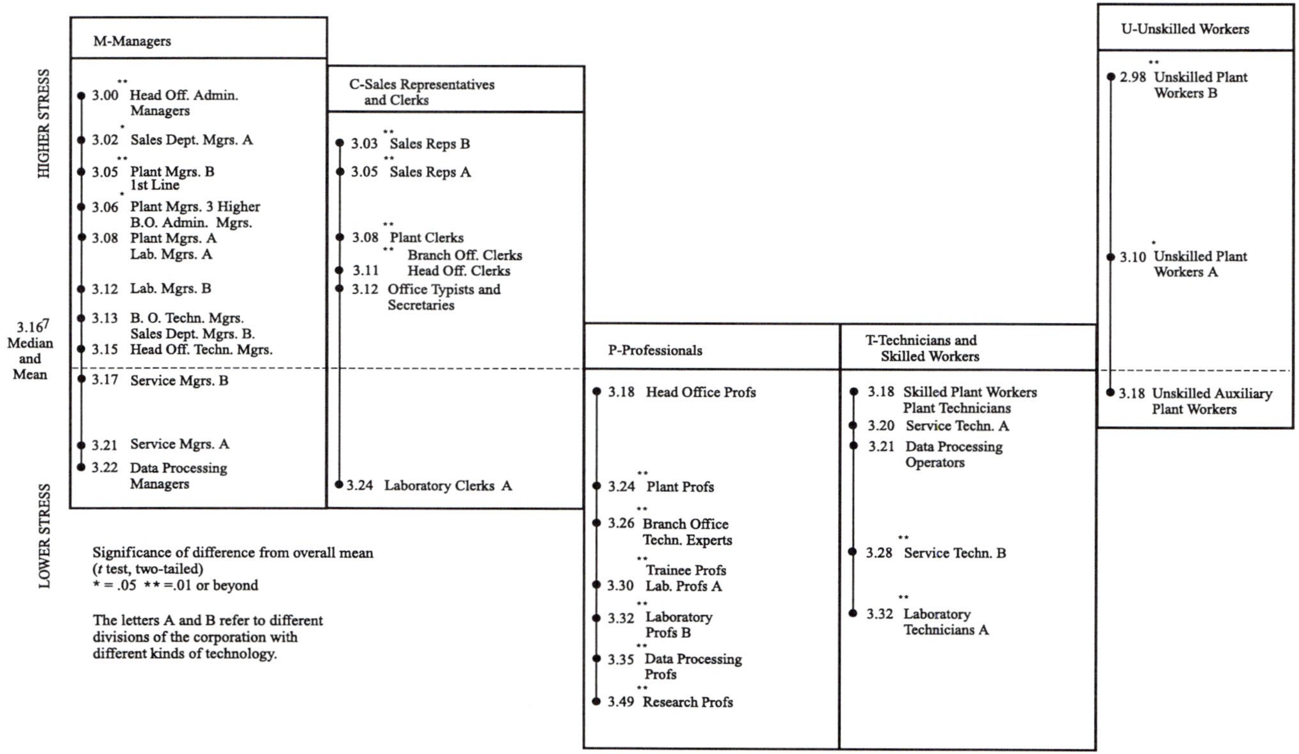

**Figure 4.1.** Subjective Stress Across 38 Occupations

**M-Managers**

- 3.00 Head Off. Admin. Managers **
- 3.02 Sales Dept. Mgrs. A *
- 3.05 Plant Mgrs. B **
- 3.06 Plant Mgrs. 3 Higher B.O. Admin. Mgrs. *
- 3.08 Plant Mgrs. A Lab. Mgrs. A
- 3.12 Lab. Mgrs. B
- 3.13 B. O. Techn. Mgrs. Sales Dept. Mgrs. B.
- 3.15 Head Off. Techn. Mgrs.
- 3.17 Service Mgrs. B
- 3.21 Service Mgrs. A
- 3.22 Data Processing Managers

HIGHER STRESS

3.167 Median and Mean

LOWER STRESS

Significance of difference from overall mean
(t test, two-tailed)
* = .05  ** = .01 or beyond

The letters A and B refer to different
divisions of the corporation with
different kinds of technology.

**C-Sales Representatives and Clerks**

- 3.03 Sales Reps B **
- 3.05 Sales Reps A **
- 3.08 Plant Clerks **
- 3.11 Branch Off. Clerks Head Off. Clerks **
- 3.12 Office Typists and Secretaries
- 3.24 Laboratory Clerks A

**P-Professionals**

- 3.18 Head Office Profs **
- 3.24 Plant Profs *
- 3.26 Branch Office Techn. Experts **
- 3.30 Trainee Profs Lab. Profs A *
- 3.32 Laboratory Profs B
- 3.35 Data Processing Profs **
- 3.49 Research Profs **

**T-Technicians and Skilled Workers**

- 3.18 Skilled Plant Workers Plant Technicians
- 3.20 Service Techn. A
- 3.21 Data Processing Operators
- 3.28 Service Techn. B **
- 3.32 Laboratory Technicians A **

**U-Unskilled Workers**

- 2.98 Unskilled Plant Workers B **
- 3.10 Unskilled Plant Workers A *
- 3.18 Unskilled Auxiliary Plant Workers

59

clearly belong to any factor (Hofstede et al., 1976, p. 23). It was weakly related to factors dealing with workload, security, physical conditions, interpersonal relations, intergroup relations, and preferring a specialist over a manager career.

For 33 different subpopulations (one occupation in one country, or one occupation across a number of countries), the first-order product-moment correlation coefficients of the "nervous or tense" scores with all other questions in the questionnaire were checked. The strongest consistent correlations were with items that in the factor-analytic study by Hofstede et al. (1976, p. 22) related to a factor called "workload." The median correlations across the 33 subpopulations between stress (feeling nervous or tense) and answers on questions associated with this factor were as follows:

Amount of work expected
    (too much/about right/prefer more)    $r = .25^{***}$
Satisfaction with personal time    $r = -.23^{***}$
Overtime (outside normal hours)    $r = -.13^{***}$

The signs of the correlation coefficients point in the obvious direction: Greater stress (feeling nervous) was associated with more work expected, less satisfaction with personal time (i.e., time for personal or family life), and more additional time spent on the job.[8]

On the basis of the literature review reported earlier in this chapter, it should be of particular interest to relate the subjective stress scores to some overall measure of job satisfaction. Kraut and Ronen (1975), in a study based on the use of the same questionnaire, related scores on subjective stress to the answers on a question on "overall satisfaction": "Considering everything, how would you rate your overall satisfaction in this company at the present time?" This question was scored on a 7-point scale from 1 = *completely satisfied* to 7 = *completely dissatisfied*.[9] Kraut and Ronen also compared the answers to the satisfaction with 14 different separate work goals.[10] For five countries and two occupations, they showed that work goals that contributed most to overall satisfaction contributed least to subjective stress and vice versa. The one work goal predicting by far the largest share of subjective stress variance was satisfaction with personal time ("sufficient time for your personal or family life").

In my own analysis of first-order correlation coefficients across 33 subpopulations, satisfaction with the following five work goals correlated consistently but weakly, negatively, with subjective stress:

| | |
|---|---|
| Personal time | $r = -.23^{***}$ |
| Cooperation | $r = -.17^{***}$ |
| Manager | $r = -.14^{***}$ |
| Security | $r = -.11^{***}$ |
| Physical conditions | $r = -.08^{***}$ |

So the relatively important contribution to subjective stress of "personal time" was confirmed in both studies.

Kraut and Ronen's finding that goals that contribute most to overall satisfaction contribute least to subjective stress does not necessarily mean that high satisfaction and low stress go together. The first-order correlations between stress scores and overall satisfaction scores show, for the 33 subpopulations, a median value of $r = -.11^{***}$, indicating a weak association of high stress with low overall satisfaction.[11] However, these negative correlations are based on scores of *individual* respondents. For the occupations pictured in Figure 4.1, I have also computed, in exactly the same way as for the stress scores, the mean occupational scores on "overall job satisfaction." These have been plotted against the stress scores in Figure 4.2, in which the letters M, C, P, T, and U correspond to the five categories of occupations in Figure 4.1. It is immediately evident from Figure 4.2 that across the 38 occupations, there is a correlation of high stress with *high* overall satisfaction.[12] This is a clear illustration of the fact that correlations between individuals within a more or less homogeneous subpopulation should not be extrapolated to correlations between subpopulation means within a larger population. This applies to occupations as well as to countries (see also Hofstede & Van Hoesel, 1976).

The dotted lines in Figure 4.2 divide the diagram across the gross mean values for subjective stress (computed from the 38 occupation means: 3.167 on a scale from 1 = *high stress* to 5 = *low stress*) and the gross mean value for overall job satisfaction (2.898 on a scale from 1 = *high satisfaction* to 7 = *low satisfaction*). In this way, four quadrants are created. The first quadrant (high satisfaction, high stress) contains 10 of the 14 managerial occupations and one group of sales representatives. The third quadrant, the opposite of the first (low satisfaction, low stress), contains six of the eight professional occupations and all six technician and skilled worker groups. The second quadrant, which seems to have the worst of both worlds (low satisfaction, high stress), contains five of the seven sales and clerical and two of the three unskilled worker occupations, plus one manager group (Laboratory Managers A). Finally, the fourth quadrant, which can be considered to have the best of both worlds (high satisfac-

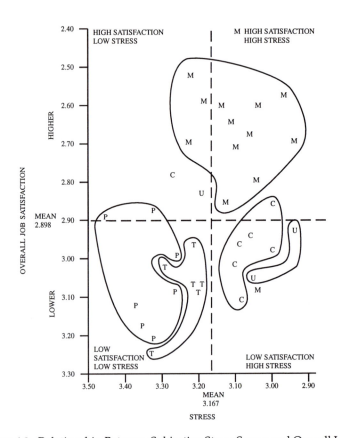

**Figure 4.2.** Relationship Between Subjective Stress Scores and Overall Job Satisfaction for 38 Occupational Categories in Three Countries

M = managers; C = sales representatives and clerks; P = professionals; T = technicians and skilled workers; U = unskilled workers.

tion, low stress), contains an odd mix: three groups of managers (Service A and B and Data Processing), laboratory clerks, unskilled auxiliary plant workers, trainee professionals, and research professionals.

## Conclusions:
## Three Levels of Stress-Satisfaction Balance

The Stress × Overall Satisfaction plot in Figure 4.2 has almost completely separated three groups of occupations:

Managers
Sales representatives, clerks, and unskilled workers
Professionals, technicians, and skilled workers

The distinction between the three groups is obviously based on the occupational role definitions and the organization structure of this particular corporation, and before generalizing to other work organizations we should be sure their role definitions are comparable. The data in Figure 4.2 come from three countries only—France, Germany, and Great Britain—but the fact that the analysis of variance showed no significant Country × Occupation interaction effect suggests that the same occupational differences can be expected in other countries as well. Because of the strong country effect mentioned above, we should still be careful with extrapolation to very different sociocultural environments.

The occupational differences found in Figure 4.2 can be compared to those in a classic study of organizational stress by Kahn et al. (1964). In this study, people in a national survey in the United States were asked to rate their changes in job satisfaction since they first started working. If the "less satisfied" were deducted from the "more satisfied" scores, the managers would have been the most positive group and the professionals and technicians the least positive, as in my findings. Kahn et al. (p. 144) also used a measure of job-related tension, but this differs from my subjective stress question; it is rather a list of areas of conflict between the individual and the organization. On this measure the professional and technical group showed the highest tension followed by managers, clerks, and salespersons. The unskilled came last. But because of the different way of measuring tension versus stress, the data from Kahn et al. complement rather than contradict mine. Because of the lesser involvement of the professionals and technicians in the organization, their greater conflict does not lead to as high a stress level as in the case of the more involved occupations.

The managerial occupations in this study include different levels. As the hierarchy forms a pyramid, the lower level managers are always more numerous than the higher ones, and as in the survey every person's opinion carries equal weight, the managers' attitudes shown in the survey are mainly representative for lower management. Only in the case of (manufacturing) Plant Managers B the data could be split into first-line (foremen) and higher level. The two categories hardly differed in stress scores, but the higher level managers were more satisfied. They were the single most satisfied occupation (2.42 against 2.62 for the first-line managers; the difference, tested with the *t* test, two-tailed, is significant at the .01 level). The higher satisfaction for the upper level managers confirms the findings by Tannenbaum et al. (1974) about the relationship between hierarchical level and job satisfaction. The high stress scores of managers can be interpreted as indicating frequent role conflicts. The negative consequences of these are partly, but probably not wholly, offset by increased job satisfaction, and less so at the first line of management than at the higher levels. The satisfaction score indicates the extent to which the aggression, generated by stress, can be constructively released in the job.

In any case, salespersons, clerks, and unskilled workers were worse off with regard to their stress-satisfaction balance than the managers. They experienced about the same level of stress, but with less job satisfaction to compensate for it. Their jobs offered fewer opportunities for stress release. It is in this group that the highest frequency of physical and mental health problems can be expected. The psychological situation of the sales representatives in this corporation was particularly unfavorable as they dealt with considerable uncertainty as to whether customers would buy or not, which affected both the organization and their own income and career prospects. Also, their workload fluctuations were negatively correlated with the success of the business: The worse the market situation, the harder they had to work and vice versa. This is the reverse of the work situation of the professionals and technicians whose workload fluctuations were positively correlated with the success of the business, a psychologically healthier state of affairs.

The problematic work situation of clerks and unskilled workers has of course been recognized in many countries and organizations and their work has been the object of attempts at humanization of work, like "work (re)structuring" and "job enrichment" (see Chapter 3). If successful, this should make their jobs technically more rewarding and move them over to the side of the technicians, that is, to the left in Figure 4.2. Another trend has consisted of attempts at "industrial democracy," at least the shop floor version of it: increasing workers' participation in decision making and thus giving them greater power. This would make their situation more similar to that of the managers, a move upward in Figure 4.2. However, we should not underestimate the amount of restructuring of the entire organization necessary to really eliminate the problem aspects of certain jobs. Wisner (1974/1975), a French ergonomist, has warned that jobs that are physiologically and psychologically burdensome will not become less so by "humanistic disguising." A comparison of the stress and satisfaction scores of Unskilled Plant Workers B and Unskilled Auxiliary Plant Workers shows that the latter are better off in both respects. The main distinction between workers from the two groups is the production pressure to which the former are exposed. It is unlikely that as long as the labor of some is a measurable bottleneck in the production system their jobs will move out of the high-stress corner.

The professionals, technicians, and skilled workers are in a different situation. They are clearly under lower stress and role conflict, and there is evidence that they suffer less from psychosomatic health hazards (see, for example, Kasl & J. R. P. French, 1962, p. 69). Their lower stress level allows them a lesser involvement with the organization, which explains why their lower satisfaction level does not harm them. Hall and Mansfield (1971) show how development engineers coped with increased pressure from the organization by increased alienation from it. Their tasks, however, allowed them this alienation: They could take pride in the tasks themselves and identify with their profession rather than with the organization. Their value system protected them against an excess of anxiety caused by forces within the organization (Levinson & Weinbaum, 1970).

The happy few occupations in the upper left fourth quadrant of Figure 4.2 (high satisfaction, low stress) contain three groups of managers of professionals or managers of technicians, in a helping role toward others inside or outside the organization (service and data processing). The psychologically favorable position of the customer service function in this corporation was also revealed in another study (see Chapter 7 of this book). The quadrant further contains the trainee professionals, who will undoubtedly shift toward the attitudes of their senior colleagues afterward; the research professionals, who are a small and privileged elite; and interestingly, the unskilled auxiliary plant workers and the laboratory clerks. The latter two groups probably use other unskilled workers and other clerks as reference groups and recognize that they are better off. They are marginal groups in their own work environment: None of the large occupational groups is found in the upper left quadrant.

The mapping of occupations by stress level and satisfaction level shows again one of the truisms of organizational life: that you can't have your cake and eat it too. If you want high satisfaction, be a manager; but you will have to pay for it in higher stress. If you want low stress, be a professional or technician; but you will have to pay for it in lower overall satisfaction. If you are quite unlucky you may neither have your cake nor eat it, which means you will get both higher stress and lower satisfaction. To avoid making this conclusion too pessimistic, I should remind the reader that the actual experience of a person in an occupation depends to a large extent on factors outside the organization as well. Fortunately, humans are very adaptable animals and many of us cope extremely well with less than ideal occupational conditions.

## Discussion Questions

1. What does this chapter suggest about assembly line work?

2. Why do higher level management jobs tend to be healthier than first-line management jobs?

3. Professionalization means providing a group of workers with a professional identity and professional norms. What does this chapter suggest for the effect of professionalization on (a) job satisfaction and (b) job stress?

4. Why is the correlation of the scores of individuals within a group different from the correlation of group means within a larger population?

## Notes

1. This is shown, for example, in the U.S. studies by Hollingshead and Redlich (1958; re-analyzed by S. M. Miller & Mishler, 1970), by Kasl and J. R. P. French (1962), and by R. D. Caplan, Cobb, J. R. P. French, Harrison, and Pinneau (1975); a review is given by Zaleznik et al. (1970).

2. Chi-square = 41.3*** with 12 degrees of freedom.

3. Spearman rank correlation coefficient rho = .49*.

4. Spearman rank correlation coefficient rho = −.48*.

5. Holding age constant, the correlations between "nervous or tense" and seniority vary between −.12*** and −.13***, which was statistically significant, but weak. The correlations with age, holding seniority constant, were virtually zero.

6. The differences between the extreme groups are statistically significant in spite of the small size of the groups (9 and 13 persons; difference of means tested by $t$ test, two-tailed, significant at .05 level).

7. The same occupational categories have been used for various comparisons in Hofstede (1980, e.g., Figure 2.6 on p. 79) for comparing response set in answers to "work goals" questions.

8. The significance of these correlations has been determined by the sign test: In all three cases the correlations carried the same sign for all 33 subpopulations.

9. This is the same question as used in Chapter 3 for determining the strength of correlation between work goal satisfaction and overall satisfaction (Table 3.1B).

10. These are the same work goals on which the importance rankings in Chapter 3 were based (Table 3.1A and B).

11. A similar finding (a correlation of −.26***) has been reported by R. H. Miles and Petty (1975), but their measure of stress also included other items.

12. Spearman rank correlation coefficient rho = .44**.

# 5

# Case Study

## *IBM Typewriter Assembly*

This case describes the development of the production methods in a part of the IBM manufacturing plant in Amsterdam from 1969 to 1977. Short-cycle tasks involving little skill and initiative were changed into much more complex ones, exercised in semiautonomous "miniline" groups of 20 people. Next to remarkably positive effects on productivity and quality, the change-over had a dramatic impact on the behavior of the employees. However, in the long run some of the innovations were abolished because the need for stable groups conflicted with the plant's strategy of volume-planning flexibility. Nevertheless the case is a successful example of humanization of work.

## The IBM Typewriter Plant
## in Amsterdam

One Tuesday night in December 1969, the lights were burning in the office of Ad Bakker, Mechanical Products group manager at the IBM typewriter plant in Amsterdam, the Netherlands. Six men sat around the

This chapter was intended to be used as a basis for class discussion rather than to illustrate effective or ineffective handling of an administrative situation. Reprinted with the permission of INSEAD. Copyright © 1974 CEDEP (European Centre for Continuing Education) and INSEAD (European Institute of Business Administration), Fontainebleau, France.

table—Bakker and the five managers reporting to him (see the organization chart in Figure 5.1). As most of the plant worked only the day shift, they had chosen the evening for a quiet discussion. Ever since April, they had met virtually every Tuesday night in this way, and some of their meetings lasted long past midnight.

They were talking about the future production methods and internal organization of the Typewriter Assembly department, considering both present problems and future production requirements. Bakker had taken over the management of the Mechanical Products group as of January 1, 1969. He was 33 at the time, with a degree in mechanical engineering and 7 years' experience with IBM. He had worked for 5 years as an engineer on typewriter assembly problems, and for 2 years he had managed the assembly department of the Electronic Products group of the plant. When Bakker took over Mechanical Products, he had brought with him a new production control manager and one of the assembly managers, Wim Smits. Smits was 30 years old with an engineering background very similar to that of Bakker. The other members of the management team had been with the group longer.

International Business Machines, or rather its Dutch subsidiary, Internationale Bedrijfsmachine Maatschappij N.V., founded its plant in Amsterdam in 1950. During its first decade, the plant assembled a variety of IBM machines, mostly for the local market. In 1961, IBM redistributed its production internationally on a product-by-plant basis. The Amsterdam plant, then employing 600 people, became the main European production center for IBM's Office Products division. The products were typewriters—in particular the IBM 72 model with rotating "golf ball" type head—composers, magnetic tape typewriters, and magnetic tape composers. Typewriters and composers together represented the plant's Mechanical Products group. The composer was a large typewriter of complicated design used mainly in the printing industry, which could produce left-and-right adjusted text before computer word processing had been introduced. Both types of magnetic tape machine were produced in the plant's Electronic Products group. They consisted of typewriters connected to a small electronic system that recorded the typed text on magnetic tape or cards and allowed automatic duplication and local corrections without retyping the entire text.

The plant grew fast. It moved into new buildings twice, in 1959 and in 1967. Both buildings were located at the southwestern outskirts of Amsterdam, near the road to Schiphol airport. In mid-1969, the plant employed about 1,600 persons.

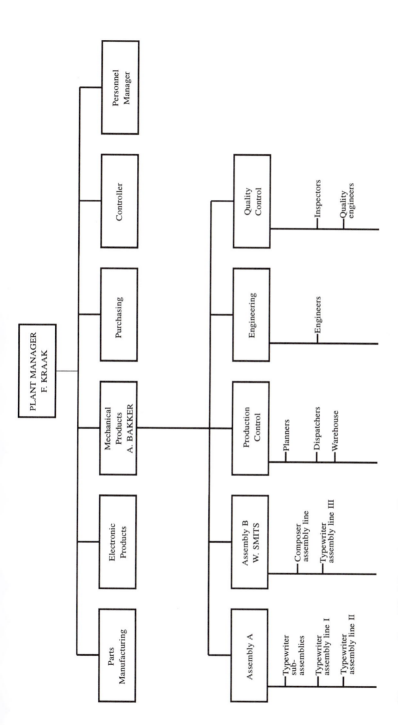

**Figure 5.1.** Simplified Organization Chart of the IBM Amsterdam Plant in Mid-1969

## Dilemmas of the
## Typewriter Assembly Lines

Typewriters were, both in numbers of machines and in money value, the plant's main product. The IBM 72 typewriter consisted of about 2,500 distinct parts, some produced in the Parts Manufacturing department of the plant, some imported from other IBM plants, and some subcontracted to independent vendors. Assembling the parts into a complete typewriter took 4 to 5 person-hours of direct work per typewriter; 90% of the assembly cost was labor cost. The Typewriter Assembly department employed, by mid-1969, about 280 people in direct (i.e., production) jobs, together assembling about 350 typewriters per day.

When Bakker was named Mechanical Products group manager, he knew that in the Typewriter Assembly department he was inheriting a problem. Over the past year the department had lagged behind production targets in both quantity and quality. Absenteeism due to illness had reached a record level of 6.5%, in itself not extravagant, but higher than ever before. Labor turnover was at an unprecedented level of 30% per year. Bakker inferred that employee morale was low. The composer assembly line, on the contrary, seemed to enjoy high morale, but unfortunately this line employed a much smaller number of people. Working methods in the Typewriter Assembly department had originally been modeled after the IBM Office Products division mother plant in Lexington, Kentucky, in the United States. Operators sat at tables on either side of a long roller conveyor, on which products in process were pushed forward to the next person, leaving a buffer of some machines in between. Engineers had divided the total assembly operation into a number of elements of, as far as possible, the same duration, corresponding to the number of operators. When this system started in 1962 there had been about 40 operators on the line; at that time each operator had to work about 30 minutes on each machine. The total assembly time per typewriter had been close to 20 hours. Subsequently, production had grown enormously. Part of the increase had been obtained by methods improvements affecting both the design of the machine and the way of assembling, reducing the assembly time from 20 to 4-5 hours per machine. The number of operators along the line had also been increased. Consequently the cycle time of the job of each operator had been decreased drastically. The short cycles allowed the use of less skilled personnel and decreased the learning time for new operators.

In 1969 the assembly department operated with 2 long lines of 65 to 70 operators each (Lines I and II in Figure 5.2) with cycle times of about 3.5 minutes and a learning time for new operators of about 3 months. In

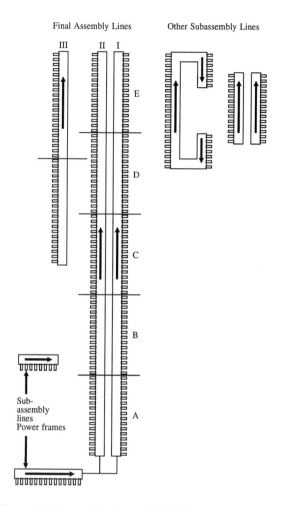

**Figure 5.2.** Layout of Typewriter Assembly, 1969

addition there was a third line (the most recently created one) of 40 operators. For managing purposes Lines I and II were each divided into 5 sections (A through E). One foreman (at IBM always called "first-line manager" or just "manager") was in charge of both A sections (from Line I and Line II), another of both B sections, and so forth. In this way not only the operators but also the foremen were specialized at a limited number of assembly tasks. Line III was managed by two foremen. The department also included three subassembly lines for three basic sub-units of the machine, with even shorter work cycles than the long final assembly lines. These were usually staffed by women. The simplest subassembly line had a cycle time of 1.5 minutes, and among operators it was informally known as the "idiots line." Each subassembly line had its foreman. Each foreman in the assembly department was assisted by his own "key man," the IBM term for a charge hand.

## The People
## in the Assembly Department

The assembly operators were a very mixed group of people, ranging in age from 18 to 55 with both sexes (altogether, about 25% were female) and varying kinds of work experience. Some were housewives, some had worked in other industrial jobs, some had been in small business for themselves. Labor union membership was low, probably not more than 10%-20%. The operator group also included migrants, either from the former Dutch colonies or from Mediterranean countries, but nearly all spoke the Dutch language fairly well. A few had a technical school training and aspired to be promoted to higher qualified jobs; others attended evening school. Most of the foremen had come from the ranks. The normal promotion procedure was that people started working in Section A where operations were simplest and the better performers would be promoted in the direction of Section E. Operators who succeeded in learning various operations could be promoted to "relief operator," which meant that they would be switched around to replace absentees. A next step on the ladder would be to become a "repairman," to correct the errors made by others. Most repairmen were located at the end of Section E. Repairmen could be promoted to "key men" or assistant foremen, and these to foremen.

Operators were paid fixed monthly salaries that compared favorably with what other companies in the area paid. Salary level depended on job class according to a classification based on a nationally accepted point system, but individual salary increases were given on the foreman's recommendation based on work performance, up to the maximum salary for the given job class. The plant had good employee benefits and a well-equipped cafeteria where employees of all levels and departments, including the plant top managers, sat democratically together.

Work on the assembly lines was supported by a number of auxiliary functions. The Quality Control department had about 15 quality inspectors who were located at the end of each section of each line and who sent back machines with defects. The Production Control department was in charge of supplying the operators with the parts they needed. A "dispatcher" belonging to this department worked for each section of each line, watched the stock of parts for each operator, and fetched new parts from the central warehouse when necessary. If parts were missing in the warehouse, dispatchers were supposed to speed up their delivery to the warehouse, for example by pushing them through the Parts Manufacturing departments or alerting Purchasing. The engineering department was in charge of a number of assembly engineers, who would look after production methods, tooling, layout, routing, time-and-motion study, and setting of time standards. Time standards were not used for pay incentives, but they determined the objectives for the quantity to be produced. A very important function of the time standards was the "line balancing": Every operator along the line had to have set of operations with, as near as possible, the same total standard time. The longest set of operations determined the target speed of the line as all shorter operations left time unused and therefore represented losses. Every time that production was increased and therefore the number of operators was expanded, a whole new balancing had to be done. The same was true in case of technical changes in the product.

Another complication was that every typewriter had to be built according to a different specification. All machines were built on customer order, and any combination of 18 basic models, 25 special models, 100 different keyboards (for different languages), 9 colors, and a variety of different electric motors and safety provisions (because of country regulations) could be built in. This situation resulted from more than 90% of the production being exported to one of 75 different countries. In the mother plant in Lexington, which worked largely for the U.S. market, such diversity had never existed.

## Quality Assurance

IBM typewriters were the highest priced of their kind on the market, bought for quality, service, and prestige. Quality of products was surveyed by a Quality Assurance department operating independently from plant management, which subjected samples from regular production to heavy laboratory tests. Consequently quality demands on the assembly line were high, and minor deviations from standards led to a need for rework and repair. Problems in one section of the line were sometimes discovered late, because the number of unfinished machines on a line could be as large as 200-300. When the error was detected and the defective machines had to be reworked, this would lead to a workload peak for the repairmen and sometimes for others as well. This workload peak, which mostly had to be resolved by overtime, would tend to further endanger quality, and so on. Other problems were caused by parts arriving late: A single missing part out of the 2,500 could mean that the line would get stuck and production targets would not be reached.

Computer-processed control systems had been designed to supervise productivity and quality. Operators filled out time cards on which time lost had to be explained by one of several codes, for example "training," "doctor's visit," or "no parts." From the data on these cards the computer produced daily lists for the foreman and the Accounting department. A system of quality reporting had been developed for which once a day the quality inspectors along the lines had to type the kinds of defects they had found into one of several computer terminals situated in the department. From these data another set of daily lists was made that reached the foremen the next morning.

## Engineers as Interviewers

None of the problems in this production system were new to the department, and until 1968 they had been resolved more or less successfully. What really precipitated a crisis in 1968 was the unprecedented growth rate of production, which had to increase by 60% from 1968 to 1969. All this meant new people who had to be trained, continuous rebalancing of the lines, more difficulty in parts supply, and a constant threat to quality. Nor was this the end of growth. Bakker in 1969 expected another 25% increase for 1970. The first months of the new management team in 1969 were taken up by a lot of fire-fighting to resolve at least the most urgent immediate problems. "We wanted to grind our axes but we had to chop with them in the meantime," said Bakker. One step that was taken in February and March was to conduct a series of discussions with all assembly line operators, in order to find out what they saw as their main problems. Bakker and Smits, both ex-engineers, decided to ask the help of the engineers for this job, and so it happened that 10 engineers from the department set out enthusiastically to interview 214 operators, taking two at a time. The interviews, for which a whole morning or afternoon was available, had a pedagogic as well as information-gathering purpose. All interviews included a private excursion through the plant to see what other people and departments did, of which most operators were not aware. Engineers also used some of the time to explain how time standards were set. The operators expressed a number of complaints: irregular parts supply, conflicting instructions from relief operators and key men, noise, heat or cold, quality of the music. Some of the interviews reported more fundamental problems: "Mr. So-and-so has previously had his own business. He cannot get accustomed to all decisions being made for him here," or "Those small operations do not give satisfaction, the job has become too boring—we don't make a real product anymore," or "The Personnel department had said that some technical qualification was necessary, but for this kind of work one need not be skilled at all," and "We are treated like children. After working hard we are not allowed to relax with a cigarette and chat with a colleague."

In late April, when production was running somewhat more smoothly, the group's management team met for a day to discuss longer-term developments. Out of this meeting, the Tuesday evening sessions in Bakker's office were born, which lasted for more than half a year and during which time all aspects of the development of the department were discussed step by step. The starting point of the discussions was that almost certainly production demands would continue to increase and quality demands would remain high. In the foreseeable future assembling would remain handwork, so the department would depend on the assembly operators and their motivation. It was also believed that the social climate of the environment would affect people inside the department and even more the new people still to be hired. Amsterdam was and always has been the socially most involved city of the Netherlands, with the highest percentage of Communist voters, residents quick to engage in riots, and founders of provoism and similar movements. Amsterdam people seldom hesitate to vent their opinion on any subject. Ideas that were in the air like "participation," "decentralization," "escape from alienation" were felt even more in Amsterdam than elsewhere in the country.

By December 1969, the long Tuesday evenings spent together by the six-man team began to yield a clear consensus about the direction in which further development of the department had to be sought.

## The Miniline Project

There was a consensus among the management team of the Mechanical Products group that for the future the long assembly lines were undesirable. They had been struck by the fact that within the same group the assembly line for the composer machines, which was shorter and had longer work cycles, always showed lower absenteeism and less labor turnover than the typewriter assembly.

The idea now was to redivide the Typewriter department into self-contained units of 20 persons, called "minilines." Each miniline would have its own foreman and would build a complete typewriter, which meant a cycle time per machine per operator of about 10 minutes. The transfer to minilines was supposed to have the following advantages:

1. Planning and operating flexibility
2. Job enlargement (longer operating cycles), making for more interesting work
3. People closer to end product, making for more involvement
4. Group of a "human" size with more contact, participation
5. Better quality through shorter feedback cycle of errors
6. Productivity gain through reduction of product handling time (20 times off and on conveyor instead of 60-70 times)

The disadvantages foreseen were:

1. Longer learning time for a 10-minute operation than for a 3-minute operation, with more damage if someone should leave and high initial training cost for everybody.
2. More tools needed (more people now doing the same operations).
3. The average job class of the operators would increase somewhat, which would lead to a higher wage bill.
4. More difficult task for foremen: They would technically have to master the whole machine (rather than just a section of the assembly process). Also, it was likely that working with small, self-contained units would call for more social leadership.

When the management team had arrived at its conclusion it became necessary to act quickly, as a new expansion of production capacity was due in spring 1970. Wim Smits, assembly manager, and Jan Kruis, a senior engineer, undertook to design the look of the miniline. Foremen were asked for ideas and some of them decided to consult their operators in turn. A few operating groups became so enthusiastic about the project that they spontaneously stayed evenings to work on it. Smits and Kruis had originally thought of a U-shaped line, but the operators objected that in this way the distance between people would still be too large and proposed an M shape (see Figure 5.3). Miniline teams would be composed of 12 regular operators, 3 relief operators, 1 test person at the end of the line, 1 quality inspector, and 3 repair people, a total of 20 team members; in addition, there would be one key man and one manager per team.

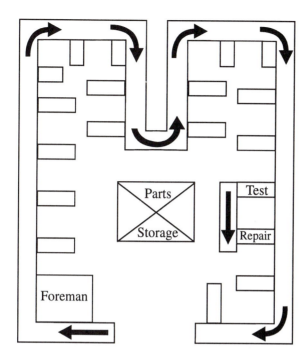

**Figure 5.3.** The M-Shaped Miniline Layout

In February 1970 Bakker took the miniline proposal to Frans Kraak, the plant manager. Bakker wanted to freeze the existing longer lines at their present size and to expand production through the creation of minilines: the first in April 1970, the second in September. Then, if all went well, Long Line III (the one with 40 operators) could be split into two minilines, and finally in 1971 the others could follow.

## The Pilot Phase

Plant Manager Kraak watched Bakker's miniline presentation with some doubt. "Well, Ad," he said, "if you and your people want to stick your necks out and try this, I will not stop you. I will give you permission for setting up two minilines. Let us see what happens."

So, in April 1970, Miniline 1 was created. Its people were selected by the foremen from the different sections of the long lines. Some refused and were replaced by others. The miniline foreman was chosen for being the technically most qualified man, one of the few who knew all operations.

Miniline 1 had a slow start. Foremen had been asked to make average performers available for the experiment, neither their star performers nor their worst, but the result was a group of mediocre capabilities. When in September Miniline 2 had to be started—there was no other choice, the production was needed—Miniline 1 still produced at a slower rate than the old system.

In the meantime the interest of the people in the department had been aroused by the miniline experiment, and for Miniline 2 there were lots of volunteers from the long lines. However, it was decided to staff Miniline 2 mainly with newly hired employees (12 of 20), although this meant a slower start-up. The learning time for a 10-minute operation was about 6 months.

Assuming the plant manager's tacit agreement, Bakker and Smits (who, due to the illness of his colleague had, in the meantime, become manager of all assembly operations) largely on their own started a massive training program of all operators for a total transfer to the miniline system, in spite of the lack of tangible production improvement so far. They were helped by an economic recession in 1971, which meant that production leveled off (it never really decreased) and also that labor turnover diminished as people could less easily find other work. The training was labeled "cross training": It meant that all operators on the long lines had to learn the operations before and after them. Next they would start to work in parallel, so that instead of three workers each doing a different 3.5-minute operation, all three would now be doing the same 10-minute operation. Most cross training was done in overtime hours. Line III, which had always been shorter and therefore operated with longer cycle times, had finished its cross training in January 1971 and was then with little difficulty converted into Minilines 3 and 4. People reacted positively on the cross training, except for a few who had earlier been promoted from simple to more complicated tasks and now had to include some of the simple operations again. In spite of the fact that some people got jobs clearly belonging to higher job classes, wages were not immediately adapted, but a promise was made that all wages would be revised when the new system was in general use. This caused remarkably few problems. Most people were happy to move to the new system in spite of the lack of immediate monetary gain.

Bakker had asked the help of the Plant Education manager, Jan Lievestro, for the retraining of the foremen, especially for their new social role. Lievestro suggested an "organization development" approach that would involve not only the foremen but also Bakker and his five department managers, as well as the engineers who worked with the foremen.

Three groups composed of department managers, foremen, and engineers spent 4 days each in "group behavior training" in a country hotel, with an outside consultant as a trainer. They were so enthusiastic about its effects that they asked to develop another group behavior training for the operators. This was done, and some groups of operators were so trained, but it soon appeared that only those already working on the minilines really benefited from it. As the long line operators did not work in groups yet, the training was not relevant to them, and it was discontinued.

## The Big Changeover

The plunge came in 1971. Miniline 1 was still operating at a fairly low efficiency level; 2, 3, and 4 did somewhat better than the long lines. So far minilines had been built up quietly in a free space before the people were transferred. Now the two long lines of 60 people each had to be converted into five new minilines, but at the same spot where they had been before, so that the whole transfer had to be done at once. It was decided to use the 3-week summer vacation period for this.

Previously internal moves and layout changes had been carried out by an outside transport company. It was difficult to obtain this outside help for the vacation period and somebody suggested that the department could just as well move itself. This was decided on. A group of 15 operators volunteered to take their vacations at another time, and with Bakker, some foremen, and some technicians they effected the change. When people returned from their vacation the department was reconstructed into 9 minilines situated around a central power-driven conveyor system (see Figure 5.4). It had been planned that production should reach the old level after 3 months, and this planning included a week-to-week learning curve to get there. The first week after the vacation showed disappointing results: Production lagged way behind the learning curve, and the managers became nervous. The second week was much better, the third week exceeded all expectations, and at the end of 1 month, long before the planned date, production returned to the prechange level. In September 1971 production was 18% above the prechange level; in December, 22%; one year later, in December 1972, 35%; and in December 1973, 46%.

The sources of the production gain were:

1. Less product handling time, as foreseen (taking the machine 20 times off and on the roller conveyor takes less time than doing it 60-70 times).

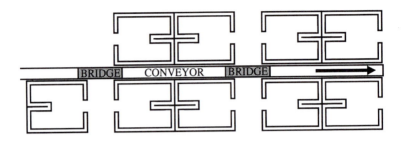

**Figure 5.4.** Layout of Typewriter Assembly, 1971

2. Sharply decreased number of errors. Very soon the entire group was made responsible for quality, and the quality inspector job could be eliminated. The repairmen then could be used for production instead of repairing.

3. A large part of the assembling time consisted of fine adjustments. In a short work cycle, many of these adjustments had to be done again and again after new parts have been placed. In the longer cycle, the effort was needed only once.

4. Less time lost for line balancing. If somebody had finished his/her own operation, (s)he would help a colleague who was overloaded. People would switch so that more skilled people would take more complicated, time-consuming operations and less skilled people could take easier, shorter operations. The line, in other words, balanced itself, not based on a hypothetical "average performer" as when the balancing had been done by time-and-motion study, but according to people's real capabilities.

5. In a similar way, temporary absence of people on the line could be handled with a minimum of disturbance for others.

Besides the gain in direct productivity, the new structure reduced the need for auxiliary jobs. For example, less administrative work was needed, because the daily computer reports on productivity and quality could be eliminated. Operators no longer needed to fill out time cards; the foremen simply recorded the number of hours worked and the number of machines produced.

Fewer engineers were needed, because the whole problem of line balancing, which had consumed a lot of engineer time, had disappeared. Layout changes were planned by the groups themselves, with the engineers in a consultant role. Time-and-motion study was maintained, but only for planning purposes.

Dispatchers used to watch each operator's stock of parts and supplement it when necessary. Now, operators were given responsibility for watching their own stock and ordering a supplement through their key

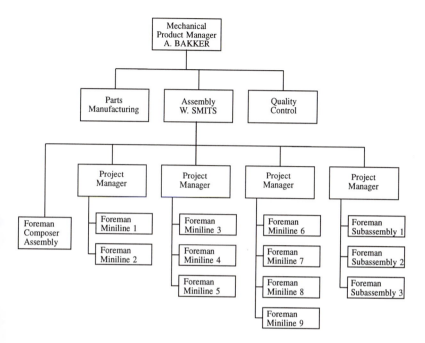

**Figure 5.5.** Organization Chart of the Typewriter and Composer Assembly Departments in Late 1971

man when necessary, counting on a delivery time of 2 days. The key man would then pass the orders for the whole group to the warehouse. This led both to a labor saving on dispatchers and a reduction of waiting times due to late delivery of parts. The organization chart after the changeover to minilines is shown in Figure 5.5.

## Effects on the People

The early miniline groups created before summer 1971 had a strong sense of cohesion. This was partly reinforced by the group training they went through, the first time this kind of training had ever been given to rank-and-file workers. Partly it was stimulated by a "Hawthorne effect"[1] of being the pioneers—others looking up to them. Some began to bring posters and flowers to make their miniline domain more attractive.

At the time of the big changeover in the 1971 summer vacation, some people had suggested using part of the free space obtained for decorative plants and flowers. Bakker had been unwilling at the time to ask Kraak for a budget for this purpose. However, when people returned from their vacation, there were pots with plants everywhere. One of the foremen had personally bought over 700 guilders' worth of flowers. Kraak good-naturedly accepted the fait accompli and had the florists' bill refunded.

The example of the flowers unchained a wave of decorative creativity among the miniline population. Within a short time, other plants and flowers, tanks of fish, cages with birds, and even a bright violet-colored box with guinea pigs were brought to the factory. The new fauna led to some uneasiness on the part of the higher plant management, but Bakker defended it successfully on the grounds that as long as it did not harm production it would be unwise to interfere with people's new freedom. He trusted that the excesses would disappear by themselves, which was, in fact, the case. Within 2 years after the switch over nearly all the fauna (except the fish tanks) and many of the plants disappeared, as only a few people were prepared to deliver the necessary sustained effort for their maintenance.

Another group phenomenon was the collective coffee breaks. It soon appeared that the space inside the M-layout provided for parts storage was not really necessary: The parts could be stored under the roller conveyors. One group found some unused tables and chairs somewhere in the plant and installed their own coffee club for mid-morning and mid-afternoon breaks, at which times they all could be seen sitting together, a habit that in 1972 spread to most other groups.

When a high IBM official visited the plant there was some concern about how he would react to the coffee club during working hours, but Smits had his arguments well prepared. He explained that he preferred collective coffee breaks over individual ones because:

1. They caused less disturbance of production (no waiting of one worker for another while they had coffee).
2. In fact, although people of course discussed yesterday's soccer match, the breaks also served as informal department meetings and daily production and quality problems got resolved in the process.
3. People liked them, so they boosted morale.

This settled the matter and the visitor left satisfied. Coffee breaks had become a fact of life.

The most difficult role in the new organization was taken by the foremen ("managers"). The technical skills for which they had been promoted did not help them in many of the tasks they had to carry out now. They were still responsible for production and quality, but the way to achieve these had become much less clear to most foremen. Although the Plant Education department spent a lot of effort in foreman training, it appeared that not all were able to benefit from it. Geographically the foremen moved from an office away from the line to a cubicle in the corner of their "M." Some had even chosen to have no office at all, just a desk inside the "M."

IBM ran periodic employee attitude surveys, and in the Amsterdam plant people were asked to give their opinion to a list of work-related problems in 1970 and 1972. Some of the results obtained in the typewriter assembly department are collected in Table 5.1. Question L shows from 1970 to 1972 a shift to a more participative style of management (Managers 3 and 4), which is what most people preferred (Question K). In spite of this, in most other respects (Questions A through J) managers were perceived less favorably in 1972. They were seen as, on the average, paying more attention to production and less to people. It seemed that they were fulfilling their new role less well than their old one.

The various miniline groups also began to differentiate into greater diversity. Some changed their layout, as they were free to do, so long as they stayed within the available space. So, some lines looked more like G shapes, some like Ms turned 90 degrees; some split themselves into two 10-person microlines, each making a complete product. Some had coffee tables; others, developing a more individualistic norm, did not and people would drink coffee in small groups at their workbenches. One 35-person macroline was re-created as a training ground for new recruits and also for people for whom the 10-minute cycle evidently exceeded their capacities.

The miniline spirit also affected the subassembly lines that had originally not been changed. Jobs in the subassemblies were redistributed and layouts adapted to group taste, so a group of 24 women assembling the golf ball carriers rearranged themselves into six groups of 4, seated such that all could look out of the window.

Labor turnover decreased sharply, but it was unclear which part of this was due to the minilines and which part to the recession. The figures were: 1969, 30%; 1970, 20%; 1971, 10%; 1972, 12%; and 1973, 17%. Sickness absenteeism did not decrease much. It was in 1969, 6.5%; 1970, 6.0%; 1971, 6.0%; 1972, 6.3%; and 1973, 5.3%.

## A Letter From Department 688

In 1973 the economic recession was over and production levels increased again. Both Kraak and Bakker had moved to new jobs. In March

**TABLE 5.1**  Some Results From the Employee Attitude Surveys in the
Typewriter Assembly Department, 1970 and 1972

|   |   | 1970 | 1972 |
|---|---|------|------|
| A. | How good a job is done by your immediate manager?<br>"very good" or "good" | 72% | 65% |
| B. | How would you rate your latest appraisal and counseling interview with your immediate manager?<br>"very helpful" | 46% | 16% |
| C. | How would you rate the group meetings with your manager and colleagues?<br>"very useful" | 32% | 25% |
| D. | Your manager expects a large amount of work from you<br>"always" or "usually" | 81% | 89% |
| E. | Your manager expects work of high quality from you<br>"always" or "usually" | 92% | 99% |
| F. | Your manager is up-to-date on the technical side of his or her job<br>"always" or "usually" | 72% | 58% |
| G. | Your manager is able to help you out when you have a problem on the job<br>"always" or "usually" | 73% | 66% |
| H. | Your manager is concerned about helping you get ahead<br>"always" or "usually" | 67% | 53% |
| I. | Your manager is willing to listen and act on your ideas and suggestions<br>"always" or "usually" | 70% | 64% |
| J. | Your manager builds team spirit among his or her people<br>"always" or "usually" | 72% | 52% |

of that year the new plant manager, Ger Prins, received a letter signed by all 20 members of Department 688. Department 688 was a subassembly group created during the 1971-1972 recession to do simple work that previously had been subcontracted. About 30% of the department population consisted of people with health or psychological handicaps who did not perform very well elsewhere. Yet as a group they had functioned

**TABLE 5.1** (Continued)

The descriptions below apply to four different types of managers. First, please read through these descriptions:

Manager 1    Usually makes his or her decisions promptly and communicates them to subordinates clearly and firmly. He or she expects them to carry out the decisions loyally and without raising difficulties.

Manager 2    Usually makes his or her decisions promptly, but before going ahead, tries to explain them fully to subordinates. He or she gives them the reasons for the decisions and answers whatever questions they may have.

Manager 3    Usually consults with his or her subordinates before he or she reaches decisions. He or she listens to their advice, considers it, and then announces a decision. He or she then expects all the workers loyally to implement it whether or not it is in accordance with the advice they gave.

Manager 4    Usually calls a meeting of subordinates when there is an important decision to be made. He or she puts the problem before the group and tries to obtain consensus. If he or she obtains consensus, he or she accepts this as the decision. If the consensus is impossible, this manager usually makes the decision alone.

|  |  | 1970 | 1972 |
|---|---|---|---|
| K. | Now, for the above types of manager, please mark the *one* which you would prefer to work under: | | |
| | Manager 1 | 6% | 5% |
| | Manager 2 | 18% | 15% |
| | Manager 3 | 20% | 17% |
| | Manager 4 | 56% | 62% |
| L. | And, to which *one* of the above four types of managers would you say your own manager *most closely corresponds*? | | |
| | Manager 1 | 14% | 14% |
| | Manager 2 | 24% | 17% |
| | Manager 3 | 14% | 20% |
| | Manager 4 | 25% | 38% |
| | None of these | 22% | 10% |

very well and their absenteeism had dropped from about 20% to 10%. Now that production was going to increase again, it had been announced that the simple subassembly work would go back to subcontractors, to free the people for other jobs; the company was still very careful about hiring new people, and Prins was tied to strict budget controls in this respect.

The letter from Department 688 ran as follows:

After the meeting of 28th February, 1973, where we were told that our work will be subcontracted, many of us reacted negatively. Most of us object to the subcontracting and our consequent transfer to other departments. In a number of discussions the following objections were raised:

1. During the past year and a half, we learned a lot about cooperation and we want to continue to cooperate as a department.

2. We were the first department of its kind to do our own quality inspection, with good results.

3. We learned to organize our work so as to supply our products to the next departments in time, even when we ourselves suffer from parts shortage, by creating buffer stocks of sensitive items.

4. Several of us could not perform satisfactorily in other departments, but they are doing well with us: These people are afraid of becoming ineffective again when they will be transferred. One of us even used the word "disaster."

5. Most of us do not want to leave our manager and key man, who treat us humanely and understand our difficulties. We feel free to talk with them and they tell us when we are doing well or not so well.

In our present department we come to work with pleasure, even on days when we do not feel so well. Before, in such cases, we would report ill and stay at home. Now we know that together we can keep things running smoothly. In 1972 our sickness absenteeism was very low and we believe this is because we like our work here.

We hope that our department will remain together, because we feel at ease here. We do not mind if the subassemblies we make now will be subcontracted, if only we can stay in a group and do something else together. We hope that you will understand our problems and find a good solution.

The employees of Department 688
(20 signatures)

## Four Years Later

In February 1977 the case writer revisited the IBM manufacturing plant in Amsterdam. Since 1973 the buildings had been enlarged. The typewriter assembly department had moved to a new hall. It looked spacious; walls, partitions, and columns were painted in bright colors.

An overhead conveyor system ran along the different sections to supply the kits of parts to be assembled and to collect the finished typewriters. The department had grown faster than the rest of the plant: It now employed about 470 people in direct jobs, or roughly 25% of total plant personnel. It was divided into 15 minilines and 5 subassembly lines, led by 20 foremen and 4 project managers. The minilines still showed a variety of internal layouts, but most of the former furnishings in the form of posters, flowers, and fish tanks had not survived the move to the new hall.

"The miniline philosophy functioned well until the end of 1973," says Personnel Manager George van der Woude. He has been in this job since 1970, so he has been able to follow the project's history closely. Several managers involved have since changed positions inside the company. Bakker left the department in 1972 and Smits in 1973. The new men who took their places had not lived through the miniline development experience. Van der Woude recalls:

> Toward the end of 1973 and especially in 1974, we had to deal with another explosive increase in production quantity. We first tried to fill places by internal transfers, resubcontracting subassembly work, and moving indirect personnel into direct jobs. Then we started hiring again from the outside. The number of direct personnel in the Typewriter Assembly department more than doubled between December 1972 and December 1974. Altogether, for the total plant, we had to hire about 500 people in this period, which meant we had to interview 5000. Also we hired a larger number of migrant workers who had great difficulties with the Dutch language and way of life: 170 of them, mostly Turks, Moroccans, and Portuguese.

Figure 5.6 shows graphs of the number of employees, production quantity, labor turnover, and absenteeism from 1969 to 1976.

The impact of this flood of new people on the productivity and the social structure of the minilines had been negative. Experienced workers were spread out to form the cores of new minilines, but the spirit of cooperation necessary for the functioning of the minilines had no time to grow. Moreover, the foreigners could not sufficiently participate in the verbal communication that is a very essential element in the microorganization of the minilines. The management saw itself confronted with huge problems of product quantity and quality and reinstated a certain amount of standardization and specialization. Thus the operations on the line although remaining enlarged—about 10 minutes—were standardized again to facilitate the training of new people and the inter-

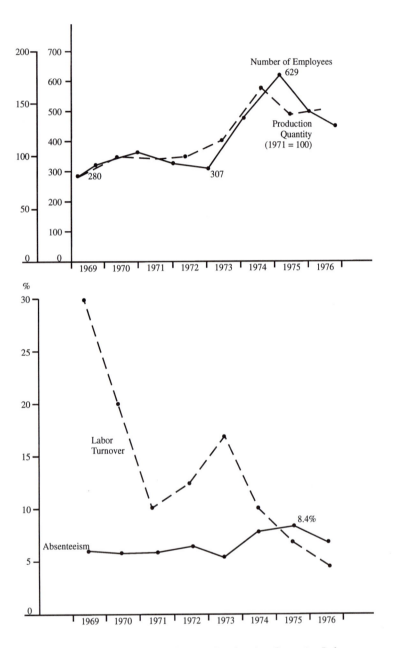

**Figure 5.6.** Number of Direct Employees, Production Quantity, Labor Turnover, and Absenteeism in the Typewriter Assembly Department, 1969-1976

**TABLE 5.2** Some Results From the Employee Attitude Surveys in the
Typewriter Assembly Department, 1970 to 1976

|  |  | 1970 | 1972 | 1974 | 1976 |
|---|---|---|---|---|---|
| A. | How good a job is done by your immediate manager? | | | | |
|  | "very good" or "good" | 72% | 65% | 53% | 49% |
| C. | How would you rate the group meetings with your manager and colleagues? | | | | |
|  | "very useful" | 32% | 25% | 15% | 19% |

NOTE: The other questions from the 1970 and 1972 surveys listed in Table 5.1 were not used in 1974 and 1976.

change between lines. The flexible interchange of people within lines was lost. The specialized jobs of quality inspector and dispatcher were reintroduced.

In spite of these measures the productivity per worker decreased in 1974 and this, together with ever-increasing production demands, forced the company to resort to massive involuntary overtime.

Again the foremen were strongly affected by the events. New and inexperienced men were promoted to foreman and they spent most of their time fire-fighting. Department meetings were neglected; new workers complained that after months they had never yet talked with their foreman. Many foremen resorted to crisis management of an autocratic type, which became evident in the results of the 1974 and 1976 employee opinion surveys (see Table 5.2).

In 1975 the effect of the overall recession was felt in the typewriter market and the production increase stopped as suddenly as it had started. A new hiring freeze was established. Labor turnover, which usually reflects the situation in the labor market, continued to drop, but sickness absenteeism reached an all-time high of 8.4% (see Figure 5.6). The miniline populations now had a chance to stabilize and the old team spirit revived somewhat. Management reminded the foremen of their duty to organize departmental meetings and conduct appraisal and counseling interviews with their people. Productivity slowly increased. In late 1975 a new program for multiple operations training was introduced to improve the qualifications of people and reestablish flexibility within lines. However, in 1976 this program met with an unexpected obstacle: Reduced output in other departments led to the transfer into Typewriter Assembly of a number of more qualified workers who had to be given the more qualified jobs, thus, at least for some time, blocking these jobs for others. The multiple operations training was suspended.

"And what happened to Department 688?" the case writer asked, referring to the subassembly department of handicapped people, who in 1973 resisted being split up and wrote a collective letter to the plant manager.

"Well, they survived as a department," said Van der Woude, "but they gradually had to absorb newcomers. But I learned something from that case. We may face the same problem again now as we start to increase subcontracting, which means transferring subassembly people to final assembly. I have made it clear that the Personnel department should have a say in our subcontracting program. We have to keep a sufficient number of simple jobs ourselves for people who are unable to do the more complicated tasks."

## An Analysis of What Happened

This case reminds one of the famous experiments at Volvo in Sweden (SAF, 1975). From a traditional Tayloristic work organization, the Typewriter Assembly department changed into semiautonomous groups. After a period of adaptation the results were excellent: Labor productivity increased by almost 50%, and quality also improved. The reaction of the personnel involved was extremely positive, and creativity and group cohesion, which had so far been reserved for people's private life sphere, started to spill over into the work environment.

Yet after a few more years only some of the innovations survived. One of the disadvantages of the new situation was that if people start behaving as groups rather than as isolated individuals, the stability of group composition becomes a constraint in planning. This was very evident in the case of Department 688, where somewhat handicapped persons had found a safe and productive haven, which they did not want to lose through a reshuffling of people.

Unlike the Volvo experiments the IBM Amsterdam experiments were not part of a companywide philosophy of social innovation. The plans for the minilines were developed at the middle management level (Bakker, Smits, and Kruis), and only sold to the higher levels of management in Amsterdam and in the United States after the fact. Structural changes in the rest of the plant, let alone in other parts of the corporation, that could have extended the lessons from the miniline experience to elsewhere, seem to have been missing. Also the planning of the production volume of the plant as a whole continued to be erratic: fast expansion followed by freezing, which killed the miniline cohesion. If the considerable forces available in group cohesion and autonomous microplanning among group members are to be preserved this implies limits to rates of growth. A group is like a plant: It needs its time to grow and if one tries to force it, it may die.

The negative impact of the changes on the way people perceived many of their foremen is one of the other remarkable aspects of this case. The importance of first-line management was highlighted in Chapter 1 of this book: For the operators on the lines, the key man and foreman may be the only members of management they ever have contacts with, and all problems in their relation with the company are projected onto these linchpin persons. The complete change in organization philosophy from the old Tayloristic long lines to the minilines demanded a change in behavior among first-line managers beyond the capacities of most of them. Further, even if a manager changed his or her behavior in the desired direction, this was not always immediately perceived and appreciated by the employees: the people may not believe it, or it may just make them feel insecure.

In spite of the backlash in the later years the IBM Typewriter Assembly case remains a remarkable example of humanization of work, as discussed in Chapter 3. It was a major success at the tactical, but not at the strategic level. If it was a revolution it was only a small one, limited in space and in time.

## Discussion Questions

1. To what extent does the case show agreement and/or conflict between IBM's corporate culture at that time and the miniline experiment?

2. Draw a comparison between the management control systems before and after the changeover, in the areas of productivity, quality, scheduling, and personnel behavior.

3. What do you think of the idea to use engineers as interviewers about people problems?

4. How can you explain changes in work methods leading to people starting to decorate the plant like their home?

5. Should a plant manager be happy or unhappy with a letter like the one from Department 688?

6. Did the plant really have a foremen problem or was this just a perceived effect from the organizational changes?

## Note

1. Named after the Hawthorne experiments at Western Electric in Chicago, between 1924 and 1940, in which some workers were isolated to form an experimental group (Mayo, 1933).

# 6

## Case Study

### Work Structuring at Philips

---

This case covers the attempts toward humanization of work in one of the production departments of the Philips Corporation in a small Dutch town between 1968 and 1977. The product is a fairly simple, low-priced electrical part (a "ballast"), and the workers are unskilled men and women. A first, rather ruthless attempt at "work structuring" fails; next, another manager proceeds much more carefully. He succeeds in convincing the engineers designing a new production technology that they should let the workers choose among three alternatives, by voting. Nevertheless, work on the new line turns out to be hardly more rewarding than on the old one. In the meantime the department introduces "shop floor consultation" according to a package prepared by the company head office. The support of the various staff groups is a major requirement that is not always met. At the end of the case, the next technological changeover appears at the horizon. All in all, the long march toward humanization of work is a pilgrim's progress.

---

## Philips's Concern for Humanization of Work

By the end of 1976, N.V. Philips's Gloeilampenfabrieken in Eindhoven, the Netherlands, was one of Europe's largest private employers. Its total

---

Originally written under the title "A Problem of Work Structuring," this chapter was intended to be used as a basis for class discussion rather than to illustrate effective or ineffective handling of an administrative situation. Reprinted with the permission of INSEAD. Copyright © 1977 CEDEP (European Centre for Continuing Education) and INSEAD (European Institute of Business Administration), Fontainebleau, France.

personnel added up to 391,000 in about 60 countries around the world, with 87,500 in the home country, the Netherlands. Total sales were $12 billion. Philips's main products were high- and medium-technology electrical and electronic products, for example, a full range of domestic appliances. The manufacturing process was highly mechanized, but it still demanded a lot of unskilled and semiskilled human work.

The traditional image of Philips in the Netherlands was that of a progressive employer with a strong concern for employee welfare. Internationally, Philips allowed considerable autonomy to its subsidiaries to determine their own personnel policies, so that its image in personnel issues varied from country to country. Still, there was a flow of ideas on personnel matters from the head office to subsidiaries. The company put a high value on maintaining good relationships with labor unions.

The company employed a number of Dutch industrial sociologists and psychologists who stimulated management interest in creating wholesome work situations. In Chapter 3 we already met the pioneering work of Kuylaars (1951), who condemned short-cycle repetitive work for its alienating effect on the workers. This and later studies in other countries inspired some enlightened line and staff managers at Philips in the later 1950s and early 1960s to experiment with forms of job enlargement and job enrichment. In the meantime, another stimulus came from the company's top management, which became increasingly concerned over the difficulty of attracting and keeping competent employees in a period of fast company growth and a tight labor market. After 2 years of work, a task force composed of members of the Personnel and Work Study departments in 1963 published an internal company report, *Work Structuring for Unskilled Workers*. The term "work structuring" became the company jargon for what elsewhere was later baptized "humanization of work" or "quality of working life." The main conclusion of the 1963 report was that "monotonous short-cycle jobs are out of tune with the workers' increasing needs for responsibility and a meaningful place in society." The report recommended small-scale experiments with various forms of work structuring.

Between 1963 and 1968, 40 such experiments, with varying degrees of success, were reported within the Dutch Philips organization. In 1968, the directors of Personnel and of Work Study jointly issued an attractive booklet evaluating these experiments and propagating their continuation. The booklet was widely distributed within the company in the Netherlands. It distinguished three levels of work structuring:

1. The level of the *work environment* (more attractive buildings; factory visits by the public; design of personnel advertisements; design of work stations

and machines; humidity, heat, and noise control; music; work clothes; toilets; smoking rooms; vending machines; etc.). In popular parlance, this level of work structuring was called the "flower pot level."

2. The level of the *work itself* (job enlargement, job rotation, and job enrichment).

3. The level of the *departmental organization structure* (forming small, semiautonomous work groups and flattening the hierarchical pyramid by the elimination of levels of management).

## The Kieldrecht Plant, Its Products and Its People

Kieldrecht[1] was one of about 50 locations in the Netherlands in which Philips operated a manufacturing plant. It is a provincial town of approximately 45,000 inhabitants with a variety of medium-sized industries and a history of poverty, poor working conditions, and distrust of employers by labor. In 1968 the Philips plant at Kieldrecht employed about 1100 people from the town and the surrounding countryside, mostly in unskilled and semiskilled jobs. The plant produced frames and accessories for fluorescent lighting.

The main accessories produced were "ballasts" for fluorescent lamp circuits. The ballast, sometimes erroneously called a transformer, was a copper self-induction coil wound around a heavy iron core. It served to limit current surges that would otherwise destroy the lamp. Ballasts were made in a range of sizes for anything from miniature lamps to giant outdoor lighting. The most common were the 40- and 65-watt models. The weight of a 40-watt ballast was around 500 grams, of a 65-watt ballast around 1 kilogram.

Until 1969 ballasts were assembled in batch production by about 190 semiskilled workers. About 40 of these were female, mostly young married women who would quit when they had children. Among the men a majority came from families in which most members also worked for Philips or one of the other local industries. Others were small farmers who lost their jobs because of the rationalization of agriculture in the region. Finally there were about 20 migrant workers from Spain, who had adapted reasonably well to life in Holland; almost all spoke some Dutch. For those who joined Philips immediately after elementary school, which was often the case, the company provided additional general education (the so-called life school) and vocational training. Many of these people would gradually move on to more skilled jobs.

The main production phases (corresponding to different jobs) were:

1. *Coil winding:* copper wire was wound around a square hollow paper coil on a coil winding machine. This was often done by women.
2. *Iron core inserting:* the wound coils were fitted between two piles of E-shaped iron plates so that the middle legs of the Es would slide inside the coil from either side and the outer legs would meet outside the coil. The outer legs would then be welded together.
3. *Fixing the housing:* the coil plus iron core were fitted into a metal housing.
4. *Filling:* the empty space in the housing would be filled with a molten plastic filling.
5. *Testing and stamping:* applying a rubber stamp specifying the electrical properties of the ballast.
6. *Packing.*

Labor turnover among ballast assembly workers was about 20% per year, absenteeism about 10%. These figures were higher than in other industries in the same region, in spite of better working conditions and fringe benefits at Philips. Within the Philips Kieldrecht plant, similar percentages were found for the other production departments, but much lower turnover and absenteeism existed in indirect departments such as those in charge of maintenance, warehouses, and transport.

## Ballast Production:
## Layout and Organization in 1968

At Philips the responsibility for the design, building, and maintenance of production machines rested with a staff department that reported to the management of each product division and was called Plant Mechanization. In 1968, the Plant Mechanization group designed a semi-mechanized production line for the 40-watt ballasts (see Figure 6.1). It was to employ 25 people per shift in two shifts (a total of 50) and obtained a considerable increase in production per person compared to the previous batch system. The 65-watt model was to be produced in a less mechanized line, by 35 people working day shifts. The other models would continue to be produced in batches (60 people). These numbers do not include people performing indirect tasks and replacement for absentees. The new production line was gradually installed in 1969.

The line organization of the Kieldrecht plant in 1968 formally had six levels above the production workers (see the organization chart in Figure 6.2), but in the Ballast Assembly department the function of assistant department manager had been vacant since 1967. The department manager, Mr. Zielhuis, was an old-timer who had been promoted from

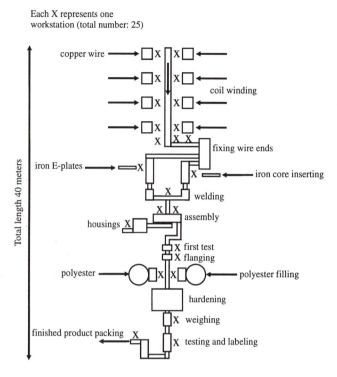

Each X represents one
workstation (total number: 25)

**Figure 6.1.** The Semimechanized Production Line for 40-Watt Ballasts as Designed in 1968

foreman. This was exceptional: most department managers at Philips in the Netherlands were people with a secondary general or technical school education who did not come through the ranks but were hired as assistant department managers. Foremen and assistant foremen were usually promoted from the ranks. Workers interested in promotion could attend an evening course that would make them eligible for assistant foreman if a vacancy occurred and they were otherwise judged capable by their superiors.

## The First Attempt: Imposed Work Structuring

In 1968 the product manager, Mr. Timmerman, created a temporary new job of assistant product manager to which he nominated Mr. Jan Van

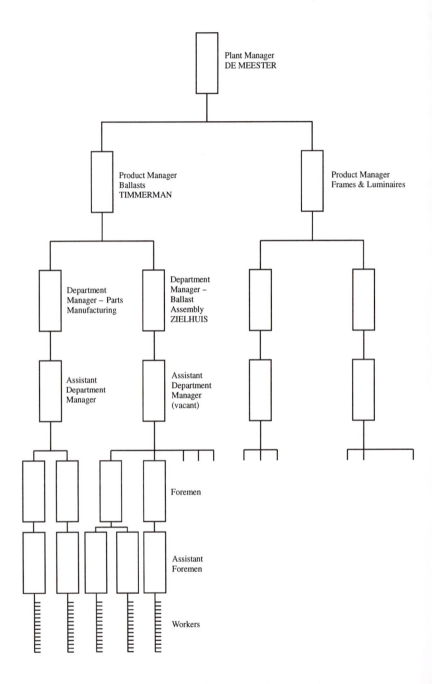

**Figure 6.2.** Plant Line Organization Chart in 1968

Dikhout. Van Dikhout was 36 years old at the time and had been a management development officer in another Philips division. He was requested to look especially into the Ballast Assembly department, the results of which were not judged satisfactory. In particular, the Sales department complained that competitors' products were sold at a price below Philips's factory cost. The new mechanizations should be able to partly overcome this problem, but Timmerman wanted also to improve other aspects of the department's organization.

Van Dikhout suggested moving the department manager, Zielhuis, to another position and leaving the department manager position vacant while he, Van Dikhout, carried out the necessary reorganizations. This was done. It was at this time that the *Work Structuring* booklet appeared. Van Dikhout quickly grasped the potential significance of a form of work structuring for the ballast department. He was an ambitious man who liked fast results. Largely on his own, but with the support of Timmerman, he planned two major changes:

1. At the level of the *work itself,* on the new semimechanized production line for 40-watt ballasts, a certain number of administrative and maintenance tasks would be transferred to the workers who would receive official training for this purpose. This was a form of "job enrichment."
2. At the level of the *departmental organization,* the hierarchical pyramid would be flattened by the elimination of the jobs of foreman and assistant foreman, replacing them by one simple level of "group leaders."

In spite of the fact that Van Dikhout had not involved the Personnel department in his reorganization project as would be the usual approach the plant manager approved the proposed reorganization. The changes in the hierarchical structure were carried out within a few weeks in 1969. Of 14 foremen and assistant foremen, 9 were made group leaders. Of the five others, first one and later another resigned from the company, one went back to a production worker job, and two were moved to other departments. Assistant foremen who became group leaders received sizeable salary increases.

An expert from the head office Work Study department was made available for 3 weeks to help introduce the change. Workers assigned to the new semimechanized production line were trained to carry out certain administrative and machine maintenance tasks themselves. As a consequence several jobs moved into a higher job class, which meant higher pay. The collective agreement with the Philips labor union distinguished eight job classes for blue- and white-collar workers. In the Ballast Assembly department, three quarters of the workers were in Job Class 2 (counting from below), most of the remainder in 3, and very few in 4. Now, more could move into Class 3.

On January 1, 1970, Van Dikhout replaced Timmerman as product manager. The latter was promoted to a job in another plant. Two new department managers for the Ballast Assembly department were named, one for the semimechanized 40- and 65-watt products, and one for the remaining batch-produced products. The new manager of the semimechanized department was Mr. Paul Hoekstra. He was 32 years old at the time and had for the past 7 years been a member of the Plant Mechanization staff group, responsible among other things for the design and installation of the semimechanized 40-watt production line. His basic training was in engineering.

Hoekstra noticed that the job enrichment project on the 40-watt production line did not seem to be working. One problem was that the administrative tasks transferred to the members were not stable. The requests for information from the floor by the Administration and Personnel departments were in a state of constant flux. It was impossible to pass all these changes on to the workers, so that the group leaders carried most of the administrative burden. Before long the administrative tasks of the workers had shifted to the group leaders completely. Another problem was the high labor turnover (about 30% per year). The initial teams on the 40-watt production line had been well instructed in their administrative and maintenance tasks, but for the new people coming in as replacements the same training was not immediately available. Thus these people had to be helped in their maintenance work, and to prevent deterioration of the machinery, the specialized maintenance crew from the Plant Mechanization department gradually took all its previous tasks back.

Hoekstra also noticed considerable resentment among group leaders and even among workers about the reorganization of the departmental hierarchy in 1969 and the elimination of the jobs of five foremen and assistant foremen, which had fallen like a thunderbolt and created feelings of uncertainty among their remaining colleagues. Eight years later some people still referred to this event.

## Starting Anew With New Technology

In 1971 Van Dikhout in turn moved to a job elsewhere in the company, and a new product manager, Mr. Everts, was named. Hoekstra had in the meantime become more familiar with the production and social problems of his department. He had observed that within the 25-person teams running either shift on the 40-watt line those working at the front end of the line (coil winding) did not know those working at the back end (testing, etc.). Hoekstra's wife was a social worker and they had frequent discussions about the impact of the factory situation on people's private lives.

At that time the management of the Lighting division of Philips, to which the Kieldrecht plant belonged, invited its Dutch plant managers to consider what long-term changes in organization and production methods would be necessary in order to keep the company both economically and socially viable against the background of a level of employment that was no longer growing. Philips in the Netherlands reached its maximum personnel strength in 1971 and gradually reduced it thereafter. Plant Manager De Meester created a six-person task force for "organizational innovation," consisting of the two product managers, the managers of the local Personnel and Work Study departments, the local industrial psychologist, and an employee representing the Local Works Council (a body elected by the employees, compulsory in the Netherlands by law). One of the ideas discussed in this task force was the creation of semiautonomous groups of production workers, and someone suggested that the semimechanized Ballast Assembly department might be suitable for this purpose. Hoekstra welcomed the suggestion. While he was considering how to proceed without repeating the mistakes of the past, a new event occurred.

Even after the installation of the semimechanized 40-watt line, the divisional Sales department had not been satisfied with the factory cost of the product, which still was not considered competitive. Plant management felt the threat that one day the company might decide to withdraw the product from the market altogether. Besides, there were quality problems: customers complained that a certain percentage of Philips ballasts after some time in use would start producing a disturbing humming noise and have to be replaced. In early 1972 the division's Product Development department launched a revolutionary new product design for the 40- and 65-watt ballasts, the so-called high stack model (because it used stacks of E-plates that were much higher than the former design). This new product would be qualitatively better (hum proof), use less expensive materials, and—provided certain technical problems could be solved—be simpler to make. The Plant Mechanization people got involved in designing the new production line, which was urgent not only because of the pressure from Sales but also because several of the old machines were due for replacement.

Hoekstra was informed by his former colleagues in Plant Mechanization about the high stack project and he immediately realized that here was a possibility to apply the semiautonomous group idea. He insisted that the design should be for a group of not more than 20 people. "It was sheer luck that I came from Plant Mechanization myself," he said. "Normally they would have involved me only after the design was all done."

Everts, Hoekstra's boss, supported the idea of smaller production units, but for different reasons: first, he expected that the smaller units would give more flexibility in planning; second, he was also responsible for the supply of production know-how to Philips plants abroad, and he expected that a standardized smaller unit would be more readily accepted by smaller production plants in other countries.

## Worker Consultation in the
## Design of the High Stack Units

A coordinating task force led by Everts and no less than five other task forces composed of line and staff experts was created to study the different technical, administrative, and organizational aspects of the high stack production units, which were to be operational in an unusually short time, by mid-1973. Hoekstra served on three of these task forces, one of which was created at his request. He had raised the issue of involving the workers in the department in the design of the new production organization, and this had led to the creation of a task force on "worker consultation." In this task force, besides Hoekstra, the staff departments of Personnel, Work Study, Plant Mechanization, Production Engineering, and Safety were represented, with the industrial psychologist as an additional expert.

The Worker Consultation task force had only 4 weeks to propose a consultation procedure. The Plant Mechanization group was asked to develop different alternatives for the high stack production unit layout that would be technically and economically acceptable, from which the workers could choose the one that best fit their ideas. Of five alternatives considered, two were rejected on technical or economic grounds. The three alternatives accepted were:

1. A long line (about 40 meters)
2. A Z-shaped layout
3. A square layout

In February 1973 all workers and group leaders who would be involved in the new production units received information on the three alternatives from Hoekstra in the presence of a member of the Works Council. Of 106 persons involved, 94 were present; they were divided into five groups of about 20 people each. Hoekstra explained in each group that the new technology would determine the nature of the work in the department for the next 5 years or thereabouts. Whereas the design of the product and of the production machines were imposed by outside forces and could not be discussed due to the great urgency of the need for a new product, the departmental layout and the internal organization of the working groups could be decided partly by the workers. The departmental layout would have to be decided on within the next 2 weeks whereas the internal organization of the working groups could be discussed at greater length. Start of production on the new machines was planned for October 1, 1973.

For the layout choice Hoekstra showed small-scale models of the three alternatives. Each worker received an 18-page document with a description of the new product; a specification of the various jobs to be performed; drawings of the three alternative layouts; and lists of expected technical, social, and economic advantages and disadvantages. After reading the information document, the workers were invited to participate in smaller discussion groups on the subject.

Seventy-four persons volunteered to participate in the smaller discussion groups. They were divided into 9 groups with an average of 8 persons per group. Two groups were composed of Spanish migrant workers who would otherwise have language difficulties. The groups were led by a member of the Personnel department; a second member of that department acted as a secretary; and a member of the Works Council was present as an observer. The discussion about the layout alternatives was most vivid in the early groups. It was evident that the later groups had their minds made up beforehand. Comments on the consultation procedure were very positive, and a strong interest was shown in continuing such sessions. The open-ended discussion in each group tended to move on to issues of departmental organization, especially the distribution of jobs over Job Classes 2, 3, and 4. At the end of the discussion group meetings a vote was taken on the three layout alternatives. The 73 votes were distributed as follows:

    Square:  64
    Line:     9
    Z:        0

The square layout was accepted by management. Figure 6.3 shows a sketch of this layout.

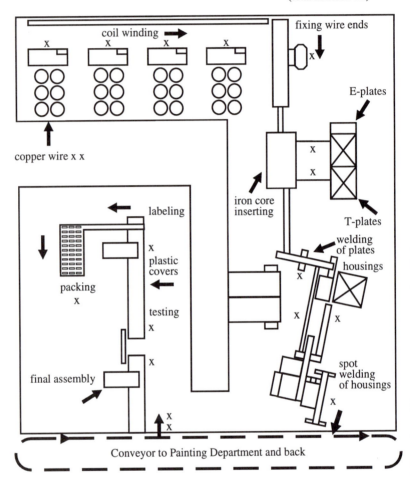

Each x represents
one workstation
(total number: 19)

**Figure 6.3.** Layout of the Square High Stack Ballast Production Unit Chosen
by the Workers in 1973

## Organizing the Tasks
## in the New High Stack Units

Start-up of production on the high stack units met with considerable
technical problems. Not until September 1974 was the production of 40-

and 65-watt ballasts completely transferred to the three new high stack groups and the old production lines discontinued. A fourth high stack group was installed in December. Compared to the old lines, work on the new units was more mechanized and left the workers less discretion to determine their own activities. In addition, two of the units had to operate in two shifts to meet production targets. Most workers who had not worked shifts before refused to do so, so the Personnel department was asked to recruit new shift workers. Shift work was particularly unpopular in the Kieldrecht area. The only candidates available in the labor market were Turkish migrants who had worked in other local companies and applied as husband-and-wife couples. Their conditions were that husband and wife would be employed in opposite shifts so that they could take turns looking after the children. As the same arrangements had been allowed to Dutch couples before, the Personnel department saw no reason for refusal. For the Turks, the shift premium and the employment of both spouses meant a considerable increase in family income, which fit well with their objective to save as much as possible as quickly as possible for their planned return to their home country.

The number of people on each high stack unit was initially 19. Later on, other mechanizations were introduced that reduced the number of people per unit to 15, divided over 6 different jobs.

During the information meeting Department Manager Hoekstra had promised consultation about the internal organization of the working groups before the start of production on the new machines. This turned out to be difficult to implement. The task force that prepared the worker consultation on the unit layout had been replaced now by a Unit Organization task force consisting of Hoekstra and representatives of the Personnel and Work Study departments, plus the industrial psychologist. When this task force first met in May 1973 it formulated a number of premises to avoid the errors of the abortive job enrichment project of 1969:

1. Transfer to the workers of nonproduction tasks such as maintenance, quality control, and administration was desirable, but could not be successfully realized without the wholehearted commitment of the staff departments involved and of higher plant management.

2. Changes in task structure should be made gradually, planned and tested carefully, and done in consultation with the workers. The latter presupposed a well-functioning consultative structure, which had so far been missing and would take time to develop. In the past, certain problems had been discussed with elected representatives of the workers, but the communications between representatives and workers had been poor. The task

force felt that for changing the task structure, a full-scale consultation system involving all workers would be necessary.

## The Shop Floor Consultation Drive

At that time, the personnel department at Philips's head office was actively promoting the idea of "shop floor consultation" in the form of regular discussion meetings of all workers with their foreman or group leader. The task force decided that any attempt at re-enriching tasks in the high stack production units should be preceded by developing shop floor consultation. This was discussed with the five group leaders reporting to Hoekstra in October 1973 during an evening meeting. They were asked to attend a four-evening training course in shop floor consultation themselves, which should enable them to subsequently train their own people.

The group leader training took place between October and December 1973. It used course material prepackaged by the head office personnel department. During the last session it was agreed that two groups working in shifts would start with the training of workers. For this, too, a training package prepared by the head office was available. The two groups selected were supposed to be the most coherent and employed fewer foreigners (Spaniards and Turks) than the other two shift groups so that language problems would be less. All the same, the group leaders asked for help in carrying out the training, if only to reinforce their self-confidence in this unfamiliar field.

The Personnel department was able to engage an industrial psychology student trainee, who was in his last year at university, as a temporary change agent from February to November 1974. Between February and April the two group leaders gave their course. The course took four 2½-hour sessions during working time and was given to half of the groups (about 10 people) at a time, so that each group leader had to teach eight sessions. Hoekstra himself was present during the first sessions and did some of the teaching. The student trainee attended most course sessions, and after each session, discussed its results with the group leaders. He summarized the effect of the course as follows:

1. Participants had learned essential skills, such as making an agenda, arriving at a group decision, making commitments, writing reports. Participants themselves were satisfied with their learning.

2. The course was at the right level of sophistication for most participants, except for the foreigners (and in particular the Turks). Both language and cultural barriers reduced the value of the course for the Turks, who felt threatened by it (they even refused to attend the last session).

3. The course contributed to the cohesion of the groups (except for the Turks) and to the confidence of the people in their group leader, as well as to the latter's self-confidence.

4. Some participants expressed a fair amount of suspicion as to the support of higher local management, their real intentions with the shop floor consultation, and whether they would allow it to continue.

In March 1974 Hoekstra announced to his group leaders that from now on he would conduct his meetings with them according to the rules of the shop floor consultation procedure (agenda, group decisions, etc.). He subsequently discovered that switching to a new relationship with his people was not so easy. Group leaders were hesitant to take more initiative and he himself had great trouble in taking less. A feedback session in which the group leaders commented on his style of leadership proved helpful in changing this.

*Shop Floor Consultation in the High Stack Units.* The two production groups trained in shop floor consultation held their first consultation meeting in May. Because the problems to be discussed involved the entire group, it was decided that these meetings should be held with the entire group (19 persons plus replacements) in spite of the difficulty of communicating in so large a group. Hoekstra and his new boss, Mr. Jansen, were present during the first meeting, the latter to try to overcome people's suspicion about support from higher management.

At about the same time technical problems in the high stack production units (which were still not fully operational) led to serious backlogs in product deliveries. Some staff people suggested that under these critical circumstances, a time-consuming activity like shop floor consultation should be temporarily discontinued. The Unit Organization task force immediately reacted by stating that discontinuing the consultation meetings at the present time would be disastrous and would destroy the little bit of confidence that had been built. The consultation meetings, on the contrary, could be used to overcome the problems.

Hoekstra succeeded in convincing his superiors to support the consultation experiment. The workers were told about the delivery problems and asked for an extra effort. They reacted in a calm and positive way, as it was clear that no one was trying to blame them for the problems, which were essentially technical. Only the Turks, who still felt very uncertain, misunderstood Hoekstra's appeal as a critique of their own performance. It took a lot of patience from some of their colleagues to correct the misunderstanding.

The first two consultation meetings in each group dealt mainly with two types of issues:

1. Problems of internal organization that could be, and were, resolved internally, such as demarcations between different jobs, scheduling of breaks, job rotation. Both groups decided to experiment with job rotation. A clear argument in favor of this was that people expected that in this way those in the lowest job classes (2 and 3) could be promoted to a higher class. The job class differences within the group were felt as a major problem.

2. Relatively small technical or organizational improvements that could not be resolved within the group, but needed intervention by staff departments, such as supplying tools and work clothes, small changes on machines, moving a machine. After two meetings it became clear that somehow the resolution of these problems via the communication chain of group leader, department manager, and staff departments did not function well; most problems remained unresolved. One example was a request for a small ladder across the conveyor belt to enable workers to reach the other side of their machine in case of technical breakdowns. The first request for such a ladder dated from November 1973; it was finally built in September 1974. The lack of response on these problems was felt by the consultation groups as extremely frustrating. At the third consultation meeting, in July 1974, one of the groups revolted and decided to send a delegation to the department manager with an ultimatum: they would stop participating in the consultation meetings if their requests were not handled more diligently. Hoekstra promised his utmost support to resolve the problems as soon as possible.

In July 1974 the production backlogs were overcome and deliveries were back to normal. In September and October the trainee psychology student conducted an interview survey among line managers and staff people and a questionnaire survey among workers within and outside the shop floor consultation groups about their opinions about the consultation system. His main conclusions were:

1. Line managers and staff people expected shop floor consultation to contribute to the workers' motivation to a better performance by satisfying their needs for information, responsibility, and independence. Workers, however, did not feel that their information, responsibility, or independence had improved. Those involved in the consultation meetings did not

perceive increased contact with management or increased influence in what went on in the department.

2. Workers had become less hesitant to approach their superiors. They asked more direct questions of group leaders and department managers, from which the latter could not easily escape. This meant that the workload of group leaders and department managers increased. Workers in the consultation groups had become more critical toward their group leaders and department managers than those in the groups without consultation.

3. Shop floor consultation was not integrated in the established organization structure of the plant. Neither line management, nor in particular, staff departments had integrated it into their organization concepts. It was still a foreign body.

4. Language and cultural differences prevented the integration of foreigners, especially Turks, in the consultation process.

5. Workers in the consultation groups strongly expected that the consultation system was there to stay, but as yet there were no signs of a dispersion effect to other departments. Nowhere else in the plant had anybody claimed shop floor consultation.

In the high stack production department two more production groups started shop floor consultation in early 1975. The Unit Organization task force, which had been reinforced by the new product manager, Jansen, at that time reviewed the situation. The high stack groups had become operational and four of them had started shop floor consultation. Nevertheless, little advance had been made toward the original goal of work structuring. The only type of work structuring that was possible within the groups was job rotation, and this was tried; but the tasks themselves remained uninteresting and subsequent mechanizations only tended to make them even less interesting. The integration of nonproduction tasks (maintenance, quality control) met with little enthusiasm from staff groups. In introducing shop floor consultation the task force had adopted a ready-made solution offered by the company head office. They now realized that this solution, however desirable for other reasons, did not resolve the problem of alienating tasks. The Unit Organization task force wondered how it should go on from here.

## Back to the
## Work Structuring Problem

In 1975 the divisional top management of the Lighting products division of Philips issued a policy statement encouraging the plants to use shop floor consultation: exactly what the task force had just been working on. But the task force had arrived at the conclusion that for the moment the subject of shop floor consultation in the high stack production department had received enough attention. It wanted to return to its original objective of work structuring. To proceed in this direction, two things were necessary. One was mobilizing the active support of higher plant management, so that from the plant manager downward the changes to come would be integrated into the total organization structure. The other was careful research into the real possibilities for work structuring, to be carried out with the help of the staff departments. This research would determine to what extent tasks now undertaken by staff departments—such as Repairs, Preventive Maintenance, Quality Control, Planning—could be reintegrated into production operations, taking into account the particular technological conditions of the department.

For this research the help was obtained of a sociologist from the Work Study department at the divisional head office. He was made available for 2 days a week for 6 months beginning January 1975. He first surveyed all managers of all staff departments about their views on the transfer of tasks to the production department, using a checklist of sociotechnical job design criteria. In a second round of interviews he contacted all staff employees directly involved with the production units. Based on these interviews he could draw a detailed sociotechnical picture of the production system and its supporting departments. That is, he could show both the technical and the social processes at work, as well as their interfaces and conflicts. This picture suggested that there were some possibilities of transferring staff tasks to operators, as had been tried before: some maintenance, some quality control, some planning. In other cases information could be provided to operators, enabling them to draw their own conclusions rather than being told by others what they should do. However, technical constraints and the necessity for organizational coordination put rather narrow limits to the amount of work structuring that could be expected.

The interviews led to some immediate action from the Plant Mechanization people. In informal contacts with the production groups they started to transfer certain machine maintenance and repair activities to the production operators. After some initial squabbling this went smoothly and the production workers took a more active role in maintenance. Also, machine resetting in case of product type changes (about once a month) was now done in close collaboration between Plant Mechanization and production personnel. In other cases more preparatory work had to be done before the transfer of tasks could even be discussed. Problems of cooperation among departments had to be re-searched; also, more factual information was needed, especially a systematic inventory of the causes of machine downtime.

A two-step plan for the transfer of staff tasks to the production workers was finally accepted by all parties in 1977:

1. For autumn 1977: transfer of additional maintenance tasks, including cleaning of machine parts, scheduled preventive maintenance, repair of small breakdowns, direct signaling in case of larger breakdowns. This implied training of the machine operators in technical skills and knowledge by the Plant Mechanization people.
2. For autumn 1978: transfer of quality control tasks, including control of input materials, process specifications (measurement tolerances, finish appearance after each step in the process), and output control (electrical performance).

Although within the production groups workers continued to practice some job rotation, it also turned out that some people did not want to rotate, and these were not forced to. The initial purpose to get all workers into the highest job class (4) was not achieved. According to a group leader, some people were unable to do more skilled work than Class 2. The department included many older workers, over 50, and several of them were considered to have reached their ceiling of qualification. The job classification system fixed by companywide collective bargaining was clearly felt by the groups as a roadblock to a new way of group functioning. The Turks had become less of a problem. Some had left and others became more integrated. The men among them (not the women) would even speak up in consultation meetings.

## Toward the
## Next Round of New Technology

The Unit Organization task force in the meantime began to direct its attention toward the sociotechnical design of an entirely new technology for ballast production that was supposed to become operational in 1980. As preparation, the task force asked the Personnel department to make a long-term forecast of the labor market situation; this was completed in January 1977. It predicted that the current high rate of unemployment in the Kieldrecht area would probably continue, but this unemployment touched the skilled and white-collar workers much more than the unskilled, of whom there would be a scarcity. The skilled and white-collar applicants would not consider the present type of work on ballast assembly as suitable. The task force therefore suggested going for a new technology in 1980 in which unskilled labor would be eliminated as much as possible and the remaining personnel would have a process control type role. It was expected that such a role would be more attractive to more qualified job applicants.

At the request of the Unit Organization task force, the management team decided that in the design and implementation of the new technology social and organizational aspects should be given equal treatment to economic and technical factors. This was to be reflected in the composition of the project group to be created for designing the new technology.

## The Long March
## Toward Humanization of Work

This case shows a kind of pilgrim's progress toward humanization of work, or work structuring as it was called at Philips: two steps ahead, one step back. Over a period of almost 10 years little real progress was made in spite of endless meetings, committees and task forces,[2] the active support of head office staff departments, and creative and even courageous actions by several persons, especially Paul Hoekstra. Market and technological developments had an obvious priority, and they left only limited room for modifying tasks.

The first attempt by Van Dikhout in 1969 was a disaster. He tried a quick-and-dirty steamroller approach, and the scars left in people's sense of security remained after 8 years. Any change in an organization has two aspects: its content and its process, that is, the way it is introduced. Van Dikhout failed completely on the process side, and therefore the content could not be a success either.

Hoekstra was much more careful and better prepared. His action to get the workers to vote on the layout of the new high stack units was unique and spectacular. Unfortunately the effects of such an action have only a limited time span: because of labor turnover, those who arrive later find the layout all set up and have as little influence as anybody had before the changeover. Still, the action was worthwhile, also because it impressed on both the production workers and the specialist designers that introducing a new system needs the ideas of both groups.

Having a layout on which people had voted did not mean their new jobs were more humanized than their old ones. Because of the changes in technology the net effect on the tasks was zero at best. What was recognized was the interest of the workers to move into a higher pay category, one of their priorities according to Chapter 2 of this book. But the constraints of a collective labor agreement and the limits to the learning capacities of some of the workers made the goal of Class 4 pay for everybody unattainable.

The shop floor consultation drive appears to be somewhat of a red herring in this case, but it shows how much impact top management and head office ideologies have at the bottom of the organization. The ballast production units were caught in two humanization efforts at the same time: work restructuring (from right to left in Figure 4.2) and shop floor consultation (from bottom to top in Figure 4.2). Neither completely succeeded, but the case pictures the hurdles that had to be overcome. One conclusion is a confirmation of the moral of Chapter 3: the values of the people whose jobs are to be humanized are not the same as those of the humanizers or the power holders.

One evident conclusion from the entire process is that one cannot change tasks of direct production workers without changing tasks of indirect workers and staff departments. Unwillingness of staff departments to give up part of their domain has been a major roadblock to work restructuring. Therefore, the active support of the plant manager to whom both line and staff report is essential.

An interesting role in the case is played by the migrant workers who had become a regular component of the unskilled work force in the Netherlands, first Spaniards and later Turks. The progressive acculturation of these people to the Dutch way of life and consensus relationships is recognizable. The Spaniards participated in the discussion about the new layout, but in their own groups for language reasons. The Turks were very suspicious at first, but by the end of the case at least the men among them had started to play the game the Dutch way; the women needed more time, but there is little doubt that given this time, they would eventually follow.[3]

The case ends with a perspective on the next round of technological change, but the company has learned a lesson—which is by no means the case for all companies—that in the project team for the new technology the social and organizational viewpoints should contribute on equal footing with the technical and economic ones.

## Discussion Questions

1. What did Van Dikhout do wrong? Could his approach have been the correct one in another environment?

2. What were the benefits of having the production workers choose from three new layouts? What expected benefits were not achieved? What were the costs of this approach?

3. There seems to be a conflict between progress toward humanization of work and the recruitment of immigrant workers (see also Chapter 5). Why is this so? Can anything be done about it?

4. Both Chapters 5 and 6 deal with attempts at humanization of work in the Netherlands in the 1970s. Why were the results so different? What role was played by the different corporate cultures, the large city versus small town environment, the different products and production technologies, the different personalities?

## Notes

1. This is a fictitious name. The names of persons in this case have also been changed at the request of the company.

2. The leading principle of management in the Netherlands has been described by a French researcher as *consensus* (d'Iribarne, 1989). This case is a vivid illustration.

3. See a study about the acculturation of Italian and Spanish migrant workers in the Netherlands by Hofstede and Kranenburg (1974).

# PART II

# Power and Control in Organizations

The six chapters of Part II consist of three articles, partly data based, partly essay, and three case studies from different European countries: France, French-speaking Switzerland, and the Netherlands.

Chapter 7 is a data-based study that links the concerns of Part I of the book (the impact of jobs on people) with those of Part II (power and control). It looks at the job situation of managers, professionals, and clerks in an international and in national headquarters operations of a multinational, and reveals considerable alienation in terms of Part I. The extent of this alienation appears to depend on the relationship of a headquarters department with subsidiary parts of the organization. Toward subsidiaries, headquarters departments exercise control and/or give support. The chapter relates these to the alienation felt.

Chapter 8 is an essay concerned with one particular form of management control—budgeting—and which factors make a budget control system an effective tool of management. It is inspired by my 1967 doctoral thesis *The Game of Budget Control*, but in particular, I try to analyze the potential of quantitative methods to improve the effectiveness of a budget system. I conclude that this potential is quite modest, as quantitative

115

methods tend to make the systems less user friendly. Examples are given of how certain aspects of the people side of budgeting can be quantified, indicating areas for improvement more likely to be successful.

Chapter 9 is another essay on management control, in which I explore the limits of what can be controlled by a budget system. Budget systems are typically designed in a cybernetic fashion, that is, based on the assumption that feedback about results will lead to improvements the next time around. The chapter explores alternative paradigms for budget control and for management control in general. The control of nonroutine, nonindustrial-type processes is unlikely to benefit much from a budget system; it is basically a political process. This issue is very topical again in the 1990s, in view of the discussion about "accountable management" in the public service of industrialized countries.

A very political process is described in the first case study, Chapter 10. It relates the rise and fall of Boimondau, a French worker-owned business company, which the author visited both in its heyday (1955) and immediately after its demise (1972). It is the story of an honest attempt to share power in an organization and of the limits that economics, culture, and maybe human nature set to such an attempt. It is an archetypical case of the confrontation of utopian vision with real-life practice, as George Orwell immortalized in *Animal Farm* (1945).

The next case study is not from a business, but from a school setting, not far from the scene of the previous case. Chapter 11 describes events that happened very close to me and my family, in Lausanne, French-speaking Switzerland, in 1972. It is a case of attempted reform, rebellion, and repression, and it illustrates vividly the resistances to changing the power relationships on which the establishment of a society is historically based.

For the last case, Chapter 12, we are back in the Netherlands. This case, based on unique insider information, pictures the events around a successful consumer boycott in 1972 of Douwe Egberts, the largest Dutch coffee and tea firm, organized by a civic action group concerned with the conditions at the coffee plantations in Angola, then still a Portuguese colony. It shows the dilemmas of a management team confronted with unsolicited new stakeholders, who assume power and undermine the management's control because they succeed in mobilizing the consumers by raising the right issue at the right time. Power in organizations is limited by events in their environment, which should be recognized in time if management wants to retain control.

# 7

# Alienation at the Top

Survey data about opportunities to contribute to company success are used to demonstrate that in one large multinational, managers, professionals, and clerks at the European headquarters and to a lesser extent at the various country headquarters often considered their jobs to be meaningless. This was less the case in the various local sales offices with direct customer contact. Conversely, the image among managers of the company as such grew from the sales offices via the country headquarters to the international headquarters. This is interpreted as a form of alienation due to company bureaucracy. In another survey, country headquarters personnel were asked about the amounts of support and control they experienced from their counterparts in the international headquarters. It appeared that personnel in international headquarters departments seen in the countries as providing support did not perceive their own jobs as meaningless. On the other hand, the perceived amount of control wielded was unrelated to headquarters alienation. These findings are used for an exploration of the phenomena of power and control in a bureaucracy; forms of "executive job enrichment" are suggested to reduce headquarters alienation. These can be sought in reflecting, recruiting, rewarding, and restructuring.

## Big Company Bureaucracy

A large multinational corporation suffered the resignation of three key executives in one of its subsidiaries within 2 months. Distressed by these losses, which were totally unexpected, the international vice president asked a consulting psychologist to conduct postexit interviews with the

This chapter was originally published in *Organizational Dynamics*, 4(3), Winter 1976, pp. 44-60. It was reprinted in M. Ghertman and J. Leontiades (Eds.), *European Research in International Business*, Amsterdam: North-Holland Publishing, 1978, pp. 307-330; and in D. A. Kolb, I. M. Rubin, and J. M. McIntyre (Eds.), *Organizational Psychology: Readings on Human Behavior in Organizations* (4th ed.), Englewood Cliffs, NJ: Prentice-Hall, 1984, pp. 514-528. Reprinted with permission from *Organizational Dynamics*.

three men. Were the three resignations in any way related? Did they signal a serious crisis of which the vice president was unaware?

The three men all met with the psychologist very willingly. In fact, they appeared eager to supply this kind of feedback-from-a-distance to their former employer. The interviews revealed that on a direct cause-and-effect level, their almost simultaneous resignations were a coincidence. They had not been influenced by each other, and their new jobs were with different companies.

At the same time their three cases were strikingly similar in many ways. All three men were in their early 40s—an age that normally is the peak of a man's working life, when he has both a past to build on and a future to look forward to. All three so far had spent virtually their entire career with the same large employer, had liked their jobs, and had been highly successful. All three had been very well paid, and prospects of improved earnings in their new jobs were minor or nonexistent. Job security was less in the new jobs than in the old. All three were quite positive about their former employer: "It is a great company. What I am now, I owe to them." However, all three complained about being increasingly frustrated by company bureaucracy as they moved up, and all three moved to new positions that involved a bigger job in a smaller company.

No specific organizational crisis, then, caused these executives to resign; instead, the cause was a midcareer crisis in their personal orientations toward their work—a common feeling of frustration, meaninglessness, and powerlessness that seemed to have grown in tandem with the increase in their formal power as measured by their hierarchical position. They felt less and less able to make the impact on the company that they wanted to make, and for this they blamed not particular individuals but a conglomerate of impersonal forces generated by "company bureaucracy."

## The Alienation Phenomenon

The ambition to make a meaningful impact, however modest, in one's life environment is common to most people. Many worry nowadays about the state of mind of industrial and office workers who have to do simple, repetitive tasks devoid of any meaning to them. The word *alienation* is used to describe the effect of these jobs on people.

Alienation is a term borrowed from sociology and used by different authors to include different attributes,[1] but it always centers on individuals' feelings of powerlessness and meaninglessness, their inability to influence or even understand the forces on which their life and happiness depend. This feeling is by no means limited to industrial workers. For example, the term has also been used to describe the state of mind of students at U.S. universities. Feelings of alienation may be found, to different extents, at all levels within bureaucratic organizations.

The word *bureaucracy*, in popular parlance, has acquired a strong negative connotation—but in its original sociological context it refers to any formal system for simplifying the management of large and complex activities. As such it applies to public as well as private organizations, the shop floor as well as the executive suite. Bureaucracies are born of necessity; without them, large-scale human activities would be unmanageable. The paradox is that by their very existence they generate forces that defeat their own ends (Perrow, 1972). The main problem appears to be that the models of people on which bureaucratic structures are built are too different from real people. Bureaucracies ask people to behave in standardized ways, whereas real people never do. If they are forced to behave as if they were standard, the consequence is alienation. The three executives who blamed their move on bureaucracy in the large corporation moved to escape the alienation they had increasingly experienced.

## Alienation as
## Reflected in Attitude Survey Scores

Evidence of employee alienation was found in the European part of a large multinational corporation. This corporation marketed its products through a subsidiary in each country. It operated sales offices in the major cities, which were coordinated by a head office in each country. All country head offices in Europe reported directly to a European headquarters.

In 1968 and 1969 this corporation conducted a series of attitude surveys of all its employees and managers. These surveys seemed to show an alienation problem at a surprising place—within the corporation's European headquarters. Moreover, this alienation problem affected not only the headquarters rank-and-file employees but also its managers. In fact there were reasons to consider the problem more serious for headquarters managers than for other categories of employees.

Attitude survey results, far from being dull statistics, can reveal fascinating secrets about the functioning of organizations, as the following tables will show. In composing the survey questionnaire we believed that one yardstick for determining the meaningfulness of a job would be a person's felt ability to make some contribution to the overall company

**TABLE 7.1** Satisfaction With Opportunity to Contribute to Company Success

| | | Percentage Scoring | | |
| | Number of Respondents | Dissatisfied or Very Dissatisfied | Neither Satisfied nor Dissatisfied | Satisfied or Very Satisfied |
|---|---|---|---|---|
| **Managers in:** | | | | |
| Sales offices | 1,277 | 5 | 18 | 77 |
| Country head offices | 896 | 9 | 31 | 60 |
| International headquarters | 106 | 14 | 39 | 47 |
| **Professional employees in:** | | | | |
| Sales offices | 7,096 | 6 | 32 | 62 |
| Country head offices | 1,144 | 16 | 36 | 48 |
| International headquarters | 49 | 24 | 50 | 26 |
| **Clerical employees in:** | | | | |
| Sales offices | 1,811 | 14 | 40 | 46 |
| Country head offices | 4,133 | 17 | 42 | 41 |
| International headquarters | 143 | 21 | 46 | 33 |

result. We therefore asked (among other things): "How satisfied are you with your opportunity to make a real contribution to the success of the company?" In Table 7.1 the distribution of answers to this question is shown for three groups of employees: managers (anyone responsible for coordinating the work of others), professional employees (college-educated, specialized personnel such as salespersons, engineers, and accountants), and clerical employees (non-college-educated, administrative personnel). Results are also divided according to three kinds of work locations: sales offices (within countries), country head offices, and the European international headquarters.

Table 7.1 reveals that for all three categories of employees—managers, professionals, and clerks—there is a consistent decrease of satisfaction from the sales offices to the international headquarters. Also, managers were more satisfied than professionals, and professionals more than clerks, except within the international headquarters, where clerks were more satisfied than professionals. In fact, the satisfaction level of managers in the international headquarters (47% satisfied) was almost exactly the same as for professionals in the country headquarters (48%) and for clerks in the sales offices (46%).

That managers are more satisfied with their opportunity to contribute to the company's success than clerks was to be expected because, by definition, they have a more central role in the organization. But although the international headquarters also has a central role, its satisfaction level was *lowest*. This level increases as we go to the country head offices and from there to the sales offices. Dissatisfaction indicating alienation thus was least present at the sales offices and reached a peak at the international headquarters.

## Other Survey Results

The attitude surveys also showed that satisfaction with opportunity to make a real contribution to the success of this company tended to go hand in hand with satisfaction with other aspects of job content. In a statistical analysis of the survey scores for each of the various categories of employees, a close correlation was found between satisfaction with opportunity to contribute and the answers to two other questions: "How satisfied are you with the challenge of the work you do—the extent to which you can get a personal sense of accomplishment out of it?" and "How satisfied are you with the extent to which you use your skills and abilities on your job?" The three questions together form a statistical cluster that indicates, in general, satisfaction with the *intrinsic nature or content of the job*. The close relationship between these three questions implies that the two other questions should show differences between managers and others and between sales offices and headquarters similar to those shown by satisfaction with opportunity to contribute. Table 7.2 allows us to verify this (for simplicity's sake only percents satisfied are shown).

Table 7.2 reveals the same kind of differences between managers, professionals, and clerks and between sales offices, country head offices, and international headquarters as Table 7.1. However, the differences in Table 7.2 tend to be smaller than in 7.1. Especially for managers, there are greater differences between sales offices and headquarters in satisfaction with opportunity to contribute than in challenge or use of skills. This suggests that the differences in managers' feelings of challenge and use of skills may be the *consequence* of their different satisfaction with opportunity to contribute.

## The Subjective Importance of Contributing to Company Success

Satisfaction with opportunity to contribute is subjectively more important to managers than it is to other organization members. This was disclosed in the above-mentioned attitude surveys by a parallel set of

**TABLE 7.2** Intrinsic Job Interest

| | Percentage Scoring Satisfied or Very Satisfied | |
| --- | --- | --- |
| | Challenge of the Work | Use of Skills and Abilities |
| Managers in: | | |
| Sales offices | 77 | 65 |
| Country head offices | 66 | 61 |
| International headquarters | 56 | 55 |
| Professional employees in: | | |
| Sales offices | 71 | 57 |
| Country head offices | 53 | 48 |
| International headquarters | 39 | 37 |
| Clerical employees in: | | |
| Sales offices | 53 | 46 |
| Country head offices | 46 | 42 |
| International headquarters | 34 | 36 |

questions to the satisfaction questions. These parallel questions tried to elicit the *importance* of various work goals to the employee. Instead of "How satisfied are you with . . . ?" the questions began with "How important is it to you to . . . ?" (for example, have a job that allows you to make a real contribution to the success of your company).

In the most extensive version of the survey there were 22 importance and 22 satisfaction questions. The 22 items covered the entire field of the relationship of people to their job—such as earnings, impact on personal life, learning, security, interpersonal relationships, and advancement opportunities. The importance questions allowed us to rank these 22 items in order of the importance attached to them by a certain category of employees. Rank 1 would be given to the item that on the average received the highest importance score; Rank 22, the lowest. The relative importance attached to contributing to company success by our various categories of employees is shown in Table 7.3.

Table 7.3 proves what was stated above: managers distinguished themselves from others by attaching a much higher importance to contributing to company success. Whereas for professionals and clerks this issue ranked from 12 to 18 out of 22, for managers it ranked fifth in the sales offices, third in the country head offices, and second in the international headquarters. In the international headquarters, the only work aspect managers rated more important than contributing to company success was challenging work. In the country head offices, managers

**TABLE 7.3** Importance of Contributing to Company Success

|                                    | *Average Rank Order* |
| ---------------------------------- | :------------------: |
| Managers in:                       |                      |
|   Sales offices          | 5                    |
|   Country head offices   | 3                    |
|   International headquarters | 2                 |
|                                    |                      |
| Professional employees in:         |                      |
|   Sales offices          | 14                   |
|   Country head offices   | 15                   |
|   International headquarters | 12                |
|                                    |                      |
| Clerical employees in:             |                      |
|   Sales offices          | 16                   |
|   Country head offices   | 18                   |
|   International headquarters | 18                |

NOTE: Rankings: 1 = *most important*, 22 = *least important*.

viewed challenging work and a good working relationship with their own manager as being more important than contributing to company success. In the sales offices, the four items rated more important by managers were, in order of importance, challenging work, considerable freedom to adopt your own approach to the job, an opportunity for advancement, and training opportunities.

If we compare the satisfaction percentages (Table 7.1) and the importance rankings (Table 7.3), we can see that the problem of alienation—not making a real contribution to the success of the company—was particularly acute for the international headquarters managers by a combination of high attached importance (ranked second) and low satisfaction (only 47% satisfied). It was much less pressing, for example, for clerical employees, who although not very satisfied, indicated by their low importance scores that to them many other aspects of the job compensated for the lack of satisfaction with opportunity to contribute to company success. This way out is not open to most managers.

## Images of the Organization as Such

Alienation, according to these data, does affect one's self-image, but not necessarily one's image of the organization one works for. In fact the two may be negatively correlated. The surveys also contained a question about the image of the company as such (not in terms of one's personal

**TABLE 7.4** Success of the Company as Such

|  | Percentage Scoring | | |
|---|---|---|---|
|  | No Feeling or Dissatisfied | Satisfied | Very Satisfied |
| Managers in: | | | |
| Sales offices | 18 | 53 | 29 |
| Country head offices | 15 | 52 | 33 |
| International headquarters | 11 | 45 | 44 |

contribution to it): "How satisfied are you with the extent to which this company is regarded as successful?"

The results for managers are shown in Table 7.4. As the overall level of answering was very favorable, we have taken the cutoff point between "very satisfied" and "satisfied." It is clear that in this case the highest success ratings were given at international headquarters and the least high at the sales offices. This is the opposite of the trend for the question about the managers' personal contribution to the company's success. It seems that the lack of satisfaction of the international headquarters managers with their personal contribution is partly compensated by a sense of pride in the company—"Never mind my job, but it is a great company to be in."

## Motivational Consequences of Red Tape

When they were presented with the survey data, some people were surprised: they had expected that respondents in the subsidiaries would be the *least* satisfied because they would be frustrated by interventions from headquarters. This expectation was based on the implicit assumption that bureaucratic systems ("red tape") are invented by people in headquarters who obviously must like what they are doing. Our data show this assumption to be wrong. In fact, it is a gross oversimplification of the origins of bureaucracy. The surveys did address the issues of the relationships between subsidiaries and headquarters. Managers and professionals in the country head offices were asked how frequently (if at all) the following problems occurred:

- International headquarters doesn't give people in our country head offices enough support.
- International headquarters interferes too much.

**TABLE 7.5** Distribution of Responses to the "Support" and "Interference" Questions

| | From Country Head Office | | | | From International Headquarters | | | |
|---|---|---|---|---|---|---|---|---|
| | Not Enough Support | | Too Much Interference | | Not Enough Support | | Too Much Interference | |
| | Very Frequently or Frequently | Seldom or Never | Very Frequently or Frequently | Seldom or Never | Very Frequently or Frequently | Seldom or Never | Very Frequently or Frequently | Seldom or Never |
| **Managers in:** | | | | | | | | |
| Sales offices | 32 | 24 | 27 | 27 | 13 | 59 | 7 | 72 |
| Country head offices | — | — | — | — | 31 | 29 | 26 | 42 |
| **Professional employees in:** | | | | | | | | |
| Sales offices | 30 | 27 | 23 | 34 | 5 | 75 | 3 | 83 |
| Country head offices | — | — | — | — | 25 | 34 | 21 | 47 |

NOTE: Expressed in percentages. The percentages of those answering "sometimes" are not shown.

People in the sales offices were asked the same questions with regard to *both* international headquarters and the country head offices. The answers are summarized in Table 7.5, from which we can read:

1. Those answering "very frequently" or "frequently" never exceed one third of the managers or professionals questioned.
2. Sales offices had few problems with international headquarters (these were dealt with at country head office level), but they had about the same level of problems with their country head office as country head offices had with international headquarters.
3. In all cases, problems were somewhat more frequently seen as "not enough support" rather than as "too much interference."
4. In all cases, problems were somewhat more frequently felt by managers than by nonmanagers.

A more important finding (not visible in Table 7.5) was that the answers to the questions on support and interference were statistically only weakly related to those about other aspects of the managers' or professionals' job satisfaction. Feeling a lack of support or too much interference, although frustrating, did not seem to affect too much the way people felt about their work. In the total picture of the attitude of

toward their jobs it stayed at the level of a minor irritation. The
of alienation that we related to not feeling able to make a real
ّution to the company's success goes much deeper. There is no real
adversary to blame: the system in which one is absorbed is unclear and
individuals feel they are wasting their time, although working very hard.

## The Price of Alienation

The price an organization pays for the alienation of its employees will
vary from company to company, job to job, and individual employee to
individual employee. In general alienated employees will lower their
aspirations to perform because they see their performance as meaningless anyway. They are less likely to exert an extra effort. As an illustration,
surveyed managers in country sales offices reported spending considerably more voluntary overtime on their jobs than did managers in country
and international head offices (observation of managers in action confirms that sales office managers do spend longer hours working). In spite
of this, sales office managers did not claim to be overloaded any more
frequently than did head office managers. A considerably greater frac-
tion of sales office managers would accept these longer hours without
feeling overloaded.

Other things being equal, employees with higher skill and education
levels expect more intrinsic satisfaction from their jobs and have a
stronger need to use their skills as fully as possible. They are, therefore,
more likely to quit if they feel alienated and if alternative jobs are
available. People who have experienced success in the past are more
frustrated by alienation than less successful people.

This fact was demonstrated in a study within the same company in
which 326 participants of an in-company executive training program
were followed through their careers after training (see Chapter 15 of this
book). The average time span between training and follow-up was 4
years. During this period, 20 participants had left the company (a very
low turnover rate). Of these 20, however, 16 had been rated by their
trainers as being among the top third of their class. This means that the
one third most successful trainees were eight times as likely to quit as
the two thirds less successful ones.

Even if we discount the fact that trainers are not infallible in their
judgment, it is still a reasonable assumption that these more successful
trainees would also tend to be the better performers in their day-to-day
jobs. The careers study therefore shows how alienation may lead to
selective employee turnover: the more successful people tend to leave.

The departure of the three executives mentioned in the introduction to this article upset the vice president because they, too, were star performers. There is a real danger that a company headquarters by this process may become stuck with a residue of disillusioned low achievers, who in turn expand the bureaucracy of which they themselves are the victims.

In the previous paragraphs the assumption has been made of a potential need to achieve and to make a contribution to the company's success in all people. The situation rather than the employees was blamed where this contribution was missing. At the same time, persons and even entire cultures differ in their need for achievement and their need to contribute. Jobs with a low potential to contribute to the company's success will by a process of natural selection attract persons for whom the need to contribute is low. Our data suggest that such people are more likely to stay in headquarters jobs; strong achievers try to avoid these jobs.

## Job Enrichment
## for Headquarters Executives

On the shop and office floor the danger of alienation has been recognized and efforts have been made to restore humanity to jobs dehumanized by the bureaucratic process (see the case studies in Chapters 5 and 6). These efforts are often called "job enrichment" (Herzberg, 1966). Traditional job enrichment focuses mainly on the structure of individual jobs, the dominant trend in the United States. In Europe, especially in Sweden and Norway, humanization of work has concentrated on changing group tasks rather than individual jobs (see Chapter 3).

Is job enrichment possible in the headquarters of large corporations? It is unlikely in this case that restructuring individual jobs will be sufficient, because the entire bureaucratic system of the organization is involved in the forces that lead to alienation. Job enrichment approaches here should include not only individuals but also groups and the role of entire departments.

The jobs we usually find in headquarters show a great variety: there are the top executives with their personal staffs; those who deal with the outside on behalf of the corporation; those who plan ahead for the short and for the long term and those who look after the execution of these plans by the various subsidiaries; those who write policies for the corporation and those who check whether these policies are being followed; those who coordinate the flow of funds, materials, people, orders, and ideas between the various subsidiaries; and those who possess unique expertise or perform unique services that the subsidiaries are not in a position to do by themselves. The bigger the headquarters becomes, the greater the number of those necessary to keep the headquarters itself running.

Why, then, in our multinational corporation would alienation be so much lower in the sales offices than in such a headquarters? What is different about jobs in sales offices? At least two differences are noteworthy:

1. Sales office jobs compared with headquarters jobs contain much more direct feedback about results—one knows whether one has worked successfully or not.
2. Sales office jobs more than headquarters jobs involve a direct client or customer relationship—there is a visible person, the customer, who is either satisfied or not.

Both *direct feedback* and a *client relationship* are recognized by job enrichment experts to be among the key requirements for an "enriched" job. Headquarters jobs, on the other hand, usually receive little or no feedback on their success, and it is generally less clear who their client is—the subsidiary offices, higher management . . . or do they have clients at all?

It is evident that, with headquarters containing such a mixed bag of roles, the alienation phenomenon will not be the same among all headquarters activities. In fact, the employee attitude survey recorded that among these activities, the satisfaction with "contribution to company success" varied from 70% to only 20% of personnel scoring "very satisfied" or "satisfied" (taking managers, professionals, and clerical employees together). We should therefore further investigate who in headquarters felt alienated and who did not, and why. For this purpose the results can be used of still another project, the Headquarters Effectiveness Study.

## The Headquarters Effectiveness Study

In the same multinational corporation that supplied the alienation data, the European vice president, after the employee attitude survey, decided he wanted feedback on the effectiveness of his international headquarters operation. He asked the corporate Personnel Research department to carry out a study of how people in country head offices looked at the job done by their international headquarters counterparts. This survey, carried out 6 months after the employee attitude survey, became known as the Headquarters Effectiveness Study. In this project the departments of the international headquarters were divided into seven main functions (such as market research, finance, and personnel) and then subdivided into 49 departments or activities. For each activity the person acting as the main "customer" in each country head office was identified and presented with a written questionnaire to be returned to the corporate Personnel Research department. Anonymity of answers was guaranteed unless "customers" expressly wanted their identity to be known. Of the more than 1100 questionnaires mailed out, more than 800 (73%) were returned. The questionnaire contained some forced-choice questions along with a number of write-in questions. The responses to the latter were assembled for each of the 49 international headquarters activities and sent to the person responsible for that activity.

Among other things, the forced-choice questions tried to get the "customers" to rate the headquarters activities on the two dimensions of *support* and *control*. Support was defined as "advice and counsel, help with specific problems, expert answers, and information that helps you to do a better job." Support given by the international headquarters activity in the past 12 months was evaluated by the country head office "customers" from the points of view of quantity and of quality. Control was defined as "staff supervision: monitoring country practices, policies, and procedures; international coordination; auditing, and so on—all aimed at ensuring a high level of overall performance." The "customers" were asked how they felt about the amount of control received from their international headquarters counterpart over the past 12 months.

The results revealed that quantity and quality of support generally went hand in hand, making it possible to compute a support index for each activity of the international headquarters, including both quantity and quality. Control and support were less strongly related (if at all, control was related to quantity of support but not to quality). Some headquarters activities were seen as high in both support and control and some as low in both support and control, but others were high in support and low in control, or low in support and high in control.

## Relationships Between Perceived Support and Control and Headquarters Alienation

As the Headquarters Effectiveness Study (in which people in the country head offices rated the international headquarters) followed closely after the employee attitude survey (in which people both in the country head offices and in international headquarters rated their

**TABLE 7.6** Comparison of Outcomes of Two Surveys

| Headquarters Main Functions | Employee Attitudes Survey[a] | Headquarters Effectiveness Study[b] | |
| :---: | :---: | :---: | :---: |
| | | Support Index[c] | Control Score |
| A | 1[d] | 1 | 2 |
| B | 2 | 2 | 6 |
| C | 3 | 3 | 4 |
| D | 4 | 4 | 3 |
| E | 5 | 6 | 5 |
| F | 6 | 5 | 1 |
| G | 7 | 7 | 7 |

a. Ranking of satisfaction with opportunity to contribute to company's success.
b. Rankings of ratings by country head office counterparts.
c. Quantity plus quality.
d. Rankings: 1 = *high*.

own jobs), we wondered whether any relationship would exist between the outcomes of the two surveys. In the employee attitude survey the seven main functional groups within the international headquarters varied considerably in their satisfaction with their opportunity to make a real contribution to the success of the company. Could the satisfaction or dissatisfaction of international headquarters employees with the meaningfulness of their jobs be in any way related to the way in which their function was perceived by their "customers" at country headquarters?

Table 7.6 shows the results of a comparison of both surveys. The seven main functional areas in international headquarters have been coded A through G according to the rank order of their employees' scores on "satisfaction with the opportunity to contribute to the company's success." Thus A is the function with the highest average satisfaction (low alienation) and G with the lowest average satisfaction (high alienation). The same functional areas have been ranked according to their ratings received on support and control in the Headquarters Effectiveness Study—that is, in the way they are perceived by their "customers."

The results in Table 7.6 are remarkable. Self-ratings of headquarters employees on satisfaction with opportunity to contribute run almost perfectly parallel to the ratings received on support as perceived by their customers in the country head offices. Such a similarity in ranking is extremely unlikely to occur by chance.[2] On the other hand, no consistent relationship is visible between satisfaction with opportunity to contribute and ratings received on control.

ipplying new know-how or tools and becoming aware of the problems t the same time.

This analysis would not be complete if we did not look at something that underlies both control and support—power. Control, as we described it, can be equated with *formal* power, but this is only one side of the coin. We owe to the French sociologist Michel Crozier (1964) a study of the phenomenon of power in bureaucratic organizations. Crozier relates power—quite independently of the formal organization chart— to *uncertainty*. Whenever events have become completely certain or predictable in an organization, a well-planned production process, or a perfect bureaucracy, no one has much power however high his position. Real power rests with those who command the sources of uncertainty. In the well-planned production process this may be the union leader who can authorize a strike or the personnel officer who negotiates with the union leader. In our case of international headquarters Function A (customer service), the main source of uncertainty is problems with customers. These are dealt with at the local office level. By virtue of its support relationship with the countries the headquarters staff is called in whenever a problem becomes really serious—a procedure that keeps them in direct contact with the source of uncertainty: this is the real source of their power. In the case of Function G (marketing), again the uncertainties arise mainly at the sales office level. In this case, however, the lack of a support relationship—in the eyes of the people in the countries—cuts the international headquarters staff off from the sources of uncertainty, which means they have no real power.

Power, in the above sense, is the opposite of alienation. This kind of power means the ability to make a meaningful contribution to what is going on. What our study has shown is that such power is scarcely related to control (formal power) at all, but that it depends on the existence of a support relationship.

## Strategies for
## Reducing Headquarters Alienation

Effective strategies for reducing headquarters alienation will, as shown by the previous data, at the same time make the headquarters—and through it, the entire organization—more effective. The challenge is formidable, as such strategies conflict with the essence of the bureaucratic tradition. I list four interventions in increasing order of difficulty as approaches to enriching headquarters management jobs: reflecting, recruiting, rewarding, and restructuring.

• *Reflecting* means presenting headquarters with a periodic mirror to reflect its image with the subsidiaries it coordinates. The Headquarters Effectiveness Study described earlier in this article was such a mirror. That the company's top management conducted it at all represented a recognition that the opinion of the people in the subsidiaries about headquarters did matter. A reflecting study of this kind is to the headquarters what a study of customer satisfaction is to a sales office. The Headquarters Effectiveness Study generated an enormous amount of qualitative feedback, which was further handled at the level of each separate headquarters activity. Unfortunately I do not possess data on the amount of change brought about by this feedback. An analogy with the process of change after regular employee attitude surveys (something that has been researched rather extensively) makes me suppose that the crucial factor in determining further change is the setting of priorities by higher management. This relates the strategy of reflecting to recruiting and rewarding.

• *Recruiting* of personnel for headquarters management jobs is obviously of key importance for the role that headquarters will fulfill in the organization. We have noted previously that by a process of natural selection, low achievers may be the ones to stay whereas the most successful people may leave. We have also seen the importance of the recruiting policy in the headquarters Function A case, where all managerial and professional jobs were filled by former practitioners from the service field, a practice that led to an effective support role for headquarters. If headquarters has to give support, it is essential that only people knowledgeable and experienced enough to be accepted as supporters are recruited to headquarters. This presents a conflict with two other reasons for recruiting in headquarters: training and shelving. In many companies serving a term at headquarters is an essential part of a person's training. Such trainees are usually not ideal supporters for the subsidiaries: it is often by the blunders they make in dealings with these subsidiaries that they really learn. The other reason for recruiting to headquarters is shelving: managers, especially higher managers, who have become redundant elsewhere in the organization and for whom at the time no equivalent employment is available, are conveniently stored in a headquarters position, with a job title whose length generally is inversely related to its real content.

Recruiting for a support role at headquarters means that training assignments should be well distinguished and limited to those positions where expertise is less necessary and that attempts at shelving should be vigorously resisted. Last, the length of the headquarters assignment is very important. It probably takes an average of 2 years for headquarters managers to establish the necessary personal contact with their clients. Thus they only start to be fully effective after that point. The ideal duration for a headquarters assignment, therefore, is not less than 4 years. An upper limit is less easy to mandate: 6 to 8 years may be the period after which the headquarters manager's experience gets stale and (s)he needs to have more direct on-line exposure to problems.

• *Rewarding* is a crucial aspect of the headquarters role dilemma. The formal reward structure of headquarters operations often prevents the building up of a support relationship. Headquarters people typically face upward—they are magnetically drawn toward the power center of the organization, which is physically close to them and from which they expect their rewards in the form of decisions on their careers. It is important to be visible to one's headquarters boss and to the higher bosses, up to the president.

A support relationship with the subsidiaries means a facing outward and mostly downward in the hierarchy. Many headquarters people believe—with ample justification—that they are not rewarded for that. They are not against support, but because their rewards lie elsewhere, they accord it low priority. Top management in headquarters communicates through its reward policy the kind of behavior it considers desirable. If the way to be promoted is to serve your boss ("he or she needs this report before Monday") rather than serve your clients in the subsidiaries, this will be the headquarters priority; but the price to be paid is alienation.

In a study I did of budget control systems in five Dutch companies (Hofstede, 1967), I compared the attitudes of lower line managers about cooperation with the Budget department to the Budget department's criteria for performance appraisal. The latter were determined by asking the Budget people to rank 10 possible criteria in the order in which they thought their boss used them when appraising their performance. It appeared that line managers' satisfaction with the Budget department was related to where the Budget people placed "tactfulness" as a performance criterion. In the company where the cooperation was best, the Budget people thought that their tactfulness (in dealing with the line managers) was their boss's *first* criterion in appraising their performance. In the company with the worst cooperation, tactfulness was placed fourth.

The company that placed tactfulness first had an interesting policy that I would recommend for any organization that wants its personnel to give high priority to support. For staff or headquarters jobs, this company determined who the clients were the staff was supposed to serve. When it was time for the yearly performance evaluation of staff, the boss was to call these clients and ask their opinions about the staff performance. Staff-line communications in this company were the best of the five companies studied.

- *Restructuring* is the hardest way to reduce headquarters alienation; it may also be the most effective one. It means that in any case where a headquarters role leads to alienation, it should be determined whether or not this role can be eliminated completely (cf. Thorsrud, 1976). If managers think they do not make a meaningful contribution to the success of the company, maybe their jobs should not be done at all. In the cases of the headquarters Functions A and G we saw that *size* has something to do with alienation—not so much the size of the entire organization, as the size of the units in which people work. Making a meaningful contribution is easier in a small group with face-to-face contact than in a large one. The needs for coordination, which detract from the contribution itself, increase disproportionately with the number of people. It is therefore important to keep headquarters groups small and to reduce their coordination with other groups to the minimum necessary. From a study of organizational stress in the early 1960s, Robert L. Kahn of the University of Michigan and his colleagues drew a number of conclusions on how to limit the need for coordination in organizations:

> Treat every coordinative requirement as a cost, which it is. For each functional unit in the organization, ask how independent it can be of others and of top management. For each position, ask how autonomous it can be made, what is the minimum number of positions with which it must be connected, and for what activities and purposes the connections are essential. . . . The advocacy of minimal coordination contrasts sharply with the notions of centralized leadership, with the idea that ultimate and maximum control must originate from a central source and maximum information return to that source. Coordination only when justified by functional requirements or systemic risk also points up a common fault of management, a preoccupation with organizational symmetry and aesthetics, and an emphasis on the regularities and beauties of the organization chart. The organization which follows this principle of coordinative economy would not necessarily be small, but it would not have grown haphazardly and it would not regard size as an unmixed blessing. It would be decentralized, flat and lean, a federated rather than a lofty hierarchical structure. (Kahn et al., 1964, pp. 394-395)

In such an organization, the risk of headquarters alienation would be greatly reduced.

## Conclusion

This chapter has been based on data collected in a private business enterprise. The increase in alienation when we move from the periphery to the center of such organizations makes us recognize that business and public organizations, after all, are not so different. The stereotypes of the civil servant do apply to many a headquarters executive in business. Large organizations have problems in common, regardless of who owns them. But business organizations do have a tradition of greater flexibility. It is easier to experiment with new forms of organization in business than in government.

If we do not want to adopt the pessimistic view that our entire society is doomed to increasing bureaucratization with consequent alienation, such experimentation with less bureaucratic organization forms is essential. We cannot stop with enriching the jobs of manual and office workers. In fact, some of the failures of job enrichment projects at those levels may stem from an absence of a job enrichment philosophy in the entire organization—including its headquarters management.

## Discussion Questions

1. This chapter compares the results of two surveys: an employee attitude survey, and a headquarters effectiveness survey. Who were the people participating in either survey, and what kind of questions were asked? What was the conclusion of a comparison of the results of both surveys?

2. In what way do jobs in the sales offices differ from jobs at the same level in international headquarters?

3. On what basis does the chapter argue that a feeling of not contributing to the success of the company is more damaging to managers than to non-managers?

4. Do the recommendations at the end of the chapter imply turning the headquarters into a service business?

5. What resistances will these recommendations have to face?

## Notes

1. In Chapter 1, note 5, a reference was made to a conceptual paper by Seeman (1959). This paper recognizes five aspects of alienation, that is, powerlessness, meaninglessness, normlessness, social isolation, and self-estrangement. In the present chapter, the stress is on meaninglessness, although parts of the other aspects can be recognized. Nisbet (1966/1970, pp. 264-312) reviews the history of the term in sociology.

2. Spearman rank correlation coefficient rho = .95, significant at the .001 level.

# 8

# People and
# Techniques in Budgeting

This chapter is an essay on what makes a budget control system an effective tool of management. Budget control is described as a sociotechnical subsystem of the organization. To function properly, both the social and the technical elements in this subsystem must be developed. Research data from my doctoral thesis, *The Game of Budget Control*, show that techniques actually play only a modest role in determining the success of a budget system. The technical side is reinforced by the increased availability of quantitative, computer-assisted methods. These are not necessarily an improvement, as they offer a temptation to focus even more on techniques at the expense of their application. The chapter suggests how quantitative methods can be used to assess the social elements in the budget system.

## The Effectiveness
## of Budget Control Systems

For my doctoral thesis (Hofstede, 1967) I studied budget systems in five well-organized companies in the Netherlands in 1964 and 1965. My research covered the methods and procedures used, the information produced, and the impact of the system on the organization and its members. It started from the premise that budgeting is meant to be an active process—it should affect the way the business is run, and for the better. The effectiveness of a budget system, then, should be measurable

This chapter was originally published in C. B. Tilanus (Ed.), *Quantitative Methods in Budgeting*, Leiden, Netherlands: Martinus Nijhoff Social Sciences Division, 1976, pp. 10-22. Reprinted with permission.

through its impact on the efforts of the organization members to achieve better economic results. It is too big a step to relate it directly with results themselves, because these depend on so many other factors as well.

The conclusions of this study, which focused on operating budgets rather than capital budgets and on manufacturing plants rather than sales or administrative operations, were that the effectiveness of a budget system depends only to a limited extent on the methods and techniques of the system. These methods and techniques should of course be within the technical competence of the budget department, so that the system can be operated smoothly. The methods should allow budgets to be ready in time (that is, before the new budget year begins, which is often not the case), and variance reports should be regular, timely, and free of errors. If budget revisions are frequent, there should be a way to handle these with minimal disturbance of the system. Within these rather obvious constraints different methods of budgeting appeared to function equally well. For example, of the five companies studied, three used a method in which individual plant departments were handled as full profit centers buying from and selling to each other. The other two used a method in which (indirect) expenses of the plant departments were budgeted, but direct production costs were handled through standard costing, outside the budget system.[1] Both methods had identifiable advantages and disadvantages, but the effectiveness or ineffectiveness of the budget system was only marginally affected by the choice of method.

What really made the difference in determining the effectiveness of the budget system in the five companies studied was the way the budget was used by operating management, because the managers—especially those at the middle and lower levels—were the people who had to be motivated to act on the budget information for the system to be effective. The crucial problems were communication problems, between the budget department and operating management, and even more within the management hierarchy itself. A budget is unavoidably a yardstick of managerial performance and the communication pattern that develops between the *budgetee* (the manager responsible for a budget) and his or her direct superior determines whether the budgetee will take this yardstick seriously, whether (s)he will apply it to him/herself or try to escape its use by playing company politics. Even as far as the communication between the budget department and operating management goes, the bottleneck is more likely to be the person-to-person verbal communication than the written parts in the form of budget variance reports and the like.

The conclusions of the study can be summarized in a few words: Budgeting is much more than an administrative technique—it is a way of managing. The key role in a budget system is played by top line management—the role of the controller with the budget department is auxiliary. A budget system is a sociotechnical subsystem of the organization it tries to control and which itself is a more complicated sociotechnical system. It appears that the trouble with budget systems lies more often within the social than in the technical processes involved.

Might it be that the particular sample of five Dutch companies used and the time at which the study was done (1964-1965) affected the results to the extent that these conclusions do not apply for other situations? Both older and more recent[2] publications from the United States and Great Britain report similar results, and discussions with managers from different countries who attended my classes in executive development courses confirm that the trouble with budget control systems is more often in their use than in the methods and techniques followed.

## The Forest and the Trees

All this does not mean that the issue of budgeting methods and techniques is unimportant. Budget control systems do need good techniques in order to function at all. But well-chosen techniques, efficiently administered, do not guarantee an effective budget control system, if line management does not use the system properly. Poorly chosen or poorly administered techniques, on the other hand, do assure the failure of a system. The role of the techniques—and more generally, the role of the controller's department in budgeting—is therefore "hygienic" (Herzberg et al., 1959). As in the case of hygiene in relationship with health, techniques in budgeting are a necessary but not sufficient condition. In fact, focusing too much on techniques in a budget control system may do harm, because it makes the system less understandable for the managers who should be the main users.

In one company in my study there was a very complete data collection system for budget variances. The budget department produced a monthly report containing 19 different well-designed tables and graphs. When asked, line managers supposed to be the users of this information indicated that only 3 of the 19 tables were read by more than 25% of the addressees. It is known from psychology that overinformation has the effect of limiting a person's ability to distinguish what is important in a communication: It is the noise that detracts from the message. The error made by the budget department in this case was to assume that because the 19 tables could technically be made, they should be reported. One budget analyst commented that line management could not see the forest for the trees, but it was rather the budget department that mistook the trees (the available techniques) for the forest (the purpose of the budget control system).

In another company budget variances were reported monthly, divided into volume variances and other variances. Volume variances are gains or losses versus the budget caused by a larger or smaller sales or production volume than foreseen, leading to an over- or underabsorption of fixed costs. Other variances included efficiency variances (due to a more or less efficient use of direct labor and direct materials), expense variances (due to differences in unit costs or overhead expenses), and accounting system variances (due to changes in accounting procedures). The distinction between these types of variances is essential for line management to understand the causes of gains and losses shown. In the particular company studied *nobody* among the first- or second-line management receivers of the budget variance reports was able to explain the difference between volume and other variances. In this case the budget department had failed to verify that its techniques (in themselves perfectly sound) were understood by those people whom they were meant to serve. Again it saw the trees, but not the forest.

Both cases are examples of a suboptimization of the technical part of the budget control system at the expense of the optimization of the entire (sociotechnical) system, which includes the effective understanding and use of variance information by line management. Optimization of the sociotechnical system, however, demands a general management rather than a functional-technical point of view. Unfortunately our way of thinking is influenced by the work we do and for which we were trained: People in functional-technical jobs tend to think in a functional-technical way. One of the basic problems of organizations is integrating the efforts of people and groups who are induced by their tasks to think in different ways.[3]

An illustration of the differences in thinking between budget people and production managers can be found in a study I did of managers participating in executive development classes. Between 1970 and 1973, 372 managers from 40 countries at the IMEDE Management Development Institute in Lausanne (now IMD) scored what they saw as their work-related values on a standard values test, L. V. Gordon's Survey of Personal Values (Hofstede, 1976a). Table 8.1 shows the scores of the 262 respondents over 30 years of age divided according to the occupational area in which they had spent the years of their career. The test is scored in such a way that the six dimensions together always add up to 90 points (an average of 15 points per dimension).

**TABLE 8.1** Mean Scores on Survey of Personal Values for IMEDE
Respondents Divided by Occupation (over age 30 only)

| | Scores for Occupation | | | |
|---|---|---|---|---|
| Test Dimensions | Marketing $n = 72$ | Accounting, etc. $n = 66$ | Engineering $n = 48$ | General $n = 76$ |
| P—Practical-Mindedness | 11.2 | 9.5† | 12.4† | 11.0 |
| A—Achievement | 19.3 | 19.4 | 18.7 | 19.0 |
| V—Variety | 11.1 | 9.6 | 12.8† | 10.0 |
| D—Decisiveness | 15.0 | 16.0 | 15.0 | 14.8 |
| O—Orderliness | 13.9 | 15.6 | 12.5† | 15.2 |
| G—Goal Orientation | 19.3 | 19.9 | 18.4 | 19.8 |

NOTE: Scores with † are significantly different from those for the sum of all other occupations at
a 5% level (*t* test, one-tailed).

The two occupational groups with the most different scores are Accounting (including Finance and Efficiency experts) on the one side, and Engineers (including Production) on the other. In comparison with Engineers, Accounting people scored *lower* on Practical-Mindedness (defined as to always get one's money's worth, to take good care of one's property, to get full use out of one's possessions, to do things that will pay off, to be very careful with one's money). Engineers scored *higher* on Variety (defined as to do things that are new and different, to have a variety of experiences, to be able to travel a great deal, to go to strange or unusual places, to experience an element of danger). Engineers scored *lower* on Orderliness (defined as to have well-organized work habits, to keep things in their proper place, to be a very orderly person, to follow a systematic approach in doing things, to do things according to a schedule). These systematic differences in how accountants and engineers described their own values are reflected in organizations where accounting people act as budget experts and engineers act as production managers. Especially the trade-off between Orderliness (sense of system, formalism) and Practical-Mindedness (what's the use of it?) is enlightening. These differences in thinking do cause a "differentiation" that if not compensated by an "integration" process leads to the kind of malfunctioning of budget control systems pictured in the two examples above.

But what happens if the budget department supplements traditional accounting methods by more sophisticated, computer-supported quantitative methods? If the difference in value systems between budget department and line management remains as it was, the transfer to quantitative methods only risks widening the gap between those designing and operating the budget machine and those supposed to use it. Quantitative methods in budgeting may lead to a new technical suboptimization, more powerful than before, because it is now supported by more scientific methods, suggesting measurability and reliability. There is a general danger in management science of mathematical techniques used to solve problems being more accurate than the data on which the solutions have to be based. A temptation exists to define problems by the available solutions—solution first, problem afterward. This situation applies strongly in budgeting, where basic data are almost always not only imprecise but also biased by the interests of the people playing the budget game. With a shiny new machine to handle the trees some people may have even more difficulty in seeing the forest.

## Potential Psychological Gains in Using Quantitative Methods

The previous paragraphs represent a call for modesty about the impact of quantitative methods on budget systems, and consequently I have stressed the risks more than the potential benefits. If budgeting is a sociotechnical system, this implies that changing one element (in this case, a technical element) potentially affects all others, including the social ones. I argued that in most budget control systems the trouble is on the social side, and that one should avoid making it worse by using quantitative technical methods if these are not understood by the users. Systems thinkers may now object that a better designed technical system does not inevitably lead to a worse sociotechnical system. This was the assumption of human relations theorists, who believed that all control systems were inhuman.[4] The question is whether the use of quantitative methods is really necessarily psychologically negative, or whether, armed with both quantitative-technical and psychological insight, one can design a sociotechnical system that is integrally superior. Is there a way for quantitative methods to help where the trouble is?

One problem preventing a better use of budget control systems is unrealistic assumptions about human behavior by both budget experts and line executives. In Hofstede (1967, p. 37) I listed a number of assumptions evident from the classical accounting literature on budgeting. Some of these are true to such a small extent that they must be considered as misleading:

1. The only source of control is at the top of the organization and control lines flow from the top downward.
2. The relationships of lower levels to higher levels in the organization can meaningfully be described in terms of accountability.
3. The perfect manager manages by exception.
4. People react on control systems as individuals (rather than as members of a reference group).

Some other assumptions about human behavior reflected in the accounting literature are true under certain, but not all conditions:

5. Goal setting by the organization improves people's performance.
6. Having people participate in this goal setting improves their performance still more.
7. People will take action when a deviation of an actual situation from a standard is reported to them.

E. H. Caplan (1966 & 1968) presented a more extensive set of doubtful behavioral assumptions in the traditional management accounting model of the firm contrasted with a more comprehensive organization theory. In a field study of U.S. management accountants and line (non-accounting) managers, Caplan showed that not only most of the management accountants questioned tended toward the traditional view, but also the line managers.

A system based on unrealistic assumptions cannot be expected to function properly. In the light of both empirical research and a more comprehensive organization theory, the following assumptions about budget control are more realistic:

1. Control (in the sense of determining what actually goes on in the organization) is widely distributed among the members, but different forms of control predominate at different levels and sections of the organization.
2. People will take action only if they are motivated to act. They may be motivated indirectly—because by acting they expect to avoid a punishment or earn a reward—or directly, that is, because the particular action is intrinsically rewarding to them (it carries its psychological reward in itself). The trouble with indirect motivation is that it easily leads to evasion: If people can avoid the punishment or earn the reward in another way, they may very well do so. For example, instead of trying to correct an unfavorable budget variance, managers may try to show why not they, but somebody else should be blamed for it.
3. Accountability is psychologically associated with punishment and more likely to lead to evasion than to motivation.

4. Management by exception is psychologically undesirable because it leads to focusing attention of superiors only on those aspects in the work of their subordinates that are wrong. It leads to a behavior of the superior that is seen by the subordinates as negative and punitive. It is, however, very seldom practiced as traditional theory propounds.

5. People in an organization usually belong to one or more reference groups (for example, the group of supervisors, the group of Department A) and they will react to a control system in accordance with the subculture of their reference group, which has developed over time and through experience.

6. Goal setting by the organization will only lead to improved performance of people if the goals are "internalized" by people and affect their performance aspiration levels.

7. Participation by people in goal setting will only improve performance if people are motivated to set high targets for themselves. This will be the case if they are directly motivated by the act of goal achievement. If goal achievement will lead to extrinsic reward or goal nonachievement to punishment, people will "play it safe," and in participating, bargain for goals that can be safely achieved but, by the same token, are less than challenging.

8. Managers will take action only when a deviation of an actual situation from a standard is reported to them if (a) they believe the information, (b) they understand the information, (c) they perceive it as relevant and attribute a sufficient priority to it, (d) effective action is technically possible, (e) they know how to take this action, and (f) they can motivate the others involved (for example their subordinates) to cooperate in the action. Also they must not be motivated to correct the deviation between actual and standard in a different way, for example by changing the data about the actual, changing the standard, or attributing the variance to somebody else.

There is no basic reason why, when assumptions about human behavior are corrected to be more realistic, the use of quantitative methods in budgeting should have exclusively dysfunctional effects on the social side of the system. One example of an area where quantitative methods in budgeting could be behaviorally functional is in the use of *control limits* in the statistical sense. Such control limits are common in quality control but rarely used in budgeting or cost control. Control limits define in advance a certain area of positive and negative budget variance that could occur either by random reasons, or else is consciously left to the discretion of the budgetee. The control limits are the quantitative expression of a "planned area of free play" for the budgetees within the constraints of the overall budget.

R. E. Miles and Vergin (1966) listed a number of features of the use of control limits (they use the term "variance controls") that make these look promising from a behavioral point of view:

1. They require an objective definition of performance standards, based on actual data.
2. They create a certain flexibility around standards.
3. They create control limits, within which the individual can establish his own performance targets.
4. They appear to have the potential for creating a positive atmosphere for the exercise of necessary corrective action in that management's action can be viewed by both parties as problem solving rather than punitive.
5. They are at least potentially both simple to apply and easy to understand.
6. Feedback can be both immediate and automatic.

The authors conclude that "variance controls appear to offer a potentially valuable compromise between traditional control techniques and the somewhat abstract and frequently vague control suggestions made by various behavioral scientists" (p. 64).

In consolidating budgets equipped with control limits into overall budgets, assumptions have to be made about the probabilistic characteristics of actual results within the limits. When a system of control limits is introduced people may still be conditioned by previous experience to push their results to the upper expense limit. It may take time for people to learn to truly use the free area within the limits.

Another example where quantitative methods in budgeting can be behaviorally functional is in mathematical model building for trying to understand the effect of such phenomena as overall budget cuts (or other ways of increasing overall pressure) or of the negotiation process in budget setting (using mathematical game theory). These models should of course take into account the social components in the system (Bonini, 1964; Roberts, 1964). A healthy skepticism about the relationship between such models and reality is due, because mathematical models tend to be so comfortable to work with that there is always a temptation for the modeler to stop bothering about the reality they are intended to represent.

## Quantitative Methods in Assessing the Social Aspects of a Control System

One of the reasons why the technical side of a sociotechnical system is often suboptimized at the expense of the social side is that the former is mostly tangible and measurable and the latter is not. The technical mind has a tendency not to take into account that which cannot be measured.

One answer to this problem is to make the social side of the system more measurable. The "intangibles" are often very tangible in their effects, and with proper methods of measurement they can be made visible. This means combining the techniques of the social sciences (sociology, psychology) with the techniques of accounting to assess the *integral* functioning of the sociotechnical budget control system.

Social variables that can be measured are, for example, (a) the motivation of the budgetees by the budget variances that are reported to them; (b) the extent to which the information that is reported is understood, memorized, and used by budgetees and others; (c) feelings, psychosomatic symptoms, and behavioral symptoms of stress among budgetees and others; (d) the frequency and emotional loading with which budget issues are discussed between superiors and subordinates, between budgetees and budget experts, and in various types of meetings; (e) attitudes to and behavior during budget negotiations, including hedging against expected budget cuts; (f) degree of risk accepted in the setting of budget goals. This list can probably be expanded further.

A number of the above-mentioned variables were measured in the study of budget control systems in five Dutch companies described in my book *The Game of Budget Control*. Some attempts at measuring social variables in this study were clearly more successful than others (some were outright failures). An example of a successful measurement will be described here, dealing with the *motivation of budgetees by the budget variances reported to them* (Hofstede, 1967, pp. 156ff). This motivation partly depends on the extent the budget is "internalized" by the budgetees, which means that in their own judgment of a situation they apply the same yardstick as the budget does.

The research took place in manufacturing plants. One budget item in such plants is the use of materials. For a strong motivation of the plant's managers by the materials budget, if the (monthly or weekly) budget variance report shows a loss on materials use, the managers feel unhappy about their department's materials use performance; if the budget variance report shows a gain or a breakeven, the managers feel happier. If on the contrary, we find that the managers' own feelings about how well their department is doing in materials use does not at all correspond to the budget variance reports, we can conclude that the motivation of the managers by this part of the budget is low. After all, we can only expect managers to attempt taking action if they feel a situation is in a disequilibrium, if they feel there is something wrong. If they are convinced that things are as good as they can be (whatever the budget variance report may state) they are unlikely to take any action.

These considerations led to a measurement technique consisting of asking all managers to evaluate their own department's operation in a number of aspects. These aspects were the "measurable dimensions" of their operation, basically the issues for which there were separate items in their budget. These measurable dimensions fell into the following categories:

1. Efficiency of direct labor ("direct" meaning immediately attributable to products)
2. Efficiency of indirect labor (all other, including supervision)
3. Machine-hour efficiency
4. Efficiency of direct materials use
5. Efficiency of the use of indirect materials and tools
6. Extra costs resulting from rejection or rework of products not meeting quality standards

All managers were asked to rate their operation on all applicable measurable dimensions, using the common Dutch school grading system (9 = excellent, 8 = good, 7 = fairly good, 6 = satisfactory, 5 = so-so). Where budget motivation is strong a reported loss in the variance reports should correspond with a low self-rating of the manager (5 or 6), and a gain should lead to a high self-rating (8 or 9). In other words, strong budget motivation makes for a *positive correlation* between the reported budget variance and the manager's self-rating. Weak or non-existent budget motivation will be reflected by a lack of correlation between budget variance and self-rating.

In the five companies in which the research was carried out, 90 budgetees (line managers) supplied a total of 466 ratings of their performance, an average of just over 5 ratings (measurable dimensions) per budgetee. Each of these 466 ratings was then compared to the corresponding reported budget variance over the last available period. These budget variances were coded as follows:

−2 = more than 5% loss
−1 = 1%-5% loss
 0 = even ± 1%
+1 = 1%-5% gain
+2 = more than 5% gain

The overall correlation coefficient between the managers' self-ratings and the budget variance (coded as described above) across the 466 cases was .32.[5] A correlation coefficient of 1.00 would indicate perfect consistency between self-rating and budget variance; a correlation coefficient of 0.00 would indicate self-ratings totally unrelated to the budget. The figure of .32 means an in-between situation, and is at least statistically highly significant (way past the .001 level).

However, the different manufacturing plants studied produced quite different correlation levels between managers' self-ratings and budget variance. Because for one of the five companies two plants were included, the total number of plants was six. The correlation coefficients for the six plants were .07, .16, .21, .28, .39, and .41, respectively.

The correlation coefficient between managers' self-ratings and budget variance in a plant represents an index of the motivation of the budgetees by the budget variances reported to them. For two of the plants, the correlation coefficients were not statistically different from zero (.07 and .16),[6] so that in these cases the budget variances simply did not motivate budgetees to take any action at all. Two plants showed a weak correlation (.21 and .28), and two a strong correlation (.39 and .41 is probably about as high as one can expect, in view of the many "noise" factors that affect both variance scores and self-ratings). The higher the correlation, the more budgetees will be motivated to take action, if at least other circumstances do not prevent them from doing so.[7]

This is a creative example of how the social part of a budget control system can yield a quantitative measure of a "soft" concept like budget motivation.

## Conclusion

The considerations in this chapter lead to the following recommendations as to budget control policy:

1. Budget control systems should not be made more sophisticated than their users.
2. Technically better methods of budgeting should be tested for their effect on the users, in particular on the understandability of the information generated and its motivational impact.
3. The use of statistical control limits for budgets is worth considering and trying out. In this respect budget experts can learn from quality control people.
4. Certain aspects of the social side of a budget system are as accessible to quantitative measurement as its technical aspects. In this respect budget experts can learn from behavioral scientists.

5. It is desirable to subject budget control systems to periodic audits of overall effectiveness, including impact on the social side of the organization.

The last point is just an application to budget control of a more general principle that, for any policy or system created by a manager, (s)he should try to collect some kind of feedback as to its effectiveness in total system terms. A successful application of this principle is demonstrated in the following case,[8] which may appropriately serve to conclude this chapter. It occurred in a manufacturing plant (not one of the six referred to above) that used control by standard costs. These standard costs were progressively introduced in its various departments. A periodic employee attitude survey (measurement of the social side of the system) held shortly afterward showed a considerable lowering of the confidence of workers in their foremen (first-line managers).

Rather than choose the frequent solution in such a case of sending all foremen to human relations training, the personnel department decided to analyze the data further and found that the confidence in the foremen had only dropped in those departments put on standard costs. Interviews showed that workers had lost confidence in their foremen because foremen could no longer fix a worker's production targets as they did before. These targets were now imposed by the engineers who set the standards used in the standard costs (compare my personal experiences in Chapter 1).

Plant management then decided on an experiment: In some "experimental" departments foremen obtained the right to reject standards they considered unfair to their workers, but the losses incurred by the rejection of standards were put on a special account for the foreman's department and therefore remained visible. In other, "control" departments, no changes in the system were made. After 5 months employee attitudes were measured again for both the experimental and the control departments. The productivity and quality performance of each department was also monitored.

In the experimental departments, the confidence of employees in the foremen was restored without any loss in productivity or quality. In the control departments there was also an improvement, but a smaller one, which was attributed to the indirect effects of the experiment on all concerned. On the basis of this experiment, all foremen were then given the right to reject standards considered unfair. This case illustrates both the use of measurements on the social side of a system and a skillfully conducted experiment to quantitatively assess the effectiveness of a policy decision before making it general. It is an example of using quantitative methods where the trouble is.

# Discussion Questions

1. To what extent is the budget control system an instrument of power?

2. *The Game of Budget Control* was based on operations budget systems in manufacturing plants. To what extent are these different from operations budget systems in sales organizations? In laboratories? In public services? From investment budgets?

3. If personal values of managers in accounting jobs differ from those in engineering jobs, is this due to self-selection or to socialization on the job?

4. The chapter describes one way of measuring managers' motivation by the budget system: correlating self-ratings with reported budget variances. What other ways could you think of?

# Notes

1. In the classical budgeting literature, the first approach (integral budgeting) is known as the "European method," the second (indirect expense budgeting only) as the "American method."

2. See for example, Bruns and De Coster (1969); Anthony, Dearden, and Vancil (1972); Hopwood (1973).

3. This relates to the processes of differentiation and integration in organizations, as described, for example, by Lawrence and Lorsch (1967).

4. See for example, Argyris (1952, 1953); Argyris at that time had not yet recognized that budgets may also have positive motivational consequences.

5. The regression formula for the data from all five companies taken together was $E = .29V + 7.3$ in which $E$ = manager's self-rating (5-9) and $V$ = budget variance coded as described from $-2$ to $+2$.

6. In view of the numbers of observations per plant, a correlation coefficient of .20 for a plant would be statistically significantly different from zero at about the .05 level.

7. For a fuller description of this case, see Hofstede (1967, pp. 156ff). It has also been published by INSEAD-CEDEP, Fontainebleau, France, under the title "The Case of the Twin Plants" (1976).

8. Published at INSEAD-CEDEP, Fontainebleau, France, under the title "The Case of the Disputed Standards" (1976).

# 9

# The Poverty of
# Management Control Philosophy

This chapter is an essay on the ineffectiveness of many management control systems that is attributed to the oversimplified cybernetic paradigm on
which they are based. For routine industrial-type processes the cybernetic
paradigm may apply, but a homeostatic paradigm is even more promising.
When, however, objectives are missing, unclear, or shifting; when accomplishment is not measurable or feedback is not available, only a political
paradigm applies. Attempts at enforcing a cybernetic paradigm in such cases
are bound to fail. This follows from the fact that in the general hierarchy of
systems humans are at a lower level of complexity than the human organizations they try to control.

Ja, mach' nur einen Plan!
Sei nur ein grosses Licht!
Und mach' dann noch 'nen zweiten Plan,
Geh'n tun sie beide nicht.
Bertolt Brecht, *Die Dreigroschenoper*[1]

## The Cybernetic
## Paradigm of Management Control

Anthony et al. (1972) define management control as "the process by
which managers assure that resources are obtained and used effectively

This chapter was originally published in *Academy of Management Review*, 3(3), July 1978,
pp. 450-461. Copyright © 1978 *Academy of Management Review*. Reprinted with permission.

and efficiently in the accomplishment of the organization's objectives." Others narrow this definition and distinguish "planning" (the setting of goals) from "control" (living up to the goals that were set). Whether we use the wider or the more limited definition, management control is the domain par excellence of formalized systems in organizations, and these systems tend to be designed according to a cybernetic philosophy.

By *cybernetic* is meant a process using the negative feedback loop represented by setting goals, measuring achievement, comparing achievement to goals, feeding back information about unwanted variances into the process to be controlled, and correcting the process. This is a much narrower use of the term than that advocated by Wiener (1954), who coined it to deal with the transfer of messages in the widest sense, but it corresponds more closely to its present use in practice. In spite of (or maybe owing to) its simplicity, the cybernetic-in-the-narrow-sense feedback loop has attained the status of a proper paradigm in a wide area of systems theory, including but not limited to the management sciences (Sutherland, 1975). A review of nearly 100 books and articles on management control theory issued between 1900 and 1972 (Giglioni & Bedeian, 1974) reflects entirely the cybernetic paradigm.

In the cybernetic view a management control process in its most simplified form is similar to a technical control process, for example, control of the heat of a room by a thermostat (see Figure 9.1). The model in Figure 9.1 uses only first-order feedback. More sophisticated models for which technical analogues also can be found use higher order feedbacks to control the lower order controllers. Another possible control model used in technical devices is "feed-forward," sometimes presented as an alternative for management control. Feed-forward assumes that interventions are programmable in advance as a known function of environmental disturbances—a condition unlikely to be fulfilled in most management control situations.

All cybernetic models of control have to assume:

1. There is a standard, corresponding to effective and efficient accomplishment of the organization's objectives.
2. Actual accomplishment can be measured. In Figure 9.1 the "measuring unit" is connected to the output of the process, but the measuring may include data about the input or about the ratio between output and input.

---

The ideas in this essay have been further elaborated in an article "Management Control of Public and Not-for-Profit Activities" in *Accounting, Organizations and Society, 6*(3), 1981, pp. 193-221, which has also been reprinted as Research Report 82-45, Laxenburg, Austria: IIASA (International Institute for Applied Systems Analysis), December 1982.

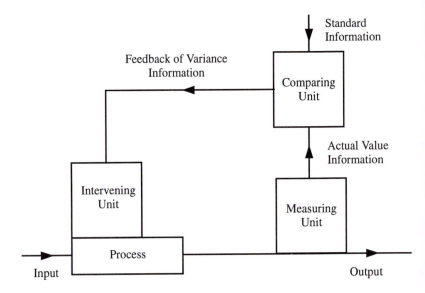

**Figure 9.1.** Technical Control Model of an Organizational Control System

For example, in an industrial production process, the quantity of various inputs (labor, materials, energy) for a given quantity of output may be measured.

3. When standard and measurement are compared and variance information is fed back, this information can be used to intervene in the process so as to eliminate unwanted differences between measurement and standard for the next round.

There is no doubt that the cybernetic model of control has been eminently successful in the design of machines, electronic circuits, or similar technical systems, but management control in an organization is a social process in a social, or maybe sociotechnical system. The "units" (see Figure 9.1) in this case are people, or even groups of people. This subjects the use of the cybernetic model to severe limitations because:

1. In many organizational situations one or more of the three above-mentioned basic assumptions necessary for the validity of the cybernetic model are not justified: Standards do not exist, accomplishment is not measurable, feedback information cannot be used. This is particularly the case for indirect (service) activities in industrial organizations and for all nonindustrial organizations, such as schools, hospitals, and public bodies. I became painfully aware of this when discussing classical industrial-type manage-

ment control (Juran, 1964) with a group of experienced management consultants working in nonindustrial settings. After finding out that the cybernetic paradigm did not apply to these consultants' daily practice, we even started to wonder to what extent it really applies in many industrial settings.

2. The three assumptions of the presence of a standard, the measurability of accomplishment, and the usability of feedback are most justified for routine industrial-type processes like industrial production and sales and the supplying of routine services to clients. But even these relatively machine-like processes are really social. The cybernetic control process as pictured by the model is only one of many interpersonal processes going on among the same people at the same time. Other processes—some of them by-products of the control system—may interfere with the control process and sometimes may even lead to an outcome opposite to what was intended by the designers of the system.

One remarkable fact about control processes in organizations that has become associated with the cybernetic paradigm is that they are usually tied to a division of labor—different units in the model correspond to different people, who are specialized in their tasks. Measuring and comparing are often done by "staff" personnel of a Controller's department, standards are set by higher "line" management, and intervening is the task of lower line management, whereas the actual process to be controlled is carried out by operating personnel (workers). In the last resort, it is usually these workers' response to the control process that determines whether the control has been effective.

Proper functioning of the control process presupposes *communication* (Wiener, 1954): The necessary messages should be sent and correctly received between the various specialized actors. It also presupposes that all will feel *motivated* to act according to the model. The proper sending and receiving of the necessary messages poses many problems, as the various persons involved have different types of education and work experience and hold different values. Their values also affect their motivation pattern.

A difference in values between people in Controller's departments and line management is evident to anyone familiar with organizational folklore. Moreover, it is illustrated by research. For example, in Hofstede (1967, p. 236) I reported that Controller's department personnel in five Dutch companies more than line managers believed that working does not come naturally to most people and that people therefore need to be controlled and prodded (a Theory X point of view; McGregor, 1960). They also showed themselves more concerned with the method of measuring than with the content of what was measured. In another study of an international group of middle-management course participants (Hofstede, 1976a; see Chapter 8 of this book), I found that those in accounting and control departments, compared to others, showed low concern for the efficiency and effectiveness of their actions, but high concern with orderliness, following a systematic approach, and doing things according to a schedule. Both studies quoted suggest that people in control departments tend to stress *form* whereas those in line roles would rather stress *content*.

In most cases the Controller's department is responsible not only for measuring and comparing, but also for the design of the entire control system. An excessive stress on form rather than content explains why at close scrutiny many management control systems do *not* supply real control, but only "pseudo-control." Pseudo-control is a state of affairs in which a system is under control on paper (the figures look right), but not in reality. There are several ways to achieve pseudo-control, for example by correcting the standards (rather than the process) whenever an important variance occurs, by choosing one's measures of performance so as to reflect the desired result (there are many ways to twist the figures without actually cheating), or by adjusting one element in the process at the expense of another that does not show up in the figures (reducing cost at the expense of quality).

The value differences between Controller's department personnel and line management are just one kind of social communication barrier in the system. We can also think of the way in which rank-and-file workers, with their particular education, work experience, and life goals, tend to react to control measures (see Chapter 1). We all know that these are often met with considerable suspicion and resistance, going counter to the desired motivation, but control systems designers have been extremely slow to take account of these facts. Jonas (1953) signaled the tendency among cyberneticians to apply two kinds of doctrine—one to the people in their models, who are taken as robots, and another to themselves: "He (the cybernetician) considers behavior, except his own; purposiveness, except his own; thinking, except his own" (p. 188). People usually dislike being taken for robots, and they will resist an organization built on such a double standard.

## An Alternative Paradigm:
## Homeostasis

Although the cybernetic paradigm, by distinguishing various "units" in the control process, has undoubtedly contributed to the division of labor in control process tasks, there can be cybernetic control without division of labor. Division of labor in control of production tasks may have been a productive innovation in the days of F. W. Taylor, who advocated in a 1906 article, "On the Art of Cutting Metals," "taking the control of the machine shop out of the hands of the many workmen, and placing it completely in the hands of the management, thus superseding 'rule of thumb' by scientific control" (quoted in Giglioni & Bedeian, 1974, p. 293). It is recognized now that the separation of tasks and specialization that Taylor defended can go too far. What, among other factors, has changed since Taylor's days, at least in developed countries, is the worker. Today's worker is better educated, and escaping from starvation is no longer his or her primary work motive, but rather, he or she can afford to look for a task with some intrinsic reward to it. Entrusting measuring, comparing, and intervening to specialized staff and line personnel implies the assumption that the operating personnel themselves cannot or do not want to adequately perform these tasks. This assumption, reinforced by the "Theory X" attitude often found among people in controlling roles, in many cases is no longer justified.

The IBM Typewriter case in Chapter 5 of this book provides an example of despecialization in a control system. Up to 1969, assembly took place in long lines of 60-70 operators each. The process was controlled by specialists in various ways. Engineers calculated time standards and divided the total assembly job into individual tasks of as equal as possible duration. For control purposes, the lines were further divided into five sections of 12-14 operators. Each section had its quality inspector to check the section's production. Quality inspectors produced computerized defect lists for the line manager, and specialized repair men repaired the defects. Five foremen, each assisted by a charge hand, supervised the five sections of two parallel assembly lines, so that each foreman was specialized in the supervision of one particular part of the assembly process. Foremen allocated workers to places, gave instructions, and watched over presence and absence. Another computerized list showed the production and the various kinds of unproductive time for each worker. Specialized dispatchers provided the assembly operators with the parts they needed.

After the reorganization in 1971 the assembly moved to semiautonomous groups of 20 operators each, who divided the total task among themselves according to each person's real capacities rather than a general standard. Quality defects were reported verbally within the group and corrected immediately. Repair men became superfluous and switched to production. Operators started ordering their own parts instead of waiting for the dispatcher. The foreman became a social rather than a technical leader who represented the group to the rest of the organization. Operators arranged the replacement for temporary absences among themselves, and the production recording was reduced to counting the number of finished machines at the end of the day. The various computer lists were discontinued. The changes led to considerable gains in both productivity and quality.

This case shows that under favorable circumstances semiautonomous groups could be created and take over most of the control roles previously fulfilled by superiors and specialists. All tasks within the classical cybernetic control loop—measuring, comparing, feedback, intervening—were carried out within the group itself. Its links to the organization's needs were mainly established through the *standards* set by others in the organization for the group's tasks. Quality standards were given by the Quality Control department based on sales and customer service requirements, delivery programs by the Production Control department, and productivity standards were present in the form of past production records. Rather than cybernetic such a control process can be called *homeostatic*. The analogy is not to a technical device like a thermostat, but to a biological system like a living cell, equipped with internal processes capable of maintaining an equilibrium in a changing environment, provided that the environmental conditions do not become too unfavorable.

Like the word *cybernetic, homeostatic* can be used to mean different things. The term is used here because of its predominantly biological connotation. Homeostatic processes are composed of cybernetic elements, but without the division of labor between controlling and controlled units; control is exercised within the system itself. Another label for these processes is *self-regulating* (Sandkull, 1975).

The switch from a technical to a biological paradigm also explains one other aspect of homeostatic control processes illustrated in the typewriter assembly case: Whereas a technical control device can quickly be put together and can be repaired if it breaks down, a cell must grow (which takes time), and it can die. Homeostatic control processes, therefore, are more vulnerable than cybernetic processes.

The transfer from cybernetic to homeostatic management control systems will demand a drastically changed control philosophy, especially with regard to the traditional division of labor tied to the cybernetic model. Those in Controller's departments involved in the design and introduction of control systems will have to widen their outlook to include a broad view of the sociopsychological processes going on between people in an organization. The homeostatic approach needs a new type of controller. It will also need a new type of information systems. Today considerable efforts are put into developing and improving management information systems, but here again the designers' basic assumptions about sociopsychological processes are often remarkably simplistic and shallow.

## Noncybernetic Processes

So far we have dealt with control situations for which the three main conditions of the cybernetic model were fulfilled: A standard exists, accomplishment is measurable, feedback can be used for corrective intervention. If we consider the full range of human organizations in which control processes occur, those that satisfy the conditions for the cybernetic model tend to be the more structured ones, those that more or less fit a machine analogue. In a criticism of the cybernetic paradigm in system theory in general, Sutherland (1975) has made applicability of cybernetic control dependent on the "determinedness" of a system. If phenomena are completely determined, cybernetic control is obviously superfluous. It becomes useful for moderately stochastic phenomena. When phenomena are severely stochastic, cybernetic control becomes either technically or economically unfeasible. When phenomena are completely undetermined, cybernetic control has become meaningless. Translated into terms of everyday organization activities, Sutherland's moderately stochastic phenomena are the more structured ones: the routine industrial-type processes referred to before. In many other organizational situations (indirect departments in industrial companies, public bodies, schools, hospitals, voluntary associations), we are in Sutherland's area of severely stochastic or even completely undetermined phenomena, and we meet with great problems in applying the cybernetic model. What we notice in practice when we try to follow a cybernetic approach is (a) objectives may be missing, unclear, or shifting; (b) accomplishment may not be measurable; and/or (c) feedback information may not be usable. Each of these three conditions is illustrated below:

1. *Objectives are missing, unclear, or shifting.* If there is to be a standard, there should be objectives from which this standard is derived. Setting of standards presupposes clarity about the organization's objectives. Social scientists have often stressed that speaking of "an organization's objectives" is unallowable: organizations cannot have objectives, only people can. We can attribute objectives to an organization only to the

extent that there is either virtual consensus among all organization members about what should be done (for example, in a voluntary fire brigade) or a dominant coalition of persons within the organization with consensus among themselves and sufficient power to impose their objectives on all others (as in many business enterprises) or a single power holder whose objectives count as the organization's objectives (as in a small owner-controlled business firm).

Many organizations do not satisfy any of these three conditions, and their objectives are therefore ambiguous. Examples are:

- Democratic institutions such as city governments in most Western countries: in this case power is deliberately distributed among several persons or coalitions who hold different objectives for the entire organization; moreover, power is partly held by elected representatives, partly by permanent civil servants. The two groups differ considerably in their involvement with and expectations for the organization.
- Universities: perhaps the extreme case of organizations in which power is widely distributed and different power groups hold very divergent views about objectives.
- Business organizations or parts thereof in which dominant coalitions are not unanimous about objectives: business employees know that objectives may shift from one day to another, depending on who has the upper hand. This becomes even more likely where societal changes, such as attempts at establishing some form of industrial democracy, bring new coalitions of organization members into the objective-setting process.

In such cases decisions, if they are consciously made at all, are based on processes of negotiation and struggle and cannot be derived from any prior organizational objective. Objectives may forever remain unclear. This may even be true if someone in the organization publishes eloquent espoused objectives for public relations purposes, such as those sometimes expressed in company charters or annual reports. The objectives in use in the real-life situation of the organization's members are not necessarily the same as the published ones.

2. *Accomplishment is not measurable.* Even in cases where objectives are clear to all involved, it is often not possible to translate them into unambiguous, quantitative output standards against which performance can be measured. How should we measure the output of a city police corps? One of its final objectives is definitely to prevent crime, so we might consider the decrease of crime rates as an output measure. This

assumes that other influences on crime rates can be neglected (which is not true) and that crime rates themselves can be measured objectively (whereas in fact they are partly derived from police reports; low reported crime rates could also mean administrative incompetence of police personnel to adequately register crimes). In such cases organizations often resort to *surrogate* measures of performance (Anthony & Herzlinger, 1975), measures that are less directly tied to the organization's objectives but more easily measurable. In the case of the police corps the number of people arrested or the amount of fines levied could be such surrogate measures.

For many organizations or activities within organizations, outputs can only be defined in qualitative and vague terms. The only thing really measurable about such activities is their inputs: how much money and other resources is allotted to them. These include most management and indirect activities in industrial organizations, including advertising, personnel, and control activities in headquarters, and research; most public bodies, such as municipal and government services; most activities in schools, universities, hospitals, and voluntary associations. In all these cases the sole control of management exists at the time of resource allocation, but the criteria for resource allocation to one and not to another activity are judgmental. The essence of the process is negotiation, a political process in which many arguments other than the effective and efficient use of resources usually play a role, including the status of the negotiator, his/her support among influential persons whom he/she might mobilize, personal relationships between negotiators, and sometimes nepotism.

One frequently used control device is whether similar funds allocated last year were really spent; its main effect is the spending of unnecessary funds. Skillful negotiators have many ploys at their disposal, and skillful resource allocators have many counterploys (Anthony & Herzlinger, 1975, p. 249). This is a part of the game of management control that has little to do with either effectiveness or efficiency of the organization, not because of anybody's evil intentions but simply because nobody is able to predict what resource allocation corresponds to maximum effectiveness.

3. *Feedback information is not usable.* The cybernetic model presupposes a recurring cycle of events, with variance information used to correct the present state of affairs to eliminate unwanted variances for the future. The model basically does not apply to one-time projects, such as most investment projects, whether in private or in public organizations. As the

project in its present form never returns, even large differences between planned and actual cost and performance have no effect on future projects.

It is remarkable that many organizations do not even attempt any project cost accounting to check whether predictions at the time of proposal were really fulfilled, a failure that can hardly be justified solely on the technical grounds that the benefits of one single project are difficult to disentangle. Once a proposal is accepted, the resources allocated to it become "sunk costs" and it is good management practice not to bother about sunk costs. This state of affairs stresses the negotiation element in the allocation of resources to investment projects even more. It is often hardly important whether the project's forecasted costs and performances are realistic—it is important only that they "look good" to the person or persons who decide about the allocation. Once the decision is made, few people worry about real outcomes. This leads to deliberate underestimation of costs. A common practice in the game of investment budgeting is, for example, to budget for the price of a machine, but not its installation costs, auxiliary tools, or spare parts. Once the machine is bought the organization is forced to spend on these other items to get it going.

A few organizations do use regular evaluation studies of past investment projects. Hägg (1974) studied these investment reviews and claims as one of their potential effects a "symbolic use." There is no change impact as far as planning of future projects is concerned, but those in command use the review procedure by, for example, referring to it as a sign of progressive management. They can do this when asked questions about capital investment activities by researchers or superiors. The review procedure can also be looked on as "institutionalized," as part of a tradition or a myth in the organization (pp. 58-59). Of course it is also possible that reviews do have a change impact, or that they have no impact at all, not even a symbolic one. Hägg notes a general lack of interest among managers in the reviews. In cases where reviews could reveal outright failures in investment decisions we can expect them to be unpopular among those who proposed and made these decisions.

## Enforcing a Cybernetic Model

With all its weaknesses, management control in situations that do meet the three basic conditions for applying the cybernetic model (presence of standards, measurable accomplishment, usable feedback) has still had a fair amount of success. In industrialized countries an increasing part of the national income is spent on activities that do *not* meet these conditions—indirect departments in private organizations and all kinds of public activities, including education and health care.

Responsible administrators have attempted to find ways to control the considerable resources spent on such activities. The success of the cybernetic model in other situations has led them to try to enforce a cybernetic approach for indirect and public activities as well. In practice this has been done by inviting successful industrial consultants to propose reorganizations for nonindustrial organizations (the McKinsey syndrome), reorganizations that have rarely been implemented and even more rarely been successful. The appointment of Robert McNamara of the Ford Corporation as U.S. Secretary of Defense in the 1960s started a movement in U.S. public agencies toward a "planning/programming/budgeting system," which became widely known as PPBS or PPB. PPBS has a number of objectives, among them control that is attempted to be executed by enforcing the cybernetic model, and in its most ambitious form is claimed to apply to any organization.

Reactions and experiences have been mixed. In 1967, C. L. Schultze, former director of the U.S. Bureau of the Budget, stated before a U.S. Senate subcommittee:

> I look forward to substantial improvements next year in terms of schedule, understanding of the role and desired character of the Program Memoranda, and, perhaps more important, in terms of their analytic content. Analytic staffs have been assembled and have had a chance to shake down; a number of data collection efforts and long term study efforts should reach fruition; and we are learning how to state program issues in a way that facilitates analysis and comparison. We have not yet by any means achieved my expectations for the system. That is partly because I have such high expectations for it. Ultimately I expect we will realize these expectations. (quoted in Anthony et al., 1972, p. 702)

In contrast, Wildavsky (1975) wrote:

> PPBS has failed everywhere and at all times. Nowhere has PPBS (1) been established and (2) influenced governmental decisions (3) according to its own principles. The program structures do not make sense to anyone. They are not, in fact, used to make decisions of any importance. Such products of PPBS as do exist are not noticeably superior in analytic quality or social desirability to whatever was done before. (pp. 363-364)

The fundamental problem of an approach like PPBS—which has spread to other countries in spite of its ambiguous results in the United

States and after it had been recognized in the United States as a failure—may be precisely in extrapolating a cybernetic philosophy derived from industrial production and sales situations to organizations of a very different nature without anyone asking the basic question whether and when this extrapolation is justified. Within the public system there are activities that meet the criteria for a cybernetic control approach, such as the quantifiable public services of garbage collection, public transport, and mail delivery. Other activities miss one or more of the fundamental conditions for the cybernetic model, and no amount of trying harder, setting up analytic staffs (with all the value conflicts involved), and data collection will overcome this.

There is a certain parallel between PPBS in public administration and another popular technique of the 1960s mainly used in private organizations: management by objectives (MBO). MBO is also based on a cybernetic philosophy (Sutherland, 1975) with objective setting (jointly between the employee, who is often him- or herself a manager, and his or her superior), performance review, and corrective action. Not unlike PPBS, MBO is supported by believers, but also heavily attacked. Levinson (1970) called it "one of the greatest management illusions" and "industrial engineering with a new name" (p. 126).

Few cases of successful implementation of MBO have been reported—that is, cases in which others than the person responsible for the implementation claim that it has been successful in improving performance. Ivancevich (1974), besides reviewing the rare literature on research about MBO, has reported on a 3-year longitudinal study of the introduction of MBO in two plants of one U.S. manufacturing company. The results were mixed, with one plant showing significant long-term improvement in performance and the other not. His study dealt with production workers and sales representatives, organization members whose accomplishment is to some extent measurable. In these cases enforcement of a cybernetic control model by MBO may not be too difficult, and if the program is well managed, it may lead to performance improvement. However, MBO is also advocated for and applied to indirect jobs in medical institutions, school systems, and government agencies. In these cases accomplishment is much less measurable, and it is rare to find surrogates acceptable to both parties. If a commonly agreed-on measurement of accomplishment is lacking the cybernetic model again does not apply, and MBO is simply bound to fail. A second reason why MBO may fail, even if the cybernetic model does apply, is that MBO is based on simplistic and mechanistic assumptions about the relationships among the people involved: It uses a reward-punishment psychology (Levinson,

1970). More goes on between people than cybernetic objective setting and feedback alone.

## Political Control

Blanket application of a cybernetic philosophy to noncybernetic organization processes can only do more harm than good. This does not mean that the advantages of the cybernetic approach *to those cases where it applies* have to be dropped. Within most organizations, even indirect and public ones, there are activities that can be controlled in a cybernetic way: those mechanized so far that people play no role in them, and those where people play a role, but there is consensus about what this role should be and how it should be executed. For cybernetic—or preferably homeostatic—control to function in these cases it is necessary that performance be measurable so that standards can be set. But often these cybernetic cases will be the exception. The more typically human and less mechanistic an activity, the smaller the chance that the conditions for a cybernetic approach will be met.

The essence of the noncybernetic situations is that they are *political:* Decisions are based on negotiation and judgment, or as an employee of a Dutch city government expressed it, on enlightenment by the Holy Spirit. Decisions often deal with *policies*. There is a well-known slogan: "There is no reason for it. It's just our policy." What this means is that policy is not merely composed of rational elements. Its main ingredients are *values*, which may differ from person to person, and *norms*, which are shared within groups in society but vary over time and from group to group (Vickers, 1973).

It makes little sense to speak of control processes here, at least in the formal sense in which such processes are described in cybernetic situations. It does make sense to speak of a control *structure,* taking into account the power positions of the various parties in the negotiations. Within this structure, we may study the control *games* played by the various actors (Crozier, 1976). Once resources are allocated there is no automatic feedback on the effectiveness of their use. The only controls possible are whether the resources were really spent or funds embezzled. Beyond that, it is a matter of trusting those in charge of carrying out the programs. The real control takes place through the appointing of a person to a task. Activities once decided on tend to perpetuate themselves. Corrective actions in the case of ineffective or inefficient activities are not automatically generated by the control system but require a specific evaluation study. Deciding on such a study is in itself a political act that may upset an established balance of power.

## Conclusion:
## The Use of Models

In thinking about organizations we cannot escape from using models. To see why this is so, I find it helpful to refer to the general hierarchy of systems first formulated in different ways by Von Bertalanffy and Boulding (Johnson, Kast, & Rosenzweig, 1963, pp. 7-9). In the general hierarchy of systems, nine levels of complexity of systems are distinguished:

1. Static frameworks
2. Dynamic systems with predetermined motions
3. Closed-loop control or cybernetic systems
4. Homeostatic systems like the biological cell
5. Living plants
6. Animals
7. Humans
8. Human organizations
9. Transcendental systems

Each successive level adds a dimension of complexity to the previous one until we get to organizations at Level 8, where the complexity is overwhelming. As the individual is at Level 7, it is fundamentally impossible for the human brain to completely grasp what goes on at Level 8. To think about organizations we must simplify, or use lower-level systems we can understand as models or metaphors for what we cannot understand. Early thinkers about organizations focused on the organization chart, a first-level model. Scientific management was often concerned with procedures, second-level models. The cybernetic control process is a third-level model, and the homeostatic "cell" model is found at the fourth level.

One consequence of the use of lower level systems as models for organizations is that we automatically consider the people in the system (at least, all except ourselves—see the quote from Jonas above) as if they were things or means to be used. The goals are supposed to be given. But in fact all organization goals derive from people: In the hierarchy of systems, the source of organization goals is at Level 7, with the individual. In an organization the individual is both *goal and means,* but the use of lower level models implies dealing with people as means. We may do this only when there is consensus over goals or goals can be imposed, and then we see these are not just conditions for the applicability of the cybernetic model, but for all lower level models, including biological ones.

In political situations, there is no consensus about goals, and replacing organizational reality by a model that treats people as means is no longer appropriate. Using a cybernetic model—such as PPBS—in such a case means a covering up of the real issues and will be perceived rightly by most people as an attempt by a technocratic coalition to impose its implicit goals on all others.

## Discussion Questions

1. Try to identify in your own environment two examples each of cybernetic control, homeostatic control, and political control.

2. What are the advantages and disadvantages of homeostatic over cybernetic control?

3. Try to identify in your own environment an example of pseudo-control.

4. What are the costs of trying to enforce a cybernetic approach for indirect and public activities?

## Note

1. Brecht's *The Threepenny Opera* may exist in an English translation, but my own imperfect translation of these German lines is:

> Just try to make a plan
> For which you pick your brain
> And after that, another plan:
> Your toil will be in vain.

# 10

# Case Study

## *Communauté de Travail Boimondau*

This case describes the entire 30-year life cycle of a worker-owned business company in the watch industry in Valence, France. The company was created with the purpose to "make men" (and women), rather than just make products or profits. From a small and adventurous start during the German occupation of World War II, the company developed successfully, although many of the social experiments tried did not succeed. Eventually the initial idealism wore off, and without this the company in the long run could not survive.

## The Setting:
## The Watch Industry in the French Jura

Around 1950, a small industrial company in the French provincial town of Valence was making history. Journalists, social scientists, idealists,

This case was written by Louis A. de Bettignies, Research Assistant at INSEAD, and the author, Visiting Lecturer at IMEDE. It was intended to be used as a basis for class discussion rather than to illustrate effective or ineffective handling of an administrative situation. Reprinted with the permission of IMD and INSEAD. Copyright © 1973 IMEDE Management Development Institute, Lausanne, Switzerland, and INSEAD (European Institute of Business Administration), Fontainebleau, France. This case appeared as an article in a special issue (guest edited by the author) on the theme "Power in Organizations" of the journal *International Studies of Management and Organization*, 7(1), Spring 1977, pp. 91-116.

and interested laypersons from many countries wanted to know more about it. Books had been written about it, both in France (Du Teil, 1949) and in the United States (Bishop, 1950), as well as several articles and brochures.

This company was Boimondau, with about 150 employees, manufacturing and selling watch cases (parts for the watch industry, the metal bodies into which the watch mechanisms are built). The reason for the renown of Boimondau was not its product, however, but its objectives and organization structure. Boimondau was the first and largest of the worker-owned and worker-managed *communautés de travail* that sprang up in France and some neighboring countries after the 1945 peace.

The watch industry in France was originally concentrated in the areas close to the Swiss border. Like the Swiss watch industry it consisted of a large number of small family firms, most of them employing fewer than 20 persons. Later on concentrations took place, but the industry remained widely dispersed. The typical firm specialized in one or a few watch parts: base plates, springs, jewels, wheels, screws, gears, dials, hands, or cases. Other firms specialized in assembling the parts into complete watches; the assemblers were the customers of the watch part makers.

Whereas assembly demanded high craftsmanship but little investment, making the parts called for a higher degree of mechanization but fewer all-around skills. The watch case production process was relatively capital intensive, and cases had to be produced in large numbers to pay for their tooling. Assemblers often worked with small quantities: 20, 50, 100 watches at a time. Case manufacturers typically designed their own models, which they subsequently tried to sell to assemblers. The case was important because it was primarily what made a watch sell, rather than what was inside.

The technology of watch and watch case production had been relatively stable. Important innovations like the use of stainless steel and the waterproof case already existed when Boimondau was founded.

In 1950, France was the world's third largest watch producer after Switzerland and the United States, with 8.5% of the total world production (4 million watches of a total of 48 million); in later years, it was by-passed by Germany, the USSR, and Japan. Watch case production in France in 1950 was divided among 26 firms, of which only 10 employed more than 100 workers. Watch cases manufactured in other countries were also imported into France.

## Boimondau's Foundation Period:
## 1941-1946

The company was founded in 1941 by Marcel Barbu, a former worker in the watch case industry who had created his own business in Besançon near the Swiss border, but fled this town when the Germans occupied it in 1939. Barbu was then in his 30s. In Valence, in the part of France that until early 1943 was unoccupied by the Germans (but governed by the pro-German Vichy government), and where he had a major client, he wanted to start again. Qualified personnel were not available, so he hired a number of young, unskilled, jobless men and taught them how to make waterproof watch cases, which were subsequently chrome plated by Mrs. Barbu in a washing machine.

The scarcity of the product (after the border with watch-producing Switzerland had been closed) and Barbu's craftsmanship guaranteed unlimited sales at good prices, and Barbu paid above-average wages. But his ambitions went further. Barbu was a devout Christian who tried to put his faith to work, as well as an unconventional thinker. He had firm convictions about the alienation of workers in traditional capitalist enterprises. Already in his Besançon venture he had experimented with forms of worker-management cooperation. Now he wanted to go even further. He called his company the Communauté Marcel Barbu and proposed that development of the full human potential of its members would be the first goal. Gradually he succeeded in gaining the confidence of the young fellows who joined his firm. He worked alongside the others; he was fellow worker Number 1, doing away with all external signs of status. His leadership was based not only on his craftsmanship, but also on his prophetic personality, his force of conviction, and his ideas.

In 1941 profits rose to a level where Barbu could expand the humble shed in which production began. He also could give everybody 10 days of vacation at Christmas, a luxury hitherto unknown. As of early 1942 regular weekly meetings with all employees were begun. At the request of his fellow workers, during 1942 Barbu started organizing courses in technical education, in French language, in music, in gymnastics, and on marriage-family problems at company expense. Half a day a week was available for these activities. As of December 1942, the communauté had 120 employees, and a strong sense of common purpose was developing.

Outside events interfered with the growth of the company. In 1942 Barbu was arrested by the French Vichy-commanded police and put in a concentration camp for 3 months because of his refusal to provide lists of employees for forced labor in Germany. In early 1943 the Germans invaded the hitherto unoccupied part of France, and the plant went underground. Production was partly continued in the stables of a mountain farm, partly in Barbu's old plant in Besançon. About 20 employees who did not want to share the hardships of underground life were expelled. In April 1944 Barbu was arrested again, this time by the Germans, and taken to a concentration camp in Germany; he was not to come back until 1945. German troops burned the farm to which the plant had moved, and the men joined the underground resistance movement. Three members of the communauté, two men and a woman, lost their lives in the hands of the Gestapo.

Before his second arrest Barbu had drafted an "act of foundation" for the Communauté Marcel Barbu in which the members would state their agreement to form a *communauté* (community), and in which he, Barbu, transferred the ownership to the communauté as a whole. This act, with some changes, was signed after his return in 1945.

In September 1944 Valence was liberated. Production was soon resumed under the temporary leadership of a relative newcomer to the communauté, Marcel Mermoz. Mermoz was 35 years old at the time. He had been arrested by the Vichy government in 1939 as a militant Marxist and spent more than 3 years in the concentration camp where Barbu met him during his own 3-month jailing in 1942. Barbu had told Mermoz about his communauté. They found they shared many ideas and started making plans together. After his own liberation Barbu succeeded in getting Mermoz liberated as well, using his personal influence with some key authorities. So in April 1943 Mermoz joined him, just in time to go underground with the others.

Mermoz was the son of a poor mountain farmer. He went to Paris at the age of 14 and successively became a valet, a photographer, a baker, and a metalworker. He read what he could, studied during the day when he worked at night, and obtained his baccalauréat (high school certificate) at the age of 27. In the underground period he soon became a leader. After liberation it was only natural that he was asked to be the formal acting chief of the communauté pending the return of Barbu. He had no experience with running an industrial enterprise, but observers at the time described him as having tremendous energy, great intelligence, and a sense of system and organization.

By the end of 1944 the company was fully back in production. When Barbu was liberated from Buchenwald concentration camp in May 1945 he could take over the leadership of a well-run organization. The Act of Foundation was signed, but Barbu never fully exercised his leadership. His ambitions went beyond this one enterprise to a reform of French society as a whole according to communitarian principles. Barbu's ideas had become widely known and other groups were following the example of Boimondau. The number of supporters was large enough to elect Barbu a member of the French National Assembly in October 1945.

The *compagnons* (companions, or community members), although they had helped elect Barbu, were not all so enthusiastic about his political aspirations. Some friction developed and Barbu, feeling the need to choose between the communauté and the National Assembly, chose the latter. He left the communauté formally in July 1946, not without bad feelings, and Marcel Mermoz was elected as the new chief of the community. The communauté was from then on called Boimondau (*Boitiers de Montre du Dauphiné*, for "watch cases of Dauphiné province"). Barbu was reimbursed for his contribution to Boimondau's capital. Much later he became an outsider candidate for the presidency of France, collecting only a few votes.

## Boimondau's Objectives and Organization Structure

The primary objective of Boimondau was stated as "making men": the full development of the human person, economically, intellectually, and morally, based on the intrinsic and irreplaceable value of humans. Boimondau and a number of other communautés de travail adopted 12 basic rules as a charter:

1. Common and indivisible ownership of the means of production, which should never become individual property.
2. A healthy economic position.
3. The supreme authority is the general assembly of all workers. The general assembly can delegate this authority wholly or in part to persons elected to be managers or to a chosen general council that assists and audits the chief of the communauté.
4. Managers are elected according to the rule of double confidence, that is, they should have both the confidence of their superior and of their subordinates.
5. The rules of the communauté are established by unanimity.
6. Information media should ensure that every compagnon is informed about the activities and problems of the communauté.
7. There should be an educational goal, that is, the fullest possible development as human beings of the members of the communauté.
8. No discrimination for political, religious, or philosophical reasons, nor on the basis of race, sex, or nationality.

9. Solidarity with society as a whole, and in particular, with all workers.
10. Compensation independent of capital contributed. Compensation not only to be based on the professional contribution of the compagnon.
11. Widely spread responsibilities, so that the results of the communauté, even though formally managed by the chief of the community or the general council, are really the outcome of everybody's fullest effort.
12. Refusal to employ anybody who is not a compagnon, except during an initiation period.

At Boimondau the communauté included all workers ("productive companions") and also their wives and children ("family companions"), at least to the extent that the latter wanted to share in the benefits and obligations of membership. All companions, after being selected on the basis of both professional ability and character, had to pass a 3-month probation period as "stagiaire" and a whole year learning period as "postulant" before being given full membership rights; moreover, they had to be accepted unanimously by all existing companions.

For a diagram of the organization of the communauté see Figure 10.1. As stated in the charter, the supreme authority was the general assembly of all companions (productive and family), which met at least twice a year. It elected the chief of community for a term of 3 years, but could withdraw its confidence from the chief at any time. The general assembly also nominated a general council, consisting of the four heads of departments (technical, commercial, financial, and social) and seven other companions, who together with the chief carried out the daily management.

All productive companions met every week in the "assembly of contact," a 2-hour information session on issues of immediate concern, like work results and plans for the next week.

The basic cells of communitarian life were the "neighbor groups." Neighbor groups included five to eight families or single companions living in the same part of town. Neighbor groups were supposed to meet twice a month in the home of one of the families. These groups served a double purpose: They were meant to discuss general problems of the communauté, according to a discussion theme suggested by the chief of the community, and they were also expected to create friendship ties and to liberate people from alienation and isolation. The results of the discussions in the neighbor groups were recorded in a notebook that circulated between the group and the chief of the community. The discussions in the neighbor groups served as preparation for the general assembly meetings. They were a vital link in the flow of information up and down in the organization. Neighbor group heads met once a month with the chief of the community.

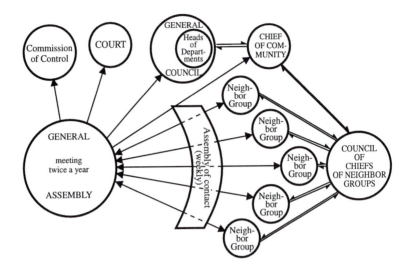

**Figure 10.1.** Organization of the Communauté
NOTES: 1. All powers belong to the General Assembly.
          2. Arrows indicate the way powers are entrusted.

In the general assembly decisions were taken by unanimity. This meant in practice that only those issues were put on the agenda for which a reasonable consensus had already been reached in the groups. A voting procedure was used in the general assembly meeting and the minority was asked to go along with the majority decision. If the minority refused, however, the proposal was considered as rejected, and a new solution had to be sought.

The organization further included a commission of control for the financial results, and a court to resolve differences of opinion and to take disciplinary actions when necessary.

Life in the communauté was divided in three sectors, and every member was supposed to participate in all three:

1. The work sector or "professional life": his or her economic activity
2. The social sector or "social life": any activity not included in the work sector that contributed to the full development of the human potential, like sports, attending courses, work on behalf of others or of society in general
3. The communitarian sector, also labeled "whole life"

The three sectors had their own hierarchies, and the same member could be found in different positions in the three hierarchies (see Figure 10.2).

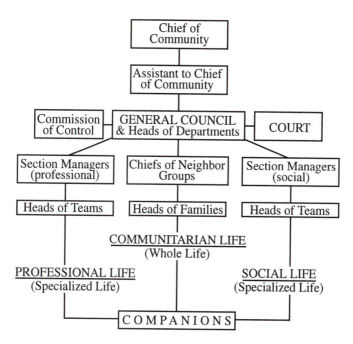

**Figure 10.2.** Hierarchy of Responsibilities

The social sector activities took place, in part, during working hours. In 1946, 8 working hours of a 46-hour week were spent on such activities, mainly on education (courses were given in the workshop itself on the most diverse subjects, such as literature, art, and philosophy) and physical exercise. The communauté had an extensive library, which was widely used. There was a rule that everybody should read two books a month, but it was said that only 10% of the companions achieved this. People could choose which social activities they wanted to participate in, but participation as such was compulsory, including for the family companions.

The social sector included membership in the "spiritual teams," which also met during working hours. Every companion, according to his or her religion or ideology, had to choose one of the spiritual teams: Catholic, Protestant, Materialist (Marxist), or "Humanist" (anybody not belonging to one of the others). The teams discussed fundamental problems of community life and met among each other to exchange views. One of the products of the spiritual teams was the "minimum morale": a common moral code to which new companions were asked to subscribe. It was subject to periodic revision.

The work sector included as an original element the "countereffort." This dated from the war years when companions went out to work on the company farm. For 4 weeks spread over the year each companion was supposed to do a completely different job; this included the family companions. Most countereffort was done at the company farm, but it also included the chief of the community working in the cafeteria and housewives working at the machines.

## Compensation According to "Human Value"

The community took a far-reaching responsibility for its members. Those absent because of illness received their full pay, but lateness in coming to work was penalized. All medical expenses were carried by the community, and all expenses for social activities as well. In addition, help was available for housewives who fell ill. The community had a kindergarten, a recreation home for housewives, and a consumers' cooperative that sold food and supplies at a discount.

Financial compensation was more egalitarian than in the surrounding world: The range of incomes from the chief of the community to the lowest paid companion was 5 to 1, whereas in the traditional enterprise it could be 10 to 1 or more. Compensation was, moreover, not based on contribution to production only. It was designed to be based on the "total human value" of the companion, which consisted of his or her professional value and his or her social value.

Total compensation also depended on the economic results of the communauté. After deduction of the necessary funds for reserves and investment, the remainder was distributed among the companions. In 1946, 50% of the compensation was distributed according to professional value and 50% according to social value.

The professional value included productive work, compensation for social risks (illness, etc.), and for those having families, compensation for the wife for her housework, for each child, and for the social risks of the housewife. Compensation for productive work was based both on job category (using the general classification adopted by the industry) and on actual performance, as rated by the worker him- or herself. All ratings were published, as was everyone's final salary.

The social value included components for all kinds of social and educational activities carried out by the companion and his or her spouse, as well as for their general contribution to the community, determined by an ingenious system of mutual ratings. The reasoning was that because the goal of the community was the maximum human development of its members, any effort at self-development or community development contributed to this goal and should therefore be compensated on a par with production work. It was also felt that self-development for a worker who had a full-time job was a very heavy task and that unless it was made part of the job itself (and compensated accordingly), not many people could be expected to devote the necessary physical and mental energy.

## The Second Five Years:
## 1946-1951

Under Mermoz's management, the communauté flourished both socially and economically. The postwar years were singularly favorable for this. At first, at least, there was a sellers' market. Everything that could be produced could be sold at good prices, and the economic prosperity in 1946 and 1947 enabled the communauté to pay for all new social activities undertaken. It also allowed it to make solid investments in plant and equipment. Boimondau got itself the most modern production machines. There was no fear that the machines would put people out of their jobs. It was said that the machines were there to liberate the people, and the time freed could be used for self-development purposes.

The number of productive employees (companions, postulants, and stagiaires) rose to 160 at the end of 1947. This was considered the optimal size. Barbu had already stated that beyond about 100 families it would become difficult for everybody to know everybody, and the communauté would lose its human face.

In 1950, with 160 employees and a production of 416,000 watch cases (27% more than in 1947), Boimondau had become the leading watch case producer of France. It made 20% of French national production and 1% of the world production of watch cases. It had a reputation for excellent quality. In 1949 it had begun exports. Sales had become fashion oriented, and the number of different models produced increased from 5 in 1946 to 46 in 1950.

The postwar years were also favorable for the development of the social activities. There was a lot of idealism and a desire to start something new. People had been accustomed during the war to making sacrifices for the common good. Shared suffering had brought them close together, and there were few opportunities for leisure activities, so people readily invested their free time in community life.

This was also the period of the greatest publicity. Visitors from all over France, but also from other countries, wanted to see Boimondau or even spend a traineeship there. This interest from outside supported the feeling among the companions of the importance of their experience. They saw themselves as "the first link in a communitarian revolution."

It has already been stated that other communautés de travail were set up. Many of them were agricultural. Some were in the building trades. A number of others were in the watch industry, and a variety of other trades were represented. Most of them were small. Boimondau remained for a long time the largest communauté de travail in France.

After Barbu's attempts to form a political movement based on communitarian principles had failed, in 1947 the existing communautés decided to form a common support organization, the Entente Communautaire. In 1950 the entente included 85 communautés, published a monthly journal, and operated a secretariat in Paris. One of the first acts of the entente was to secure a legal basis for the way of life in the communautés. According to French law the form of common ownership intended by the communauté members was not possible; legally, the ownership during the first years had been supposed to rest with the chief of the community. The entente succeeded in developing a formula according to which the communautés could be considered as a special form of production cooperative. Boimondau adopted this legal status immediately, in 1947.

The key influence of Boimondau on the communitarian movement can be demonstrated by the fact that nine chiefs of other communities were former companions of Boimondau (five others had become heads of "capitalist" firms). The general secretary of the Entente Communautaire had previously been head of the social department at Boimondau.

Boimondau had relationships not only with the communitarian movement but also with the labor movement in general. Mermoz and others were very concerned about the danger that the success of the community would lead to spiritual inbreeding, and the reactions of the trade unions to Boimondau had been not too favorable. The experiment was considered bourgeois, if not fascist. The Marxist press had maintained complete silence about the communitarian movement.

In late 1947 there were general strikes in France and some fighting in the streets. Boimondau declared its solidarity with the workers and it absorbed three of the most militant strikers who had been fired elsewhere. On this and other occasions it also subsidized strike funds. After 1947, therefore, relations with the national unions in France improved. Individual companions took active roles in unions and political parties. One capitalist supplier, who saw Boimondau as a dangerous tool of Moscow, stopped the delivery of vital materials without warning. The companions went to see the union members in the supplier's company and delivery was resumed immediately.

Finally, Boimondau greatly influenced cultural life in Valence. When Boimondau started, opportunities for cultural activities for workers were virtually nonexistent. Other workers began to show an interest in the social and cultural initiatives of the communauté. Boimondau decided to open its social activities to others, and several of them became independent of the communauté. Also, Boimondau took the initiative for a home construction association open to anyone, with the purpose of providing good housing at low prices.

In May 1948, within a few weeks the French watch case market collapsed. Sales dropped to a third of their normal volume. The postwar boom was over, normal competition resumed, and so did imports. In the watch production-distribution chain all suddenly realized that they had been overconfident and stocks were too high, so orders were canceled. Several of the smaller private watch case manufacturers had to close down.

Boimondau, having heavily invested in new machinery, found itself with an acute cash shortage. For four months no salaries were paid and the companions' own bank accounts served as a security for the communauté. Companions and members of their families were encouraged to look for temporary jobs outside doing construction, household help, fruit picking. Families helped each other and shared their modest meals.

In September 1948 the situation returned to normal. In fact, the failure of many small competitors enabled Boimondau to expand its market. The crisis had been overcome thanks to an incredible willingness to sacrifice: Only one companion had left. Nevertheless it forced the communauté to rethink its social policy: the weekly hours for social activities were reduced from 8 to 6½ and these social activities themselves, which had been compulsory before, were made optional. A year later hours were further reduced, to 3½ per week. The compensation scheme was revised. The distribution of income according to professional or social value, which had hitherto been fifty-fifty, was changed to two thirds professional, one third social. A year later, this became seven eighths to one eighth. The countereffort, which had been losing popularity anyway and had been reduced from 4 to 2 weeks a year, was stopped altogether. The budget for social activities was maintained at its precrisis level of 10% of total payroll.

Mermoz succeeded in convincing the companions that greater stress should be put on productivity. A consultant firm, Bedaux, was called in for time-and-motion study and the setting of work standards. This led to a remarkable increase in productivity. Another consultant, CEGOS, installed a management information system that for its time was very progressive. The learning period for new jobs was reduced by the adaptation of the "training within industry" (TWI) method, which had then started to penetrate Europe from the United States. All these measures bore fruit: In 1949-1951 Boimondau did very well once more.

## Developments After 1951

Marcel Mermoz left Boimondau in 1951, at his own will. He had been offered a very challenging proposition by the United Nations Refugee Fund: to create a center where political refugees from abroad could be retrained and subsequently settle down to work—all of this in the form of a "communauté." He remained in Valence and regularly saw companions from Boimondau.

A U.S. sociologist, Henrik Infield, studied the social structure of Boimondau in 1951, just before the departure of Mermoz. Infield's analysis showed the existence within the communauté of two groups: the old-timers, who had lived through the war years together, and the newcomers. The community grew less than before. The young men of the pioneer days had married and become fathers of families. The kindergarten run by the community was flourishing. But for new members of the community it was clearly difficult to feel integrated. Their potential contribution to community life was not fully realized.

On Mermoz's recommendation, Georges Matras was elected the new chief. Matras was one of the old-timers of Boimondau, who had participated in the underground period. In Mermoz's days his main responsibility had been marketing, for which he had a special talent. Matras was an intelligent and hardworking man who would have made a career in any organization. He was not the prophetic type like Barbu, nor the natural leader type like Mermoz. He belonged neither to the Christian nor to the Marxist group, but was considered a "Humanist." The technical leadership was in the hands of R. Billiet, a companion whom Boimondau had enabled to complete his engineering studies.

Economically Boimondau continued to prosper in these years. Excellent quality and good marketing had given it a good reputation with customers, and it could get good prices for its products. A new crisis in the French watch industry in 1953, when other companies suffered from overproduction, did not have a serious impact on Boimondau thanks to its exports. Boimondau emerged from this crisis economically stronger: It supplied 50% of the French watch case market.

Publicity about Boimondau diminished and the number of visitors became smaller. I visited Boimondau in 1955 and gained the impression of a well-run business operated not by idealists or dogmatists, but by pragmatic people.

One consequence of the lack of integration of the new members was that not all of the new employees wanted to become companions any more. Already during the 1948 crisis it had been decided that married women whose husbands were working elsewhere could be kept on salary, that is, not sharing the risks and benefits of the companions. During the late 1950s an increasing number of new members, not only women, remained on salary for an indefinite period, a situation that violated one of the basic rules in the charter of the communauté de travail.

The division between old-timers and newcomers was not the only one which became evident. Even within the group of old-timers there were different ideological tendencies. There were those who advocated a radical application of communitarian principles (I will call them the "communitarians"), and those who wanted to give priority to productivity and the demands of the market (the "technocrats").

Unlike his predecessors, Matras was not a universal leader. He was, therefore, unable to bridge the ideological gap. He himself was identified with the technocrats. The 1953 crisis, which caused other companies to collapse, proved the success of his approach to strengthening Boimondau's position in the market and for a period masked the ideological controversies.

An alarming development affecting the maintenance of the communitarian principles was the gradual dying out of the neighbor groups that had been conceived as the basic cells of community life. As early as 1951 the author of a series of articles about Boimondau mentioned that some of the neighbor groups appeared to have fallen asleep. Outside factors were partly responsible for this: the increase in the general standard of living and the increasing availability of alternative ways of spending free time. Private cars became attainable for workers around 1954; television came around 1956. The lack of internal cohesion in the communauté helps to explain why it became increasingly difficult to keep the neighbor groups going.

At the request of some of the communitarian companions Marcel Mermoz was asked to come back part-time in 1954, to look after social affairs. Mermoz's work with the political refugees had resulted in the foundation of two small communautés, Centralor (making gold watch cases) and Cadreclair (making watch dials). They were united in a "holding" communauté, the Cité Horlogère, of which Mermoz was the chief. Boimondau, Centralor, and Cadreclair shared various social and cultural activities. Mermoz succeeded in reviving the neighbor groups. The wife of a companion said about this period: "Thanks to the social life, to the fact that we felt at home, we could afford to exercise criticism at the same time."

Mermoz continued to function as social advisor until 1956, and as long as he was active in this role the communitarian principles were dominant, at least on the surface. A companion commented, "We were accustomed to discussing everything, and as has happened to others, we too fell into a kind of communitarian formalism. For example, we said, 'We are democratic: the best proof is that we meet seven or eight times a week to discuss everything.' We really met all the time, we discussed and discussed, and we made very few decisions, which nobody carried out anyway."

In 1957, at the request of the Entente Communautaire, a French sociologist, Albert Meister, studied the various member communities (Meister, 1958). It appeared that the deterioration of community life visible in Boimondau had happened in the other communautés as well—and to an even greater extent. The goal, full development of the human person, was gradually reduced to collective self-management of the means of production of the group. But even this limited goal appeared difficult to realize. The election of managers meant no real influence because there was no choice—only a few people had the capacities to take on the management roles. The control exercised by the general assembly tended to be nominal, because the companions lacked the knowledge to judge the acts of management. Collective self-management meant, in practice, the right of all companions to be informed.

The Meister report mentioned two main achievements of the communautés. One was the education of many companions to take greater responsibility. Virtually all people in more responsible positions had come up through the ranks. In Boimondau about one fourth of the companions held line or staff management positions in the professional sector. If we include all kinds of committees, two thirds of the companions had some kind of special responsibility.

The other major achievement of the communautés was the congenial and friendly working atmosphere they had succeeded in creating, which differed from that in the typical French capitalist enterprise. Interpersonal communications were better and there was more freedom. Said a companion, "The system is not authoritarian, one cannot order people around at Boimondau as they do elsewhere, there is a great freedom to express oneself and very easy contact, even with the managers." Another said, "I can raise hell with my foreman or my general manager even when I am wrong, while elsewhere I couldn't do it even if I were right." Still another stated, "It's a different world. We do our work, nobody is watching us. In the capitalist shop we had often a boss breathing down our neck. And it often happened that even colleagues played tricks on each other."

A snapshot of Boimondau in 1957 would have shown the number of companions had somewhat decreased to 105, although the total number of employees had not gone down—it was about 180. The average age of the companions was 37; of the noncompanions, 23.

There were still 14 neighbor groups, which met seven to nine times per year. For the rest the participation of the wives in the community affairs was small; only 12 of them visited the assembly meetings. There were 11 study groups that met 1½ hours per week during working hours. Their subject was the work itself as courses by outside teachers in the workshops had stopped. There were four creative teams during evening hours. Physical training was still given 1½ hours per week, but the hours were no longer paid. The social affairs department still employed a full-time person, and the social budget was maintained at 10% of total payroll. The "social value" component of compensation was still in existence, but it had become a small bonus on the order of 5% of the salaries, to encourage participation in educational and social activities.

Those interested could take a management development course, jointly organized by Boimondau, Centralor, and Cadreclair, which was given during evening hours and lasted 2 years. Successful completion of this course led automatically to a promotion, or at least to a salary increase.

About two thirds of the companions, but fewer than one third of the noncompanions, were members of labor unions. An agreement had been made with the unions that the General Council of Boimondau would be accepted by the unions as a "comité d'entreprise."[1]

Such was the situation when in 1957 a new economic crisis in the watch industry hit Boimondau and led to a sharpening of the "technocrat" pressure on production and marketing. Some companions left; at the end of 1957, the number of companions was 95. Meetings were held less frequently and they focused more and more on business problems. A reform led to the elimination of the unanimity rule in the General Assembly. It was replaced by a simple majority rule. The same was true for the General Council and for the Arbitration Committee, which replaced the former Court (and which seemed to function only on rare occasions). The last neighbor groups gradually died out.

The economic situation strengthened the role of the higher management group, and Georges Matras, as chief of the community, began to look more like a company president. His business contacts were largely

can be labeled "value" power: the power of raising at the right moment an issue that reflects the values of a sufficiently large number of people. Ironically, the same thing occurred in the same cathedral before—when the Reformation was preached from the same pulpit four centuries earlier. History repeated itself.

## Discussion Questions

1. How do you feel about Pierre Zwahlen's speech?

2. What do you learn from the fact that two teachers who respond to the decrees in *Vingt-quatre Heures* do so anonymously?

3. Why can't the authorities adopt a more flexible stance? (consider also the distribution of votes in the Grand Conseil).

4. What is the implication of the case for a business that will eventually employ Pierre's generation?

## Note

1. In French, this is a pun. "Le père fouettard" is an ogre, and it is also a name for the black servant of Saint Nicholas who punishes the bad children.

# 12

## Case Study

### *Angola Coffee*

A dramatic case description of events in a Dutch company that is put under pressure to change its policy illustrates how managerial behavior is subject to the prevailing climate of opinion in society. The clash of interests both inside and outside the organization and the mobilization of consumer opinion by external pressure groups compels management to revise its policy position. The case is analyzed from the point of view of the value systems of various actors inside and outside the company, and of the cultural specificity of the Dutch environment in which it took place. It is also considered as an example of "garbage can" decision making. Its consequences are explored for the management of both business corporations and civic action groups.

### Initial Contacts

On the morning of January 13, 1972, Mr. Groen, assistant to the managing director of the Coffee and Tea division of Douwe Egberts, was going through the morning mail in his office at Douwe Egberts N.V. headquar-

This case was intended to be used as a basis for class discussion rather than to illustrate effective or ineffective handling of an administrative situation. Copyright © 1973 IMEDE Management Development Institute, Lausanne, Switzerland. Reprinted with permission of IMD, successor to IMEDE. The present version of the case appeared as an article in *Organization Studies*, 1(1), 1980, pp. 21-40.

ters on the outskirts of Utrecht, the Netherlands. The following letter caught his attention.

ANGOLA COMMITTEE
Freedom for Angola, Mozambique,
Guinea-Bissau, Portugal.
Da Costastraat 88
Amsterdam 1014
Douwe Egberts N.V.
c/o Mr. Groen
Keulsekade 143
Utrecht
Amsterdam, January 11, 1972

Dear Sirs,

As you know, a large share of the coffee imported into the Netherlands comes from Angola. The Portuguese government benefits financially from these imports: a state of events that the Angola Committee deplores.

In the month of February we intend to initiate a large-scale action against the importation of Angola coffee into the Netherlands. In this context we would like to meet with you within the next few days, to investigate with you whether Douwe Egberts, as a large Dutch processor, will be able to purchase its coffee from the independent African states rather than from Angola.

We expect that the action will be carried out in more than a hundred towns in the Netherlands in February, March, and April. We also have a number of agreements with large communications media that will support the action. Through this action we want to make it widely known to what extent our country, through its purchases of coffee in Angola, is actually supporting the oppression of the Angola people. We count on the support of the Action Groups for Southern Africa, which exist in about thirty cities. In addition, a large number of Third World Shops and Action Groups of the Peace Week will cooperate. In a number of cities we will organize door-to-door discussions. Provisionally 250,000 information leaflets and 10,000 posters are being printed.

In the meeting, which we would appreciate having with you at short notice, we will be glad to further explain our aims. We will call you on the telephone soon to try to make an appointment.

For the Angola Committee

Yours sincerely,


Dr. S. Bosgra

The letter did not come as a surprise to Mr. Groen. An early announcement of the planned action had been sent by the Angola Committee in the middle of November 1971. A second letter, identical in content to the one reproduced above and dated December 29, 1971, had been received at the company's main manufacturing plant in Joure, in the province of Friesland. It was after Mr. Bosgra called the Joure plant management that he had been referred to Mr. Groen.

Mr. Groen decided to discuss the issue with the managing director of the Coffee and Tea division, Mr. Schoonhoven.

## A Profile of the Company

The Douwe Egberts company was founded in 1753 by Egbert Douwes (son of Douwe), who started a "colonial store" in the village of Joure. His descendants afterward adopted the family name De Jong. The firm gradually began to move out of retailing into production, and its main products became coffee, tea, and tobacco. Another plant was opened in Utrecht, in the center of the Netherlands, in 1919, and later the firm's headquarters also moved there. The firm became widely known during World War II, when it marketed a popular coffee substitute. After the war it was the first to reintroduce real coffee, and with most of its former competitors in bad shape, it soon became the market leader. Sales in 1971 were about 750 million guilders ($230 million). Total personnel added up to 4,100, of whom 3,500 were located in the Netherlands. About half of the Dutch employees were concentrated in the area of Joure, now a small, provincial town. In coffee alone Douwe Egberts's market share in the Netherlands in 1971 was almost 50%. The share that different products contributed to the company's overall sales figure was not published, but it was known that coffee was the main contributor to profits, followed respectively by tobacco and tea.

The firm was completely owned by about 40 members of the De Jong family. Management had been in the hands of members of the family until 1967, when differences of opinion between the two top managing directors induced them to invite an outsider, Mr. J. Boost, to become chief executive. Mr. Boost was 56 years old at the time and had been president of the Pharmaceutical division of Philips. He reorganized Douwe Egberts's management structure according to modern principles. Several professional managers were brought into upper and middle-level executive positions.

Douwe Egberts had always enjoyed good employee relations. Labor turnover was low (an average of 7% over 1971) and absenteeism had been 3.7% in 1971, compared to as much as 10% in other large Dutch companies. About 30% of Douwe Egberts's employees were unionized into one of the three national labor unions in the Netherlands: the General (Socialist), Catholic, and Protestant Unions. Unionization was stronger in Joure than elsewhere. Union relations had always been constructive. In 1969 the company had adopted a "social charter" that expressed the social responsibility of the company toward its customers, its employees, and its shareholders. This social charter had been discussed with and agreed on by the works councils and the labor unions. The works councils conformed to the Dutch Works Council Acts of 1950 and 1971. There were regional works councils in Joure and Utrecht (15 members each) and a central works council for the total enterprise (8 members). The members were elected by all employees; the labor unions had the right to nominate the majority of the candidates. A member of top management acted as the council chairman. The works councils had the legal right to receive information on the financial results of the company, to be consulted on major structural changes, and to jointly decide on internal issues such as work regulations or benefit plans.

Douwe Egberts had never tried to build an image in the outside world based on anything other than its products. Its structure as a family enterprise had allowed it to publish no business results (until 1972 no annual reports were available) and there had never been any conscious attempt at public relations. In fact, a Public Relations department did not even exist.

## Early Signs
## of the Angola Coffee Problem

In 1971 in the Netherlands, a great deal of public attention was focused on the countries of the Third World. According to World Bank data, the Netherlands was one of only four countries that in 1971 spent more than .5% of their national income on direct development aid. In fact, it came second, with .64%, to France, with .65% (most of France's aid went to its former colonies, which was not the case in the Netherlands). A sizeable share of the Dutch contribution to the developing countries came from private gifts. A popular private fund, created through self-taxation by a number of citizens who thought the government was not doing enough, had existed for about 20 years. Press coverage on Third World topics was extensive. The churches were one of the major sources of support. Special action groups, mostly consisting of young people and concerned about specific Third World problems, were frequently created.

A major issue both in the Dutch press and public opinion had for a long time been the continuation of the Portuguese colonial regime. Portugal, with 9.5 million inhabitants, was the only major colonial power that by 1971 had not yet changed its relationships with its colonies (called "overseas territories" since 1951). Portugal's overseas territories in Africa and Asia covered an area 23 times the size of Portugal, with a total population of about 14 million. In the three largest territories, Angola, Mozambique, and Guinea-Bissau, independence movements were created in the 1950s; these later started guerrilla warfare. In Angola (5 million inhabitants) the war between the Portuguese and the major independence movement, MPLA, broke out in 1961 and was still going on in 1972. Shortly after it started, a committee supporting the MPLA, the Angola Committee, was founded in Amsterdam. Its goals were "to inform the public about the events in the Portuguese colonies, to mobilize support for the liberation movements, and to oppose the Western support of Portugal." The Angola Committee consisted of a small number of young Dutch intellectuals. Its chairman, Sietse Bosgra, who had a Ph.D. in physics, had given up his university job to work full-time for the committee. In 1972, the committee, still headed by Dr. Bosgra, then 36 years old, employed three full-time and two half-time staff members at (for the full-timers) a survival salary of 500 guilders ($150) a month. The office occupied two rooms in a popular district of Amsterdam.

Over the years the Angola Committee had established good relationships with most of the Dutch press, with local Third World action committees in almost every Dutch town of any size, with church and school groups, and with some of the political parties (not with the Communists, however). The mission of the Angola Committee was to keep the public informed about the situation in the Portuguese overseas territories. In addition the committee fought against Portugal's membership in NATO and its attempts at association with the European Community, actively lobbied in the Dutch parliament at the time of the discussions on the Foreign Affairs budget, and collected money and supplies for the independence movements in Angola.

The interest of the Angola Committee in the coffee trade started in 1970. In August a discussion had taken place in the Dutch parliament about the Netherlands' role in the International Coffee Agreement.[1] In September 1970 the national Protestant newspaper, *Trouw*, had published a letter from a Dutch volunteer couple working in Zambia about forced labor on coffee plantations in neighboring Angola. The press reported that the Netherlands was a major importer of Angola's Robusta coffee. Economics students at Dutch universities made two extensive studies of the coffee trade. Another discussion about the Dutch coffee trade, this time focusing on Angola, took place in parliament in December 1970. The Angola Committee searched for more information about Angola coffee, and as relatively little had been published, it was decided in 1971 that the committee itself would publish a booklet. This booklet, entitled *Coffee for the Netherlands, Blood of Angola,* appeared in January 1972 in an edition of 15,000 copies. The booklet was illustrated with photos supplied by Portuguese conscripts in Angola.

The Angola Committee decided to use the booklet as part of an action to obtain a boycott of Angola coffee in the Netherlands. It wanted to start the action on February 4, 1972, the 11th anniversary of the beginning of the war in Angola. In December 1971, 700 local action groups were contacted to support the campaign in their particular area. Some of these groups were Third World Stores, action centers opposed to the exploitation of the Third World. Other groups were Southern Africa action groups and groups that had participated in previous actions. From these first 700 contacts about 250 local groups promised to actively support the coffee action. The number of people who were involved was somewhere around 5,000.

Douwe Egberts had been made aware by its employers' association, the Dutch Union of Coffee Roasters and Tea Packers, of the discussions in parliament in August 1970. After the *Trouw* article in September 1970 occasional letters by consumers had been received, asking the company to stop using Angola coffee, but the total number of such letters in 1970 and 1971 had not exceeded 20. In September 1971 the personnel director, Mr. N. Dohmen, had been informed by one of his younger colleagues of the plans for a national action, and he had raised the issue in a meeting with top management. The other members of the management team did not share his concern that this might seriously affect the company. Neither the mid-November nor the later December letters from the Angola Committee had been answered by Douwe Egberts.

In January, affairs had taken a different turn. Albert Heijn, the largest Dutch supermarket chain, announced in early January that it would no longer use Angola coffee. Albert Heijn was a major customer of Douwe Egberts coffee and tea, but it also produced its own blends, which made it the second largest coffee roaster in the Netherlands, with a market share of 10%. A letter similar to the one written to Douwe Egberts had been addressed by the Angola Committee to Albert Heijn. Albert Heijn's management had answered that they would gladly meet with the committee, and the meeting was held on December 27, 1971.

Sietse Bosgra, when I interviewed him, described the meeting as follows:

We knew that members of the management had already expressed their objections to importing coffee from Angola on moral grounds. We explained our opposition to the use of Angola coffee and referred to the action scheduled to begin on February 4. The management said that they had already been reducing the share of Angola coffee, but that it would be difficult to stop using Angola coffee altogether. They were busy looking for new coffee suppliers in Cameroon, Togo, and Uganda. We showed them the pictures of atrocities committed by the Portuguese on the coffee plantations, and we received the promise that the issue would be placed before the Management Committee and that we would receive a written answer to our request for a boycott of Angola coffee.

Two weeks later, the Angola Committee received the following answer:

Dear Sirs,

Subsequent to our discussion of Monday, December 27, 1971, I can now communicate to you the following. In the past year we have already started to reduce the share of Angola coffee in our mixtures. As the situation is now, we firmly plan to continue this reduction. We expect that by mid-1972 no more Angola coffee will be used in our mixtures. Our decision was based on a number of commercial considerations, among others on the fact that comparable coffee offers have become available from young African states. As the political element has not played any role in our company's decisions, we kindly request you not to use in your actions the information that we are minimizing our use of Angola coffee.

Yours sincerely,

ALBERT HEIJN SUPERMARKET N.V.
P. Ligtenstein

Albert Heijn's decision received wide coverage in the press, on radio, and on television. Mr. Ligtenstein was quoted as saying that although the decision had been made on purely commercial grounds, the political tension with respect to Angola coffee did of course have its indirect effect on the Albert Heijn decision. "If a portion of the public does not wish to be confronted with coffee from Angola, then this is a commercial fact that we have to take into consideration."

When Dr. Bosgra called Mr. Groen on January 14 he was informed that Douwe Egberts had agreed to a meeting. It was scheduled for Monday January 17.

## From Angola to Douwe Egberts

Dr. Sietse Bosgra and his colleague Frans Ernst visited Douwe Egberts on January 17. On behalf of the company, Mr. Schoonhoven and Mr. Groen, as well as the purchasing manager and the marketing manager for coffee, were present. The company people found Dr. Bosgra and Mr. Ernst to be soft spoken and polite. The meeting lasted about one hour, during which the Angola Committee people did most of the talking. They indicated that they were asking all the coffee roasters in the Netherlands for a declaration similar to the one they had received from Albert Heijn. Companies unwilling to issue such a declaration would be subject to boycott actions.

The Douwe Egberts people said that they had already reduced their use of Angola coffee. Until 1970 Angola coffee had represented about 25% of their total coffee purchases, but in 1971 it had been reduced to 16%, and more recently to 5.5%. They said that for purely commercial reasons they had been looking for some time for alternatives to Angola as a supplier, but that it would take time, and no firm commitments could be made that the attempts to replace Angola coffee by other coffee would be successful. They also said that it was undesirable for single coffee processors to make such commitments, as this could disturb their competitive positions. They maintained that it would be much better if the employers' association, the Union of Coffee Roasters and Tea Packers, could agree on a common policy. The Angola Committee people repeated their demand for a written statement, which was urgent as it affected their preparations for the next action phase, which was to start on Friday February 4.

In the meantime salespersons who had daily contact with retailers were expressing their concern. "The breeze that is now rising will become a storm and this won't do us any good," said a marketing manager.

The Angola issue led to an emotional discussion in the management committee. Mr. Boost said that he did not feel obliged to justify his decisions to the first man he met. His obligations were to the shareholders and the board of directors. He felt no inclination to follow the Albert Heijn example. Albert Heijn's letter was really insincere. Taking a position as a single company was undesirable. The management committee decided to approach the employers' association and to insist that a common position be communicated to the Dutch press.

On Monday January 31, the Union of Coffee Roasters and Tea Packers issued the following press bulletin:

During the past weeks a strong appeal has been made, by the Angola Committee among others, for the Dutch coffee roasters to adjust their purchasing policies to the political and social conditions in the producing countries. The coffee processors in the Netherlands communicate that their position on this issue is as follows:

The coffee roasters in the Netherlands depend largely on basic materials from the developing countries. Unfortunately, in these countries forms of colonialism and oppression of parts of the population still occur. The Dutch coffee roasters, with due respect for the point of view of action groups, take the position that the exclusion of certain producing countries is an issue for the parliament and the Dutch government, but definitely not for business enterprises. More so because the choice of basic materials is determined among other things by trade agreements made by the government.

The individual coffee processors therefore cannot go beyond the promise that whenever possible the desires of the action groups will be respected, to the extent that this does not conflict with their company strategies.

On February 1, Douwe Egberts wrote a short letter to the Angola Committee enclosing the union press bulletin, and aligning themselves with the point of view expressed by the union:

"With due respect for the point of view of your action committee, we therefore cannot go beyond the promise that whenever possible the desires of the Angola Committee will be respected, to the extent that this does not conflict with our company strategy."

In a letter to all salespersons the sales director, Mr. C. van Lookeren Campagne, explained the company's position. In spite of this letter, the salespersons still reported uneasiness. Mr. Campagne reported:

We told them that the company could not take a political position. On the other hand, they know that they should follow the customer—the customer is always right. This was okay as long as the customer was only interested in the taste of coffee. Now, for the first time, the customer expressed an opinion about something very different. Our salesmen were not prepared for this.

In the meantime the press had reported that first one and then two other supermarket chains, competitors of Albert Heijn, had written to the Angola Committee that by the middle of 1972 they would process no more Angola coffee. On Wednesday February 2 several newspapers published articles about the working conditions at the coffee plantations in Angola, obviously based on the booklet *Coffee for the Netherlands, Blood of Angola.*

It also became known that on February 1 the Angola Committee had been granted a subsidy of 9,500 guilders ($3,000 at that time) from the National Committee for Development Strategy, a commission appointed by the Dutch government to further aims of the United Nations Development Strategy Decade. This commission had been given 4.5 million guilders for 1972 from government funds for making awards. The chairman of the commission was Prince Claus, husband of the then Crown Princess Beatrix.

On February 3 Douwe Egberts issued a statement to the press that was published as follows:

> The management of Douwe Egberts is unhappy about the 9,500 guilders subsidy that the National Committee for Development Strategy has granted to the coffee action of the Angola Committee. The company feels that in this way the government supports an action that is only directed against Douwe Egberts.

In an interview with the *Volkskrant*, a progressive Catholic morning newspaper, Mr. Groen was quoted as follows:

> We are quite willing to take the committee's wishes into account. For years, 25% to 30% of all coffee that Douwe Egberts processed came from Angola. In 1971 this percentage was halved, and now the share of Angolese coffee is only 5%. Our best selling coffee (Red Brand) contains no more Angolese coffee at all. We give the greatest priority to a further limitation of the share of Angolese coffee, but our company refuses to commit itself on this issue to the Angola Committee.

On Friday morning February 4 leaflets were distributed to the employees of Douwe Egberts as they arrived at work, both in Joure and in Utrecht. The leaflets showed a large photo of the body of an African with a severed head beside it, on a pile of coffee beans. The text of the leaflets was as follows:

COFFEE FOR the Netherlands—BLOOD OF ANGOLA

> On February 4 it is 11 years since the population of Angola rose up against the Portuguese colonial rule. Through a civil war of oppression the Portuguese are still able to maintain their position in Angola.
> On February 4 an action starts in the Netherlands to put an end to Dutch coffee imports from Angola. The Netherlands purchases about 30% of the Angolese coffee exports, which is more than all other West European countries together. We annually buy coffee from the Portuguese in Angola for a

total value of 100 million guilders. Of this amount at least 13 million is spent for the warfare against the Angolese population, or one guilder per inhabitant of the Netherlands per year.

The African workers on the coffee plantations are working under inhuman conditions. Wages are so low (25 guilders per month) that the Africans do not want to work for them. Therefore the Portuguese use force to get their labor. According to a report of the Catholic People's Party[2] dating from 1969, 85% of the unskilled Africans in the coffee area in the north of Angola work under a system of forced labor. Also the plantations use much child labor.

Through the coffee purchases in Angola we cooperate against our will in the oppression and exploitation of the Angolese people. Therefore we should convince the coffee companies that we do not want any more coffee from Angola. If the Netherlands redirect their coffee purchases to the independent African countries we can support these countries in building free societies. This is also the purpose of the major UNCTAD conference that will be held in Chile this spring.

As the coffee from the independent African countries is as good as Angola coffee and not more expensive the employees of the coffee industry and the consumers will not suffer from the action. Two Dutch coffee roasters, Albert Heijn and Co-op, have therefore already committed themselves to stop processing Angola coffee within six months.

Everybody can support this action by refusing to buy coffee from companies that have not made a commitment to refrain from processing Angola coffee.

If you want to know more or to participate actively in this action, please contact:

Angola Committee
Da Costastraat 88
Amsterdam, phone 020-183598
Postal account 600657
or
REFUSE ANGOLESE BLOOD COFFEE

The newspapers of Saturday February 5 as well as the following week gave wide coverage to the action. They mentioned that the main coffee producers who had not made a commitment to stop using Angola coffee were Douwe Egberts and two other "independent" (nonsupermarket) roasters, Van Nelle and Niemeyer. The minister of Foreign Affairs was interviewed on television: he condemned the action, explaining that it was undesirable "to let our economic decisions be based on political considerations." Some members of parliament spoke out strongly against the action. The minister of Development Aid refused to sign the 9,500-

guilder grant to the Angola Committee. However, the youth organizations of most political parties, including those in power, publicly supported the action. The women's organization of the Protestant party, to which the prime minister and the minister for Development Aid belonged, wrote to the latter requesting that he sign the 9,500-guilder subsidy grant.

During the following weeks an increasing number of young people stood outside shops and supermarkets, handing out leaflets and asking housewives what brand of coffee they had purchased. Posters showing a photo of a dead African were hung in the vicinity of shops. On February 12 the national Catholic newspaper *De Tijd* appeared with a 14-page supplement devoted mainly to Angola. Four pages of this supplement were reprinted and 100,000 copies of the reprint were put at the disposal of the Angola Committee. Mr. Groen was interviewed by the *Nieuwsblad van het Noorden*, a newspaper widely read in the Joure area, and had an opportunity to reaffirm the company's point of view:

> Our use of Angola coffee has decreased drastically. . . . We use it at this moment, . . . only in the very cheapest mixtures ("Pink Brand"). In our Red Brand and in the better mixtures we presently use no Angola at all. . . . It is our opinion that we cannot give in to this action committee, because other action committees are already waiting at the back door. For example, we already receive letters about the use of tea from Ceylon. If we give in to the Angola Committee—and to us this is fairly basic—what would we say to subsequent action committees? Our raw materials all come from developing countries. A number of developing countries have problems and unstable situations. There may suddenly be undesirable situations leading to the creation of new action committees. And in our own country we can expect committees for the protection of the environment, which react against, for example, plastics. One cannot determine one's own policies any more, one is manipulated. . . . The desires of the consumer are our guide. If the consumer does not want any more Angola coffee, we will not use it any more.

As a result of its concern about consumer attitudes Douwe Egberts had asked its market research agency in early February to study consumer attitudes in the Angola coffee case. Between February 7 and 11, a representative sample of 515 Dutch housewives was interviewed. A first report to the company was issued on February 17. Sixty percent of the housewives said they used mostly Douwe Egberts (DE) coffee. Of these, over 75% used "Red Brand." Only 1 out of 20 used "Pink Brand." Of the total sample 48% associated the word "Angola" with "coffee." Only 20% were unable to make any meaningful association with "Angola." Two hundred and fifty-four housewives (49%) had heard about the Angola Committee and of these, 55% supported the committee's position, and 7% disagreed with it.

The interviewers then explained Douwe Egberts's point of view:

"According to the newspapers, DE continues for the time being to use Angola coffee in its mixtures, because in this way they are best adapted to the Dutch taste. Do you think they are right in doing so, or do you think that DE should stop using this Angola coffee, although the taste will then change somewhat?" Confronted with this question 37% of all housewives agreed and 37% disagreed with DE. DE customers agreed more frequently (46%) than non-DE customers (24%). Finally, the respondents were asked whether they expected that DE users would continue to buy DE coffee if the company continued to use Angola coffee. The response indicated that 27% would either continue to buy DE coffee or that their buying decisions would hardly be affected, but 32% thought that it would affect their buying decisions. On this question there was little difference between DE customers and noncustomers.

The market study itself contributed to the publicity on the Angola coffee case. On February 14 and 15 two national newspapers reported on the study and the questions asked.

In the third week of February a new slogan appeared on stickers (see Figure 12.1) on shop windows. The action began to focus more and more on this one company.

Not all public reactions to the campaign were positive. Douwe Egberts began to receive letters from customers complimenting it for its firm attitude. A small right-wing political group (not represented in parliament) wrote an angry letter to the management of Albert Heijn for giving in to the Angola Committee: "We consider this to be treason of a NATO ally and an European brother people. . . . The members of our growing party will completely boycott your firm. . . . Some wealthy members will buy shares of your company and start a virulent action at your next shareholders' meeting . . . ."

The Portuguese newspaper *Diario de Noticias* appeared with a headline article strongly condemning the action. Quotes from this reached the Dutch press. The largest Dutch newspaper, *De Telegraaf,* politically independent but considered right wing, attacked the Angola action with a big headline on February 19: "International agreements would undermine the effect of a boycott by the Netherlands alone. . . . The situation on the plantations has nothing to do with the trade."

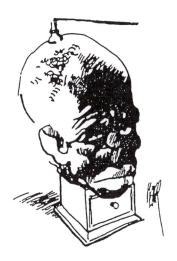

**KOFFIE voor DOUWE EGBERTS
bloed van ANGOLA**

**koop het niet!**

Angola Comité, Da Costastraat 88, Amsterdam, tel 18 35 98

**Figure 12.1.** COFFEE and for DOUWE EGBERTS, blood of ANGOLA: don't buy it!

## The Reaction Among
## Employees and Labor Unions

The Angola Committee action had been briefly discussed in a meeting of the Utrecht Local Works Council[3] on January 28. At that time management had said that the strategy was to develop a common line of action among all coffee companies through the employers' association. The next meeting of the council was on February 15. Mr. Groen was invited to explain the situation. What he said is summarized in the minutes as follows:

The point of view of the Management Committee, which the Works Council has supported, has not changed. As far as publicity goes we will not cooperate in radio or T.V. interviews. We will however explain our point of view to the press. From our consumers we have so far received about 80 reactions, 60 for the Angola action and 20 against. The consumer will continue to be our main guide: therefore we have ordered the market study. The publicity about the market study has come from the interviewees, not from us. A reliable judgment based on the results of the study can be given in about 3 weeks. The written reactions we received will all be answered. We have a guideline for answering them, which basically runs (a) perfect neutrality, (b) commercial considerations, (c) no political stand, (d) consumer behavior decisive factor.

In the subsequent discussion several members questioned the company's position as expressed by Mr. Groen: have we really been politically neutral so far? What about our statement on the 9,500-guilder grant to the Angola Committee? Is it realistic to say that the consumer decides? Can we afford to remain neutral? Shouldn't we cut down on Angola purchases until the results of the market study are available? The conclusion of the discussion was that the Works Council would go along with the official company point of view as expressed.

A similar development took place in the Joure Local Works Council, which also decided to go along with the company's point of view. In the meantime, works council members were increasingly approached with questions by employees whom they were supposed to represent. These people were themselves exposed to questions by friends and relations who knew they worked for Douwe Egberts, and they felt unable to respond. A young employee in the personnel department said: "My wife wondered whether I could continue to take the responsibility of working for such a company—one which did not seem to respond to what happened around it, which just went ahead rigidly. I began to ask myself this question, and so did our friends."

On February 16, the day after the Utrecht Works Council meeting, the Dutch Labor party[4] issued a statement supporting the Angola Committee. On February 22 the newspapers published a statement by the National Catholic Labor Union (NKV) supporting the Angola action and announcing that the union headquarters would buy no more coffee from companies that continued to use Angola coffee. On February 23 the morning papers printed a joint statement by the NKV plus the two other major national labor unions, reinforcing the NKV decision.

As soon as the union statements were published, works council members both in Joure and in Utrecht asked for an urgent extra meeting. Both meetings were held on the afternoon of Wednesday February 23. The discussion in Joure was summarized as follows:

> The Local Works Council has until recently supported the Management Committee. Now the members' point of view has changed and they recognize new aspects to the issue. Can we ignore all the publicity? We are afraid that this action will affect our sales. Some members question whether we can isolate ourselves from developments taking place in society. We think that we should ask the Management Committee to reconsider their decision.

Similar concerns were expressed in Utrecht. Some members of the Local Works Council there openly expressed concern about employees' jobs if sales were to drop drastically because of the action. After exchanges of views by telephone between the two meetings, the following letter was sent to the Management Committee:

The Works Councils of Joure and Utrecht in their meetings of February 23, 1972, have expressed their deep concern about the recent developments in the action against the use of Angola coffee. The following immediate reasons for this concern were mentioned:

- The statement of support of the three national labor unions for the Angola action, as it was published this morning
- The daily publicity around the action
- The intimidation of consumers through an increasing amount of picketing in front of shops and an increasing number of stickers "advising" them to stop using DE coffee
- Uneasiness among employees, partly for reasons of conscience, partly out of concern for their jobs at DE
- The feeling that increasingly a direct connection is made between the situation in Angola and the point of view of Douwe Egberts

Under these circumstances and especially because through the involvement of labor unions and political parties an escalation is expected, the Works Councils advise the Management Committee urgently to clarify their point of view as soon as possible. A longer silence will be interpreted as an expression of guilt or arrogance.

In the present situation the Works Councils feel that the only decision can be to follow the fairly general trend to stop the purchase of Angola coffee as soon as possible. The Works Councils advise issuing a statement to this effect at the shortest notice, if possible this week. Further delay could mean that the same statement must be issued but will be interpreted as imposed upon the company by others, which would only further damage the image of DE.

The statement to be made should be addressed to consumers and employees and it should avoid mentioning commercial considerations. It should refer to the social responsibility of our company. As the Works Councils can support the ideas of the Angola Committee but not all the means that it has used, they think it undesirable to answer directly to the Angola Committee.

As Mr. Boost and Mr. Schoonhoven were away on a trip the letter was received by the director of Finance, Mr. Landsmeer, who met with the Central Works Council on the evening of Friday February 25. It was decided that a joint meeting of both local works councils with the Management Committee would be held as soon as possible.

## The Climax

On February 26 the newspapers announced that three more smaller coffee roasters had decided to stop using Angola coffee. Douwe Egberts, Van Nelle, and Niemeyer still stood firm. Following the statements of the Labor party and the labor unions, the city government of the Netherlands' largest city, Rotterdam, decided to boycott coffee from these companies for all public services. Other cities and public bodies followed.

An urgent meeting of Douwe Egberts's top management team of about 10 people was convened at the home of Mr. Boost, chairman of the Management Committee, immediately after his return on Saturday evening February 26. The facts were reviewed. Technically it would be possible to stop buying from Angola. Temporarily this might lead to higher costs, but in the long run the higher quantity bought somewhere else would lead to better prices there, which would balance the costs. But what kind of precedent would it be if the company gave in to an action group of a handful of outsiders without any official status, condemned by the government? Would this not encourage other groups to come forward tomorrow, attacking, for example, Brazil or Colombia? If giving in would help the company to retain some customers, how many others would be lost? What would be the effect on the company's image both with its employees and with its customers? It was clear that some decision had to be taken. The smaller competitors Van Nelle and Niemeyer had indicated that they would follow the Douwe Egberts decision.

The management team was divided. Some of its members had questioned the company's line of action earlier. Others joined them now in the opinion that giving in would be unavoidable. Some were undecided. Mr. Boost was disappointed at not finding unanimous support—it would have to be his decision.

On Monday February 28 both local works councils met in Joure with the Management Committee. Repeating the arguments in the letter the works council members strongly advised the Management Committee to change its decision and to stop using Angola coffee. Although the councils seemed to be unanimous, some members afterward privately contacted Mr. Boost to state that they did not fully agree with the contents of the letter, but that they had been unable to express their views during the meeting.

On Tuesday February 29 Douwe Egberts invited representatives of the industry branches of the three national labor unions to meet with Mr. Boost and the personnel director, Mr. Dohmen. The union people said that they did not want to discuss the question as to who was right and whether the action was justified or not. They simply had no other choice but to follow their members who supported the action. They further said that they would appreciate receiving a quick answer as on Friday March 3 there would be a meeting of union leaders where further steps would have to be decided.

Mr. Boost decided to contact the government. In a telephone conversation on Friday morning March 3, Prime Minister Biesheuvel advised him not to give in. However, no specific support from the government could be expected. The cabinet was too much involved in other problems to discuss the issue.

On the afternoon of Friday March 3, 1972, the following notice appeared on the bulletin boards of Douwe Egberts:

To all employees

After extensive consultation with the Works Councils, the Management Committee has today issued the following statement, both as an advertisement and as a press bulletin:

THE UNDERSIGNED COFFEE ROASTERS DECLARE THAT AS OF TODAY NO NEW PURCHASES OF ANGOLA COFFEE WILL BE MADE.

In the past weeks it has become clear that consumers have objections to the processing of Angola coffee. Under these circumstances we find reason to change our purchasing policy.

The Angola coffee in stock and on order will be used up shortly.

DOUWE EGBERTS
VAN NELLE
NIEMEYER

## After the Decision

After the decision to stop using Angola coffee had been taken, the situation at Douwe Egberts soon returned to normal. The stickers on shop windows disappeared. The interest of the press in the Angola coffee case was kept alive for some time by various events unrelated to Douwe Egberts. A right-wing extremist politician filed a complaint with the Ministry of Justice against the Angola Committee, accusing it of black-mail against the coffee roasters. However, a police investigation did not find any illegal practices.

The letters from consumers urging Douwe Egberts to ban Angola coffee stopped. The total count between February 4 and March 4 was about 240 letters contra the use of Angola coffee and 60 letters pro. After the company decided to stop using Angola coffee, letters were received from consumers who protested at this giving in to the Angola Commit-tee. This stream of letters was partly instigated as a counterattack against the Angola Committee by the widely read newspaper *De Telegraaf* in April. After that, the letters gradually stopped. During the 6 months following March 3 a total of about 240 such protest letters were received.

By October 1972 no significant changes in sales volume of DE coffee as a result of the action could be perceived. An initial decrease did not continue. Fluctuations were within the normal range. The time was too short to measure any long-term effect on Douwe Egberts's market position.

## Analysis:
## The Angola Coffee Boycott as a Values Crisis

I wrote the above case study in late 1972 as a teaching case.[5] The material for it was collected: (a) through the collaboration of the Man-agement Committee of Douwe Egberts, which allowed me to interview whomever I wished within the company, and which opened all relevant internal files to me; (b) through the collaboration of Dr. Sietse Bosgra of the Angola Committee, who gave an extensive interview; and (c) through an exhaustive study of documents, including the contents of all major Dutch newspapers before, during, and after the events.

The case describes a dramatic event that deeply affected one of the oldest and most respectable business corporations in the Netherlands and to some extent, for a short time, shook up a major part of the Dutch nation—at that time over 13 million people. An event like this can be interpreted in many ways, depending on the vantage point, the values, and interests of the observer. I have tried to be objective in my description of the case, but there is no such thing as objective history. I personally interpret the event mainly as evidence of a conflict of values between the company and its environment, or more precisely between the top decision maker or makers within this company and an important share of the Dutch public. This conflict of values threatened the legitimacy of the organization.

Interestingly, the events happened in a company that had not been unresponsive to environmental change. The modernization of top management in 1967 and the adoption of the social charter in 1969 reflect a serious intention to follow the trends of the time. However, not only did the values of the public change more quickly than management recognized but they also changed in an unexpected way. The social charter expressed the social responsibility of the company toward customers, employees, and shareholders. This reflects the public ethos in the Netherlands of the 1950s. Even in 1969, Douwe Egberts was one of the pioneers in the Netherlands in adopting a social charter. But by the time Douwe Egberts's social charter was completed, the public ethos had already changed. The public had become more aware of Third World problems, but neither the company management nor the works council spokespersons nor the labor union leaders had thought of covering the social responsibility of the corporation toward its Third World suppliers in the charter.

One of the inherent problems of organizations (even more of large ones than small ones) is that by the time people penetrate to top decision-making roles they are usually no longer young and their values are set. Elsewhere (Hofstede, 1980, chap. 8) I have published research data suggesting that the age up to which people continue to adapt their values to the Zeitgeist depends on their educational level: higher educated people remain mentally flexible to an older age, but somewhere between the age of 40 (for people with only elementary school) and 55 (for those with the highest academic education) most people have lost this responsiveness to environmental value shifts—obviously, with a wide tolerance margin for individual differences. This applies to business managers, to workers' representatives, to union leaders, and to politicians as well as to ordinary citizens. A younger top manager might not have been more enthusiastic about the restriction on his or her freedom of action with regard to suppliers that the events imposed on the firm, but might have recognized more quickly that he or she had to, and could, live with it, and might also have been more able to reduce the cognitive dissonance about giving in, justifying it as an act of social responsibility vis-à-vis the Third World.

## The Specificity of the Dutch Environment

I stress the influence of environmental change in this case because the case is environment specific. The event happened in the Netherlands, and we should not assume without further proof that it could have happened elsewhere. Environmental changes take place in other countries and value conflicts do occur elsewhere, but they are not necessarily the same conflicts. Far too often organization theories extrapolate freely across national borders, without taking national cultural specificities into account. One of the characteristic national features of the Dutch (Hofstede, 1975-1976) is a sympathy for the underdog. This is a "feminine" characteristic that we also find, for example, in the Scandinavian countries. In other countries, like the United States, Great Britain, and Germany, we find more "masculine" value patterns in which the primary sympathy of the public is with the successful achiever—the opposite of the underdog (Hofstede, 1980, chap. 6). In the 1960s, all wealthy countries were exposed to a considerable increase in information about Third World problems. I suggest that sympathy for underdogs among the Dutch has existed for centuries, but inclusion of the peoples of the Third World in their set of relevant underdogs as a national phenomenon probably happened in the 1960s.[6]

As things stand, few countries in the world exceed the Netherlands in their level of public interest in Third World problems. The action of the Angola Committee and its effectiveness should be seen against this background. It is no accident that the action received strong support from women's associations, even against the male leadership of their own parties. Coffee, of course, is mainly bought by women; it is a "feminine" product. By addressing itself to a value issue in the center of public interest, the Angola Committee got other organizations, such as newspapers, church groups, political party groups, and labor unions, to move on "its" issue. Although the value issues that have this power are culture specific (they vary from one country to the next, as well as over time), the fact that raising the right issue at the right time provides an organization with leverage over other organizations is, of course, universal. It has been demonstrated time and again in history, such as in the Khomeini revolution in Iran in 1978.

## The Angola Coffee Crisis as a Case of "Garbage Can" Decision Making

The Angola Coffee case provides enlightening insight into the process of corporate decision making under environmental change. A rational decision-making model does not get us anywhere in this case. It cannot, because the essence of the crisis is a conflict of values and values are nonrational—they precede and constrain the use of rationality. This case is an example of "muddling through" (Lindblom, 1959) and even more of the "garbage can" process of organizational choice (Cohen, March, & Olsen, 1972; March & Olsen, 1976). In the garbage can process, problems, solutions, participants, and choice opportunities move in, out, and around more or less autonomously, and choices are the result of the meeting of the other elements around a certain problem subjected to time pressure. This case shows in particular how new participants moved in on Douwe Egberts's decision (the Angola Committee, consumers, the works councils, other employees, the labor unions), and how the employers' association and the government moved out, until the decision took itself.

The case also illustrates the extent to which values distort information, so that on value-laden issues the role of information (a central element in the rational decision-making model) is ambiguous. The personnel director's early warning speech in September 1971 was filtered out as irrelevant by DE's top management team; so were the Angola Committee's first and second letters. The company commissioned an expensive market research survey, but its conclusions, although unusually clear, played no role in the final decision. The market research survey itself used a leading, and even misleading, question ("According to the newspapers . . . although the taste will then change somewhat"); the data in the case showed that 95% of the blend of coffee (all except "Pink Brand") no longer used Angola coffee, so that the taste would *not* change. Obviously, leading questions in market research are a waste of money (do we want to tell them or to learn from them?). It adds to the confusion that the corporate decision makers themselves still seemed to believe in the rational decision-making model: politics was ruled out as a decision premise, although at the same time, in the issue of the 9,500-guilder subsidy the company management did take an explicitly political stand.

The misperception of what actually went on in the company during the crisis was interestingly shared by its main adversary, the Angola Committee. Both company management and the committee saw their opponent as dangerous, clever, monolithic, and Machiavellian. The Angola Committee was unaware of the large differences of opinion and the confusion within Douwe Egberts's management team. On the other hand, the Angola Committee itself very much "muddled through" the action and attributed its own success mainly to luck. One luck factor was the position of Albert Heijn in the coffee market; coffee was a minor part of that company's business, so it did not want to risk a consumer boycott, which made it give in quickly; but Albert Heijn was a big enough coffee roaster *and* customer of DE to give its decision considerable leverage on DE. In addition the DE boycott provided Albert Heijn with a nice competitive advantage, but this could hardly have been foreseen by Albert Heijn.

## Management Under Environmental Change

What can we learn from this case about management—depending on which way the reader's sympathies go, the management of a business corporation under environmental change or the management of a civic action group? For corporations, the moral is that in a turbulent environment, closed-system management is dangerous. By closed-system management I mean management in which deviant values and unpopular messages are filtered out. But how can we resist the general human proclivity to trust only people with the same values as ourselves and to hear only the messages we want to hear? In the first place, the age composition of the management team is important: older people are less sensitive to value shifts in their environment than younger ones (again, ceteris paribus, and personality factors play a strong role too). In the second place, corporations may need a modern equivalent to the medieval kings' court jester, a person or team with direct access to the highest decision makers, whose institutionalized role it is to challenge values. Such a "court jester" would at the same time be involved in environmental scanning, in meeting people from different walks of life, in moving outside the closed inner circle of the corporate decision makers. The court jester could be the "external relations manager" some corporations have institutionalized, *if* this position is really taken seriously and not used as a convenient shelf for a senior manager for whom no other job is available. In the Douwe Egberts case a real court jester would have met Sietse Bosgra long before the latter had even thought about a boycott.

Finally, the management of a civic action group is not an easy affair for which there are easy rules. It is probably even more difficult than the management of a business corporation, and the rewards are of a quite different nature. Action groups are seldom successful—even in the Netherlands. The elements that brought about the Angola Committee's success were: (a) perseverance: Bosgra headed the Angola Committee for more than 10 years before the action began; (b) contacts: the Angola Committee had worked for years as an information center and the reliability of its news had provided it with good links with most of the Dutch press, and it could also rely on local committees, church and school groups, and political parties; (c) a devoted team and the ability to keep this team together (many action groups die ignominiously in internal struggle); (d) the right issue at the right moment: a finger on the pulse of public opinion; and finally, as we have seen, (e) lots of luck. The management of a civic action group is probably not too different from the management of a new, small, innovative business enterprise. The majority of these fail, but we know that the few that succeed play an essential role in the spread of technological innovations, which larger enterprises cannot do because of their own inertia. In a similar way, civic action groups can be seen as essential to the spread in society of social and political innovations that the institutional and political establishment could never generate itself.

## Discussion Questions

1. What would you have done if you were Mr. Boost?

2. Can a corporation remain politically neutral?

3. Test the public statements made on behalf of Douwe Egberts in the course of the case for consistency. There are a number of internal contradictions. What was the reason for these contradictions?

4. Could Douwe Egberts have used the values shift in Dutch society as an asset rather than as a liability? In what way should it change to respond positively to new challenges of this kind?

## Notes

1. An association of coffee-producing and consuming countries founded in 1962, whose aim was to control prices and export quotas.
2. At the time, the second-largest political party in the Netherlands.

3. In the Netherlands, companies employing over 50 persons are required by law to have an elected works council, which has legal rights of information on a wide range of company-related issues, and of joint decision making on a smaller range. Companies spread over more than one location have local works councils as well as a central works council composed of delegates from the local councils. Very large companies may have three levels of councils.

4. At that time the largest party in the country, but not represented in the government.

5. The teaching version of the case is slightly longer and contains as appendices the full text of Douwe Egberts's social charter, a document on the world coffee trade, and one on the Dutch coffee market.

6. Awareness of Third World problems in the Netherlands had its pioneers long ago. The masterpiece of Dutch 19th-century prose, the novel *Max Havelaar* (1860/1983) written by Douwes Dekker (Multatuli) in about 1850, is in fact a political document exposing exploitation of the Javanese population by the coffee trade.

# PART III

# Studies in Training Settings

Unlike the data-based chapters in Parts I and II, which used the vast data bank collected by the IBM Personnel Research department, the five chapters of Part III derive from material collected from participants during training programs with the explicit purpose of contributing to the training process. The numbers of respondents, therefore, are much smaller than in the previous chapters. Most teachers of organizational behavior in postexperience management courses try to use classroom research at times, and the results need not be significant or useful outside the classroom. In the five cases reported in the following chapters, the research yielded insights of broader importance.

Chapters 13 and 14 form a pair. Chapter 13 describes an exercise developed by László I. Rajkay asking course participants to rate their "needs for improvement" in a number of areas and subsequently to repeat the same exercise for the needs for improvement of their boss, as they perceive them. The exercise tends to show a systematic difference in the ways people look at their boss and at themselves: the boss needs to improve his or her attitude; they need to increase their knowledge. It demonstrates an attribution bias resembling the success versus failure bias in psychological attribution theory (success is due to one's own efforts whereas failure is due to circumstances). Chapter 14 reports on one occasion when this needs for improvement exercise was completed in conjunction with a high-involvement personal sensitivity training program, a so-called T-group. By accident half of the trainees took the exercise before the program, the other half after. Contrary to expectations, the T-group made participants more critical of their bosses, but not of themselves.

Chapters 15 and 16 describe research aimed at the trainers rather than the trainees in management courses. Chapter 15 uses longitudinal data on the careers of participants in an in-company program over an 8-year period, and it verifies the extent to which trainers had been able to predict career success correctly. Trainer predictions appear to have been subject to a number of biases, and in one case when the training peers also made a career prediction, they did much better than their trainers. Chapter 16 is based on data from executive course participants and from faculty members at IMEDE, who all supplied scores on two values tests. It shows that faculty values differ significantly from participant values, but also that faculty tend to give the most favorable performance ratings to participants whose values most resemble their own.

Chapter 17, finally, uses information collected in the context of in-company management courses to analyze the organizational role of one particular function: the personnel function. Both its image among other parts of the company and personnel managers' own assessment of their tasks, objectives, successes, and failures are explored. This exploration reveals considerable frustration among personnel managers, related to the ambiguity of the role that the organization allows their department to play. They often have to take the "low road," although they derive their success experiences on the "high road."

Thus the chapters in Part III illustrate that research among organizational participants in training sessions can reveal surprising and sometimes disconcerting truths about the trainees, their relationships with their superiors, the structure and role distribution of their organization, the effect of the training programs themselves, and the role of the trainers or professors. Those of us who teach others, I believe, should also be prepared to face uncommon sense about our own effects on our trainees.

# 13

## Looking at the Boss
## and Looking at Ourselves

This chapter describes a simple exercise, to be used as part of a management course, in which participants rate the improvement needs of themselves and their bosses. The results are then calculated and presented back to the class. Results typically show perceived self-improvement needs to exceed boss improvement needs in the area of knowledge, but the reverse to be true in the area of attitude. Moreover a number of other differences tend to show up on individual items in the questionnaire that point to systematic biases in perception. The exercise is used for a short essay on the influence of hierarchy on perception and the nature of learning in management development.

### The Exercise "Needs for Improvement"

One of the objectives of management training in the area of organizational behavior is usually to convey systematic knowledge of and insight into behavioral phenomena. The problem is that, unlike the case for other subjects, the trainee him- or herself in this case is part of the problem (s)he studies. There is a danger that what is learned about human behavior in organizations is only applied in a "they" fashion, that is, only

---

This chapter was coauthored with László I. Rajkay and originally published in *Management International Review, 16*(2), 1976, pp. 61-71. Copyright © 1976 by *Management International Review*. Reprinted with permission.

to others. The objective, of course, is for trainees to use their new insights reflexively and recognize "we" or "I" in what they learned.

Various methods of development try to overcome this danger by approaching people at the emotional level and supplying them with direct feedback about their own behavior in a simulated situation. Most of these have originated in the "sensitivity training" school of the 1950s (see Chapter 14 and e.g., Harrison, 1962). The cognitive content (conceptualization) of learning by these methods is often weak, and for that reason they contribute little to people's ability to generalize to other situations and apply what they have learned. Also the emotion-level exercises ask for very specific skills in the trainer and a specific rapport between trainer and trainees that are not always present; thus their risk of failure is high. Finally they assume a particular cultural context, in which direct feedback is evaluated positively. In cultures in which the maintenance of outward harmony is at a premium, they are taboo.

A category of training tools that although still operating on the cognitive level do directly involve the "we" and "I" into what is learned are those carrying out simple behavioral research in the classroom itself. We want to demonstrate such a tool, the exercise "Needs for Improvement."

The exercise "Needs for Improvement" is described in detail in the Appendix to this chapter. Developed over a period of 10 years by László I. Rajkay of IBM Germany, it asks trainees to fill out first one, then another questionnaire, on each of which 50 items potentially needing improvement are listed from which they have to choose those that most apply in their case. One questionnaire is to be filled out for the trainees' own improvement needs, and another for those of their boss, as they see them. The "improvement needs" were originally collected through open-ended group discussions in a number of management development classes. These discussions, first in small groups, then in plenary class sessions, yielded a list of about 350 items, which were subsequently classified and condensed. The needs identified, both in the people themselves and in their bosses, could be classified into five main categories: (a) knowledge, (b) experience, (c) skills, (d) attitude, and (e) personality.

The other questionnaire, composed after several cycles of trial and error, contains 10 items for each of these five main categories and is the same for "selves" as for "bosses." In each questionnaire respondents are asked to divide 100 points over the $5 \times 10 = 50$ items, reflecting the importance of these items as they see it.

## Typical Results

Results are available for 263 participants in 15 in-company management courses. Seven of these courses were held with mixed international groups, 2 with German, 2 with Swiss, 2 with Mexican, and 2 with mixed South American groups. The results for each course are roughly similar and reflect the trend of the mean scores over all 263 participants, shown in Table 13.1.

Table 13.1 shows large gaps between self and boss needs for Knowledge (self > boss) and Attitude (boss > self). The average of all scores is obviously 20 points per category (100/5 = 20). Individual respondents' scores within categories were distributed according to slightly skewed, but close to normal distributions with standard deviations averaging 10.6 points.

For the same group of 263 participants results have been calculated for individual items. The average number of points per item is 2 (100 points for 50 items). Table 13.2 shows those items receiving more than average points. This list shows many interesting differences between perceived self and boss improvement needs. We see that even for the categories of Experience, Skills, and Personality, where the totals for self and boss do not differ significantly, the individual items that are selected do differ.

The most important items selected for self (≥ 3.5 points) are:

- Knowledge of languages (4.0)
- Experience in planning and budgeting (3.6)

For boss, we find:

- Sensitivity to others' feelings and to own impact on others (4.6)
- Experience in work distribution and organization (3.7)
- Skills in decision making (3.6)
- Skills in motivating subordinates (3.6)
- Courage to make decisions (3.6)
- Skills in creating enthusiasm (3.5)

An amusing difference in the category Skills is that in "communicating" the self needs are in speaking, whereas the boss needs are in listening. Other items, selected with above-average points for boss, but not for self, are:

**TABLE 13.1** Average Points Allocated to Improvement Needs by Category
(based on data from 263 course participants)

| Category | For Participant | For Participant's Boss |
|---|---|---|
| Knowledge | 23.6*** | 16.5 |
| Experience | 18.9 | 18.5 |
| Skills | 22.7 | 24.4 |
| Attitude | 16.0 | 22.5*** |
| Personality | 18.1 | 18.1 |

NOTE: Categories marked *** show significant differences between "self" and "boss" scores ($t$ test, $t = 6.0$ for Knowledge, 5.0 for Attitude, well beyond the .001 level).

- Tactfulness, politeness (3.1)
- Experience in working with subordinates (3.0)
- Objectivity, open-mindedness (2.5)
- Human touch, sense of humor (2.1)

Of course some items in the above list reflect the particular situation in the company in which the data were collected, as well as problems common to the particular groups of managers who participated and will not necessarily be found with other groups. Experience shows, however, that with other groups too the stress for the self will be more on items oriented toward job content, whereas the stress for the boss will be more on items related to interpersonal relations and work organization.

In nearly all cases where we used the exercise the gap in perceived needs for Knowledge and Attitude between self and boss showed up clearly. Of course the fact of using an exercise based on collecting here-and-now data implies a certain risk that results may differ from what was expected. In this case the trainer should refer to the norms (previous results) as published in Tables 13.1 and 13.2 and discuss with the class why the present group showed another outcome. However, in our experience this has rarely happened.

The difference in the average scores for Knowledge and Attitude improvement needs for self versus boss does not mean that each individual participant will score them that way. The actual personalities and situations of the participants and their bosses play an important role in the individual answers. In one particular example, for a group of 60 managers:

For Knowledge:       32 (53%) scored self > boss
                     12 (20%) scored self = boss
                     16 (27%) scored self < boss

**TABLE 13.2** Average Points Allocated to Improvement Needs for Individual Items Within Categories

| *Knowledge* | | |
|---|---|---|
| *Self* | | *Boss* |
| 4.0 Language(s) | | |
| 3.1 Company's Objectives and Long-Term Strategy | | |
| 3.0 Psychology, Sociology | 3.1 | Psychology, Sociology |
| 2.9 Company's Finance, Accounting, and Control Systems | | |
| 2.7 Company's Policies, Procedures, and Organization | | |
| 2.6 Company's Products | 2.2 | Company's Products |
| 2.5 The World of Business, Economics, Labor, etc. | | |

| *Experience* | | |
|---|---|---|
| *Self* | | *Boss* |
| 3.6 Planning and Budgeting | | |
| 2.4 Work Distribution and Organization | 3.7 | Work Distribution and Organization |
| 2.0 Present Job | | |
| 2.0 Recognizing Business Trends in Time | | |
| 2.0 Presenting Results | | |
| | 3.0 | Working with Subordinates |

| *Skills* | | |
|---|---|---|
| *Self* | | *Boss* |
| 3.4 Decision Making | 3.6 | Decision Making |
| 3.0 Motivating Subordinates | 3.6 | Motivating Subordinates |
| 2.9 Communicating: Speaking | | |
| 2.8 Training and Developing People | 3.1 | Training and Developing People |
| 2.3 Convincing Superiors | 2.1 | Convincing Superiors |
| 2.3 Stimulating and Leading | 3.0 | Stimulating and Leading Teamwork |
| 2.2 Creating Enthusiasm | 3.5 | Creating Enthusiasm |
| | 2.0 | Communicating: Listening |

| *Attitude* | | |
|---|---|---|
| *Self* | | *Boss* |
| 2.9 Firmness to Stand Pressures | 2.8 | Firmness to Stand Pressures |
| 2.2 Trust in Subordinates' Capacities | 2.9 | Trust in Subordinates' Capacities |
| 2.0 Courage to Make Decisions | 2.9 | Courage to Make Decisions |
| 2.0 Willingness to Delegate | 2.5 | Willingness to Delegate |
| | 3.1 | Tactfulness, Politeness |
| | 2.5 | Objectivity, Open-Mindedness |

*(Continued)*

**TABLE 13.2** (Continued)

| Personality | | |
|---|---|---|
| *Self* | *Boss* | |
| 2.9  Creativity, Combinative Ability | | |
| 2.5  Emotional Balance | 2.0  Emotional Balance | |
| 2.3  Sensitivity to Others' Feelings | 4.6  Sensitivity to Others' Feelings | |
| 2.3  Ease in Personal Relations | 2.0  Ease in Personal Relations | |
| | 2.1  Human Touch, Sense of Humor | |

For Attitude:           31 (52%) scored self < boss
                        17 (28%) scored self = boss
                        12 (20%) scored self > boss

So in this group, one fifth to one fourth of the group answered opposite to the dominant trend and another one fifth to one fourth gave equal scores to boss and self.[1]

## Conclusions From the Exercise:
## The Impact of Hierarchy on Perception

When confronted with these results in small discussion groups or even in a plenary classroom session, most of our management trainees discovered at least some of the key messages by themselves. Our role as trainers was limited to promoting the discussion by asking good questions and drawing attention to aspects not yet covered by the class. At the end we summed up the results. What follows must be considered as such a summing up, reinforced with some additional arguments.

The most obvious conclusions from the exercise are in the area of the impact of hierarchy on perception. The data collected in the exercise show that a majority of the managers in the classes viewed their own improvement needs as different from those of another group of managers, their bosses. It is very unlikely that all these bosses had really such different improvement needs. If we could give the questionnaire to the bosses to fill out, they would very likely perceive their own needs approximately in the same way the subordinates scored for the self-questionnaire, but would perceive the improvement needs of the next higher level, their own bosses, very much as the subordinates scored the boss questionnaire. In one particular case where we were able to administer the self and boss questionnaires to a group of managers and the self-questionnaire to their bosses, we could verify this (cf. a similar phenomenon in Sadler & Hofstede, 1976).

In another case the questionnaires were answered by a group of managers for themselves and for their subordinates (rather than their bosses). We found some perception differences, but they were less pronounced; the managers perceived their subordinates' improvement needs as less different from their own than those of their superiors.

We are obviously not dealing with a real difference in improvement needs between subsequent levels in the management hierarchy, but with a law of perception or attribution that can be formulated as follows: "Managers tend to see themselves as having deficiencies in the field of knowledge, but less in the field of attitude. When looking at their superiors, however, they tend to see them not so much lacking knowledge, but more as having deficiencies in their attitude." Why this difference in perception? We offer two complementary explanations:

1. Our results derive from a general law of perception between people: We tend to see all others this way, not only our bosses. Our attitudes always look very different from the inside than from the outside, and few people have the interpersonal sensitivity to see themselves as others see them. In addition it is easier to increase one's knowledge than to change one's attitudes—and we therefore look for the solution of our problems in increase of knowledge rather than change of attitudes.

2. This general law of perception is reinforced when we deal with people in a hierarchy. The hierarchy means a formal power difference: The superior has more formal power than the subordinate. This power difference impacts communications, both the kind of messages that the subordinate will select to send upward, and those that the superior will select to send downward. Interpersonal sensitivity (seeing ourselves as others see us) can be increased by receiving feedback from others on our behavior. But in the superior-subordinate relationship such feedback rarely flows upward (and if it does, it is even more rarely accepted). It is much more likely to flow downward.

## The Nature of
## Learning in Management Courses

We have seen that managers tend to estimate their own needs for more knowledge higher and their needs for attitude change lower than those of their superiors. We have extrapolated that in the eyes of managers their own needs for knowledge will be rated higher and their needs for attitude change lower than in the eyes of their subordinates. The question is, who is right? Who has the best appreciation of managers' real improvement needs, they themselves or their subordinates?

We should distinguish improvement needs by categories. As far as *knowledge* is concerned, the managers are probably the best judges of their needs. They are unlikely to share a lack of knowledge freely with subordinates, and so the subordinates will tend to underestimate managers' needs for more knowledge.

As far as *attitude* is concerned the subordinates are probably better judges than the manager. Attitudes become operational in interpersonal contacts and determine to a large extent the effectiveness of these interpersonal contacts. In attitudes it is the perception by the other person that counts; the essence of an attitude is the way in which it is perceived by others.

For a fair estimate of managers' improvement needs it is therefore advisable to accept their own point of view as far as knowledge is concerned, but the subordinates' point of view as far as attitude is concerned. For the other categories—experience, skills, and personality—we have seen that the overall ratings for self and boss do not differ, but that ratings for individual items within these categories do. For each of these items, we should ask ourselves who is in the best position to judge managers' improvement needs, themselves or their subordinates. For example, in Skills there are some that relate to communication. The proof of the effectiveness of communication is in the receiver, so it is the subordinate who should be considered the better judge of managers' communicating skills.

So far, we have dealt with improvement needs, without considering whether and how these needs can be met. Our categories of knowledge, experience, skills, attitude, and personality are, in this order, increasingly difficult to change.

Figure 13.1 shows how efforts at improvement, mostly through training and development (on the job as well as in courses), reach first of all the knowledge level. Additional knowledge is fairly easy to supply, within the limits set by a person's intellectual capacities and willingness to learn. Increase of knowledge involves a person only superficially. Also, it will most easily be lost again. Experience is already at a more involving, deeper level. The "Needs for Improvement" exercise itself can be seen as an attempt at bringing experience into the learning process, thus increasing involvement, understanding, and retention. Skills have to be acquired through a process of trial and error. Their acquisition demands a still higher level of involvement, motivation, and energy release from

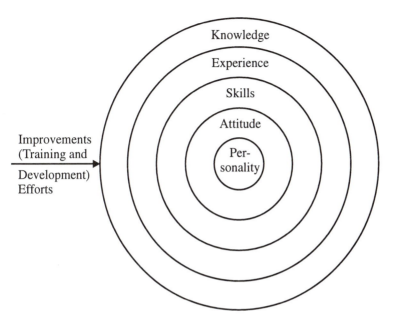

**Figure 13.1.** Five Levels of Improvement Needs

the participant. His or her innate capacities play an important role in the speed and perfection with which new skills can be acquired. Attitude involves most of the previously mentioned levels, as well as factors of education, culture, and early life experience. Personality finally involves basic traits partly inborn, partly acquired in early life, and to a limited extent adaptable in later life. Items like intelligence, creativity, or memory can be consciously developed, but only within rather narrow limits set by the basic abilities available.

As the outer layer of knowledge is easiest to reach, training and development efforts are most likely to be successful at this level. At subsequent levels—experience, skills, and attitude—training and development becomes more and more difficult, whereas at the personality level it is doubtful whether any effect of training and development can be expected at all. Unfortunately we found in Table 13.1 that improvement needs are high at the skill and attitude level. The problem is in addition frequently compounded by a lack of awareness of needs for attitude change. The dilemma of learning in management development is therefore that in the attitude area, one of those where improvement is most needed, managers tend to be least conscious of their needs and therefore least motivated to change, and even if they are motivated, change is most difficult to obtain. This explains the search for more involving approaches to training, be it through various forms of the case study method, particularly role playing, group dynamics exercises, action learning, sensitivity training, or others—all methods in which interpersonal feedback on attitudes is structurally facilitated. The same insight prompts also the trend toward organizational development, where improvement is sought not for one individual, but for a total social-organizational unit at the same time, so that people can reinforce each other in their new attitudes.

## Appendix: Description of the "Needs for Improvement" Exercise

The exercise uses two questionnaires, identical except for the headings "you yourself" and "your boss." Normally, the self-questionnaire, shown in Figure 13.2, is administered first. Filling out on average will take about 15 minutes per questionnaire. After completion of the self-questionnaire, a participant will turn this in and receive a boss questionnaire.

The administration session should start with a brief verbal explanation of the method of filling out, as explained on the questionnaires. An example may be used, but the administrator should take care not to suggest in the example that one particular set of numbers is the "right" answer. The explanation could, for example, run as follows:

> On the questionnaire you have received, you find large squares marked A to E, and labeled *knowledge, experience, skills, attitude,* and *personality.* First, please read through the whole questionnaire, so that you know what is meant by each of these labels. Now decide how you see your own improvement needs. Allow for your total needs 100% or 100 points, and please distribute these over the five main categories. For example, you may give 20 points to knowledge, 20 to experience, 20 to skills, 20 to attitude, and 20 to personality. You may also decide that you do not need some of the categories at all, and for example, give 0 points to knowledge or to personality. However, your total points should always add up to 100, and you are not allowed to give more than 50 points to any single category, so that you must select at least two categories of 50 points each. Please use the squares in the upper right-hand corner of each category to write down the points allocated to each category.
>
> Your next step is to distribute the points allocated to the category as a whole over the 10 items within each category (the ones numbered 1-10). For these items you will find two empty columns on the right side. Use the first column to mark by a cross or tick (x)

QUESTIONNAIRE -- NEEDS FOR IMPROVEMENT

| | | | | S |

Place for 4-digit code
(Please choose arbitrarily but make a note of it for
yourself)

In what fields do you think you yourself need most
improvement to become a better manager?

1. Read the whole questionnaire carefully

2. Distribute 100 points among the five main
   catories in accordance with their importance: use
   the squares framed with thick lines. Maximum
   number of points for any of the five main

3. Mark the most important items in each category
   using the first column. Try to mark about four
   items per category.

4. Distribute the points you have allotted to each
   category between the items just marked within
   each category. Use the second column for this.

5. Check whether your points within each category
   now add up to the category total, and whether the
   category totals add up to 100.

| C | SKILLS IN: | | |
|---|---|---|---|
| 1 | Interpreting company policies | | |
| 2 | Decision making | | |
| 3 | Communicating in the spoken word: speaking | | |
| 4 | Communicating in the spoken word: listening | | |
| 5 | Communicating in writing | | |
| 6 | Creating enthusiasm | | |
| 7 | Motivating subordinates | | |
| 8 | Convincing superiors | | |
| 9 | Stimulating & leading teamwork | | |
| 10 | Training and developing people | | |

| A | KNOWLEDGE OF: | | |
|---|---|---|---|
| 1 | Your company's present policies procedures, organization | | |
| 2 | Your company's products | | |
| 3 | Your company's product markets and competition | | |
| 4 | Your company's finance, accounting and control systems | | |
| 5 | Your company's objectives and long-term strategy | | |
| 6 | Own job and specialty | | |
| 7 | Language(s) | | |
| 8 | The world of business, economy, labor, etc. | | |
| 9 | Psychology, sociology | | |
| 10 | The cultural environment | | |

| D | ATTITUDE: | | |
|---|---|---|---|
| 1 | Tactfulness, politeness | | |
| 2 | Objectivity, open-mindedness | | |
| 3 | Fairness in use of authority | | |
| 4 | Willingness to delegate | | |
| 5 | Courage to take decisions | | |
| 6 | Firmness to stand pressures | | |
| 7 | Trust in capacities and self-motivation of subordinates | | |
| 8 | Willingness to help others | | |
| 9 | Willingness to accept help | | |
| 10 | Optimism, devotion, enthusiasm | | |

| B | EXPERIENCE IN: | | |
|---|---|---|---|
| 1 | Present Job | | |
| 2 | Work distribution and organization | | |
| 3 | Planning and budgeting | | |
| 4 | Dealing with superiors | | |
| 5 | Working with suborinates | | |
| 6 | Dealing with other departments of your company | | |
| 7 | Dealing with customers, authorities, the public | | |
| 8 | Presenting results | | |
| 9 | Recognizing business trends in time | | |
| 10 | Handling emergency situations | | |

| E | PERSONALITY: | | |
|---|---|---|---|
| 1 | Intelligence, judgement | | |
| 2 | Reasoning, logical ability | | |
| 3 | Creativity, combinative ability | | |
| 4 | Intuition, vision | | |
| 5 | Emotional balance, maturity | | |
| 6 | Ease in personal relations | | |
| 7 | Human touch, sense of humor | | |
| 8 | Sensitivity to other's feelings and to own impact on others | | |
| 9 | Sense of order and system | | |
| 10 | Reliability: a good memory | | |

**Figure 13.2.** Example of a "Self" Questionnaire

which of the 10 items of this category you think you need most. Try to mark about four items per category (more or less is allowed but four is the ideal number). Then divide the total category points (written down by you in the upper right-hand corner) over the four, or about four, items that you ticked off. If the total category gets 0 points, of course, you do not need to select any items for this category.

Finally, please do not forget to check whether your points within each category add up to the figure in the upper right-hand corner, and whether the figures in the five upper right-hand corners add up to 100 points. Any questions?

The questionnaire is best kept anonymous, with participants not mentioning their names. During the discussion, it is useful to give each participant his or her own questionnaires back, so that (s)he can compare personal answers with the class average. The 4-digit code on the top of the questionnaire, chosen arbitrarily by the participant, makes it possible to return questionnaires without violating anonymity.

Although normally the self-questionnaire is given first, experiments have been made with the boss questionnaire given first and even with half of the class taking boss first, half taking self first. All these approaches produced similar results. It is essential that the questionnaire given first is collected before the second one is handed out, to avoid direct copying. It is allowable to administer the self and boss questionnaires on different days. If the self-questionnaire is used in a before-and-after fashion (to measure shifts in participants' perceived needs at the beginning and at the end of the program), the boss questionnaire or at least the feedback about it should be given after the *second* self-questionnaire, not the first, because the feedback on the boss questionnaire will strongly affect the way people fill out a self-questionnaire next time.

Calculation of the results can of course be done on a computer, but even on a pocket calculator it will only take about 3 minutes per questionnaire. Normally the questionnaire session should be planned somewhat ahead of the discussion session, to allow time for calculation and preparing the presentation of the results.

Steps in calculation:

1. Check each questionnaire for possible errors (points not adding up to 100). If errors are found, correct these proportionally (for example, if points add up to 120 instead of 100, divide all points by approximately 100/120).

2. Add up totals for each category for all participants and calculate an average by dividing by the number of participants. The five average category totals should add up to 100 points (except for the effect of rounding off).

3. Do the same for each of the 10 items within each category.

4. Make a list or graph showing a comparison of average category totals for self versus boss, and another list showing those individual items on self and boss questionnaires that receive more than average points, as demonstrated in this article.

## Discussion Questions

1. The allocation of the questionnaire items to the five categories (knowledge, experience, skills, attitude, personality) is somewhat subjective. Check whether you would allocate the items in the same way.

2. The chapter shows that only for just over half of the individual participants the scores followed the general trend. Doesn't this weaken the conclusions of the chapter?

3. The chapter points to an often-unrecognized cost of hierarchy: its impact on perception. What structural measures can be taken to reduce this cost?

## Note

1. The data presented allow testing the statistical significance of the difference between self and boss scores with the sign test. For Knowledge, the difference is at the .025 level, for Attitude, at the .005 level.

# 14

# Perceptions of
# Others After a T-Group

Sixty managers attending an executive course responded to questionnaires specifying their perceptions of the needs for improvement of themselves and of their bosses. Half of the group, randomly assigned, answered before participating in a 3-day T-group program and the other half immediately after. When the responses were compared, it was seen that the perception gap between perceived self and boss improvement needs in the interpersonal area was wider after training than before. From this finding and an analysis of the literature, it is argued that T-group programs tend to have a negative influence on perceptions of outsiders and that this effect may be functional as well as dysfunctional in organization development.

## The "Cold Shower" Effect

When I was about 16 we sang a special song when returning from a boys' camp. Translated into English, it ran something like this: "We now go back to the cold, cold, cold, cold world." After the intense interpersonal experience of camp life, returning to the everyday world was experienced as somewhat of a "cold shower." I wonder whether the participant in a successful T-group[1] does not often have a similar feeling, and does

This chapter was originally published in *Journal of Applied Behavioral Science,* 11(3), 1975, pp. 367-377. Copyright © 1975 by the *Journal of Applied Behavioral Science.* Reprinted with permission.

this have implications for the uses and users of T-group methods in organization development?

The literature on T-group research alludes to this "cold shower effect," though rarely explicitly. Harrison (1962) compared the responses of 11 managers in an experimental group after and before training. His findings showed significantly greater interpersonal sensitivity in the terms in which managers described one another after training; when describing associates outside the group, however, they showed less sensitivity (although not significantly less). Harrison interprets his findings in these terms: "The expectations of others and the demands and restrictions of an organization's structure may pose formidable obstacles to practicing the values and using the new perceptual skills" (p. 269).

Morton (1965) collected 359 critical incidents from 97 trainees in an in-company organization development program using T-groups. Seventeen percent of the critical incidents indicated "difficulty in applying what had been learned." Those in groups together with members from their own work department cited as the main barriers to application: organizational rules, resistance from outside the department, and the insufficient numbers trained. Those trained with people from outside their own department cited skepticism of the untrained and resistance and organizational barriers within their own departments (p. 66).

Zand, Steele, and Zalkind (1969) compared the perceptions of 65 managers in an in-company laboratory training program concerned with interpersonal, group, and organizational functioning. The perceptions were measured before the laboratory, immediately after, and again after 1 year. Immediately after the laboratory, perceptions of others in the work situation, including bosses, showed a significant shift toward the unfavorable. The authors interpret this shift as a change in the standards participants used to evaluate various dimensions of their relations with others.

Lieberman, Yalom, and M. B. Miles (1972) sent 209 Stanford undergraduates to encounter groups representing 10 different approaches to personal change; 69 others served as a control group. Among other assessment procedures, changes were measured by means of 73 paper-and-pencil indices, 10 of which dealt with perceptions of "significant others" (outside their training groups). Participants compared with controls showed unfavorable shifts in perceptions of significant others in all 10 encounter settings.

Bowers (1973) reports on attitude survey measurements obtained by the Michigan Inter-Company Longitudinal Study from more than 14,000 respondents in 23 organizations. Effects as measured by the Survey of Organizations questionnaire results were tested for six treatments:

Survey Feedback, Interpersonal Process Consultation, Task Process Consultation, Laboratory Training, Data Handback, and No Treatment. Changes were measured both for those actually involved in the treatment and for whole systems. Laboratory training (i.e., T-groups) was associated with a negative shift in attitudes, especially from those participating; attitude areas most affected were Managerial Support and Peer Support. Some other treatments were associated with a positive shift in attitudes.

## A Natural Experiment

This chapter will report about a natural experiment with an unpredicted outcome, conducted at IMEDE (Management Development Institute) in Lausanne, Switzerland,[2] in autumn 1971. Sixty-four participants (all male) in the 5-month Program for Executive Development, about halfway through their course, were offered a 3-day T-group program labeled "Personal and Managerial Feedback" (PMF), originally developed at IMEDE by Professor Howard V. Perlmutter. It consisted of both structured and unstructured sessions and capitalized on the fact that participants, although originally strangers to one another, had already worked together for a couple of months at IMEDE and could in a relatively short time build up the high degree of involvement expected in a T-group-type training activity.

Fifty of the original 64 actually took PMF, which was offered as an option. They were divided into four teams. As only two trainers were available, participants from one half of the class (Group B) took PMF at the beginning of the week; the other half (Group A), at the end. The unoccupied half of the class took regular courses and among other tasks completed the exercise "Needs for Improvement" described in Chapter 13. It was one of several exercises used during the Organizational Behavior course and meant to be a tool of experiential learning rather than research. Participants were quite accustomed to the use of such tools and to the discussion of their results in class.

As described in Chapter 13, the purpose of the "Needs for Improvement" exercise is to start a discussion on two issues: the impact of hierarchy on perception and the nature of learning in management development. The exercise tends to show consistent differences in how a majority of participants view the improvement needs of their bosses as opposed to their own: For themselves, knowledge and skills—but not attitude—are seen as areas most in need of improvement; for their bosses, skills and attitude—but not knowledge.

## Before-and-After
## Design and Hypotheses

The division of the class into Group A and Group B meant that Group A filled out the "Needs for Improvement" forms before PMF whereas Group B completed them after PMF. Eight persons from Group A and six from Group B who did not take PMF at all also participated in the "Needs for Improvement" exercise, making a total of 32 usable responses from Group A and 28 from Group B.[3]

The accidental administration of the exercise before PMF for one half of the class and after PMF for the rest formed a natural experiment. Recognizing this, I hypothesized that those who took the exercise after PMF would score:

1. More of their self needs in the Attitude category and in the "sensitivity" item of the Personality category (E8 in Figure 13.2)
2. Their own needs along lines closer to their bosses' needs, as a demonstration of increased interpersonal sensitivity

First, for purposes of verification, I had to test whether the composition of Groups A and B showed differences other than the PMF treatment that could account for any differences in outcome. The average ages were not significantly different: 34.6 years for Group A, 33.8 years for Group B. Group A contained 15 different nationalities; Group B, 18; 14 of these were represented in both groups. Scores had been collected for the members of the two groups on three paper-and-pencil values tests: L. V. Gordon's Surveys of Personal and Interpersonal Values (Hofstede, 1976a), and the Allport-Vernon-Lindsay Study of Values. None of the scores on the three tests show a significant difference between the two groups. So it is safe to conclude that participants were randomly distributed over Groups A and B.

The left-hand part of Table 14.1 shows the mean points for the perceived needs for improvement of the self and of the boss for both Groups A and B. As 100 points had to be distributed over the five categories Knowledge, Experience, Skills, Attitude, and Personality, the average expected number of points per category is 20. Group A (before PMF) shows more or less the expected pattern: self needs predominantly in the categories Attitude and Skills (see Table 13.1).

Hypothesis 1 was that Group B after PMF would produce higher self scores for Attitude and (some) Personality needs than Group A. This was the case, although not to a statistically significant degree.[4] Hypothesis 2 stated that scores for self and boss would be more similar after PMF. This

**TABLE 14.1** Scores on "Improvement Needs" for Self and Boss, Group B (after T-group) Versus Group A (before T-group)

| | | Mean Points | | | Group A No. of Persons Scoring | | | Group B No. of Persons Scoring | | |
|---|---|---|---|---|---|---|---|---|---|---|
| Category of Needs | | Group A n = 32 | Group B n = 28 | Dif-ference A − B | Self > Boss | Self = Boss | Self < Boss | Self > Boss | Self = Boss | Self < Boss |
| Knowledge | Self | 21.4 | 20.6 | .8 | 13 | 8 | 11 | 19** | 4 | 5 |
| | Boss | 19.3 | 13.7 | 5.6† | | | | | | |
| Experience | Self | 19.5 | 19.7 | −0.2 | 14 | 9 | 9 | 12 | 9 | 7 |
| | Boss | 16.4 | 17.4 | −1.0 | | | | | | |
| Skills | Self | 24.3 | 21.2 | 3.1 | 11 | 8 | 13 | 10 | 9 | 9 |
| | Boss | 20.7 | 21.8 | −1.1 | | | | | | |
| Attitude | Self | 16.5 | 18.0 | −1.5 | 8 | 8 | 16 | 4 | 9 | 15* |
| | Boss | 25.7 | 22.0 | 3.7 | | | | | | |
| Personality | Self | 18.3 | 20.5 | −2.2 | 15 | 7 | 10 | 6 | 7 | 15 |
| | Boss | 17.9 | 25.1 | −7.2** | | | | | | |

*Significant at .05 level (sign test).
**Significant at .02 level (Mann-Whitney test, one-tailed, for score difference; sign test for number of persons).
† $p = .07$ (Mann-Whitney test, one-tailed).

appeared to be the case for Skills and Attitude, and marginally for Experience. For Knowledge and Personality, however, Table 14.1 shows a *widening of the gap* between perceived needs of self and of boss. Group B participants (after PMF) saw their bosses as needing much less improvement in Knowledge and more in Personality than Group A. Moreover, these two unpredicted cases are the only score differences between Group A and B having less than a .10 probability of occurring by chance.

The right-hand part of Table 14.1 shows numbers of individuals rather than mean point scores. Because of the way scores are arrived at by dividing 100 points, a single individual can sharply influence an item's score by allotting a large portion of the points to it. The right-hand part of the table simply lists whether individuals allotted less, the same, or more points to their boss for an item category than they allotted to themselves. The statistical significance of the tendency to score a difference between boss and self can be tested by the sign test. Contrary to expectation, it is again Group B (after PMF) rather than Group A for which the tendency to score boss needs as different from self needs is statistically significant (for Knowledge and also for Attitude; the difference for Personality stays just above the .05 level).

**TABLE 14.2** Improvement Needs Obtaining Markedly Different Emphasis in Groups A and B

| | | Number of Times Scored | | Average Point Value Given | |
|---|---|---|---|---|---|
| | | Group A $n = 32$ | Group B $n = 28$ | Group A | Group B |
| For Self | —more in Group B (after T Group): | | | | |
| Experience | Dealing with superiors | 11 | 17* | 2.5 | 4.2 |
| | Dealing with customers, etc. | 9 | 13 | 1.5 | 2.9 |
| Attitude | Firmness to stand pressures | 11 | 15 | 1.8 | 3.8 |
| Personality | Sense of humor | 4 | 11** | 0.4 | 2.1 |
| | Sensitivity to others | 10 | 17* | 1.3 | 4.5* |
| For Self | —less in Group B (after T Group): | | | | |
| Knowledge | Languages | 16* | 9 | 4.0 | 2.2 |
| Experience | Planning and budgeting | 21 | 12 | 4.2 | 2.1 |
| | Recognizing business trends | 14 | 9 | 2.9 | 1.3 |
| For Boss | —more in Group B (after T Group): | | | | |
| Experience | Working with subordinates | 14 | 18 | 2.3 | 4.0 |
| Skills | Convincing superiors | 9 | 8 | 1.6 | 3.3 |
| Personality | Emotional balance, maturity | 11 | 14 | 1.6 | 4.0* |
| | Ease in personal relations | 13 | 16 | 2.8 | 5.7* |
| | Sensitivity to others | 17 | 20 | 3.0 | 6.0* |
| For Boss | —less in Group B (after T Group): | | | | |
| Knowledge | Finance, accounting, control | 12 | 8 | 2.7 | 1.0 |
| | Company objectives | 16* | 8 | 3.1 | 1.2 |
| Attitude | Willingness to delegate | 15 | 12 | 6.3 | 3.6 |
| | Courage to make decisions | 14 | 9 | 4.9 | 2.4 |

*Significant at .05 level ($\chi^2$ test, 1 *df* for number of times scored; Kolmogorov-Smirnov test for point values given).
**Significant at .02 level ($\chi^2$ test, 1 *df*).

Table 14.2 contains a selection from the individual items within the five categories Knowledge through Personality (Figure 13.2). The columns "Number of Times Scored" list the number of persons who allocate any points to an item (regardless of number of points), and the columns "Average Point Value Given" record the average points across all respondents, including those who did not allot any points to the item. As there are 100 points allotted and 50 items, the average expected number of points per item is 2.0. The item "Sensitivity to others" gets considerably more attention in Group B (after PMF) than in Group A, as predicted in Hypothesis 1. For both self and boss it is the most frequently chosen item by Group B participants and has the highest average point value. Instrumental improvement needs, especially "Knowledge of languages," and formal organization concepts, especially "Company objectives," are less emphasized in Group B than they were in Group A.

## Conclusions:
## The Cold Shower Effect

As described in Chapter 13, when discussing the results of the "Needs for Improvement" exercise with a class, we point out that it is highly unlikely that bosses as a group have improvement needs so vastly different from subordinates as a group. The exercise demonstrates a difference in perception rather than a difference in actual needs—managers tend to be aware of their own lack of knowledge but it takes somebody else (notably subordinates) to be aware of their shortcomings in the attitude area.

One of the main purposes of a T-group is to increase interpersonal sensitivity—"to see ourselves as others see us." Thus the perception gap between boss and self improvement needs should narrow after a T-group. The results, however, proved to be the exact opposite of our hypothesis. Whereas perception of own needs did shift somewhat in the predicted direction of more Attitude and more Personality change, perceived needs of the boss in the area of Knowledge and Personality, contrary to our expectation, shifted toward fewer Knowledge and more Personality needs. At first glance (Table 14.1, left-hand part), the points assigned to Attitude suggest a closing of the gap between boss and self; but inspection of the raw data shows that this is due to some extreme scores of Group A, and it is not reflected in the right-hand part of the same table, which includes only numbers of respondents and shows that for Attitude, too, there is a greater tendency for Group B to rate bosses' needs higher than self needs.

Careful analysis of Table 14.2 shows that after "Sensitivity," Group B rated "Experience in dealing with superiors" the second highest self need, and then "Firmness to withstand pressures"—undoubtedly at least partly understood as pressures coming from above. Bosses were seen to need, on the contrary, "Experience in working with subordinates," in addition to "Maturity," "Ease in personal relations," and greater "Sensitivity."

What distinguishes the after-PMF group from the before-PMF group, then, is greater awareness of interpersonal issues, but applied more to the boss than to the self. After the T-groups, individuals were not more but less tolerant when rating their superiors than before.

On hindsight, Hypothesis 2 was naive (when data turn out differently from what we expect, there are always good reasons why we should have known it beforehand). The results actually obtained help explain the disaster of an organization development program in one company where we trained "cousin" groups (within the same organization, but not directly reporting to one another) in T-groups during one week, and after project work during the second week, confronted them with their highest superiors. They did not succeed in establishing communication and complained bitterly about the superiors' insensitivity.

The same phenomenon is reflected in an article by Argyris (1972), in which he analyzes behavior patterns in "personal growth laboratories" and reports about participants who develop a "negative and hostile feeling about the *non*understanding that exists in the outside world" (p. 23). The references to Harrison, Morton, and others cited at the beginning of this chapter deal with similar situations.

These researches and the natural experiment described in this chapter seem to warrant the conclusion that T-groups and similar high-interpersonal-involvement programs create or increase negative perceptions of outsiders—including, but not limited to, superiors. With Zand et al. (1969), we can interpret this as the result of a shift in trainees' standards. The data from this chapter suggest that it is a shift in trainees' standards as applied to others rather than to themselves.

It may be that we are dealing with a short-term effect, as our Group B data were collected immediately after the training. Perhaps the defense mechanisms protecting our self-perceptions take more time to be torn down. Schutz and Allen (1966), who measured self-perception—using the "FIRO-B" questionnaire—before a T-group program, immediately after, and 6 months later, report that the main change took place between the measurements immediately after and 6 months after. They did not use a control group. The Zand et al. study (1969) quoted reports that after 1 year the perceptions by the T-group participants were no different from those by other managers, except that they were more optimistic when rating the extent to which managers were "facing up to conflicts" and "seeking help." Both expressions are typical T-group jargon, and the higher scores of the participants may just show their greater familiarity with this kind of terminology.

Bowers (1973) does not specify how long after the laboratory training the second measurements of the Michigan ICLS were taken. If the interval between two surveys is 1 year, the average estimated time after the lab is 6 months, and Bowers still found negative shifts in perceptions of others. The data pertaining to a possible difference between a short-term and a long-term effect of T-group training are therefore inconclusive.

## Functional or Dysfunctional?

Let us assume for the moment that the negative influence of T-groups on perceptions of others rather than on self-perceptions is not just short term. Then, should we consider it as undesirable, immaterial, or desirable? The answer will depend in part on our own values and in part on our diagnosis of the situation. Our values will determine, among other things, whether we wish the interest of the individuals or the interest of their organizations to prevail. In the executive course at IMEDE, our orientation as teachers was clearly toward the individual, yet the name "organization development" suggests that the interests of the organization should prevail. Organization development consultants are caught in a dilemma between the individual and the organization and this has consequences for the training method to be chosen. For example, our diagnosis may be that the organization suffers from excessive dependency of those in lower level roles on those in power roles. If this is the case, an increase in the critical sense of the lower level people toward others in superior positions is a desirable goal, and this particular outcome of T-groups is functional. If our diagnosis or values go in another direction, negatively influencing the perceptions of others with whom they have to work anyway may just be a source of frustration for trainees and dysfunctional to the organization. Our findings reconfirm that within the context of organization development, high-involvement techniques like T-groups are a tool to be used with good judgment and discrimination.

## Discussion Questions

1. What is a "natural experiment"?

2. What does Table 14.2 show about the "ideology" of T-group training?

3. Can you think of other experiences besides boys' camps and T-groups that produce a cold shower effect on return?

4. To what extent do you expect the changes after PMF to have lasted?

# Notes

1. Sensitivity training with its T-groups (training groups) was very much in vogue in the 1960s. Originally developed at the National Training Laboratories in Bethel, Maine (Bradford, Gibb, & Benne, 1964), they have spread widely across Western countries. The inheritance of sensitivity training movement is still present in the 1990s in various types of high-involvement interpersonal relations training using personal feedback. In this article the term *T-groups* is used, but the phenomena described probably occur in a wide range of related training situations even today.

2. Now merged into IMD, Lausanne.

3. In Group A, all members filled out the "Needs for Improvement" completely. In Group B, four members missed either the boss or the self-questionnaire, or both, so that only 28 valid sets of "Needs for Improvement" data were available. Including the responses of some non-PMF participants in both groups obviously dilutes the impact of the PMF experience on the results; differences in perception before and after a T-group would have been *more* pronounced had the design of this natural experiment not included these anonymous responses.

4. It has been argued that a few items on the "Needs for Improvement" questionnaire could belong to either category: Attitude or Personality. However, respondents saw the generic labels and it is therefore likely that they interpreted improvement need specifically in terms of the intended category. Moreover, because the main conclusions from this chapter affect both Attitude and Personality alike, the allocation of items between the two is not critical.

# 15

# Predicting Managers' Career Success

More than 300 managers from five countries participating in management
training programs run by a multinational corporation were rated on overall
career potential by their training staff. Trainer ratings were significantly
correlated with career success after the programs, but only after about 6
years. Trainer ratings were also subject to measurable biases based on participants' mother language and other factors. In one 21-manager group,
ratings by training peers were also available. For this group both peer and
staff ratings were compared with position level increase after 3½ years. Peer
ratings in this case significantly predicted career progress, whereas trainer
ratings did not.

## Selecting Leaders

The usual way of selecting leaders in business organizations is nomination by one or more superiors. If the nominees' later success depends
largely on their relationships with these same superiors, this may work
well. If success depends more on the objective capabilities of the candidates, nomination by superiors is not always an effective procedure. Not
all superiors appear to be good judges of candidates' capabilities. This
is why business (and other) organizations have sought more objective
predictors of leadership success to supplement superiors' judgments.

---

This chapter was originally published under the title "Predicting Managers' Career
Success in an International Setting: The Validity of Ratings by Training Staff Versus
Training Peers" in *Management International Review*, 15(1), 1975, pp. 43-50. Copyright ©
1975 by *Management International Review*. Reprinted with permission.

Among the more professional assessment methods used figure psychological tests (Dodd, Wollowick, & McNamara, 1970; Kraut, 1969), personal background inventories (Laurent, 1961), and management assessment centers (Bray & Grant, 1966). A solution in between professional assessment and the judgment of superiors is available where candidates take part in company-sponsored training programs. In this case, ratings by training staff and training peers, although seldom used, might be feasible predictors of candidates' leadership success.

Kraut (1973) extensively reviewed the literature on the reliability and validity of staff and peer ratings. Most of the research in this area was carried out in a U.S. military context. The fewer and mostly recent studies quoted by Kraut dealing with business applications, however, presented very similar results. Kraut's own research data, collected in a large U.S. corporation, showed that for 82 middle-level managers, peer ratings of "capacity for advancement," obtained in a training program, correlated significantly[1] with the number of career moves in the 2 years following the program. Staff ratings, although correlated with peer ratings, predicted career moves less well.[2] This superiority of peer ratings over staff ratings was also found in military studies quoted by Kraut (Gordon & Medland, 1965; Trites, 1960; Wherry & Fryer, 1949; Williams & Leavitt, 1947). In a very different setting, that is, for students taking part in encounter groups (similar to T-groups; see Chapter 14), Lieberman et al. (1972) found that for predicting which participants would suffer negative long-term effects from the group experience, peer judgments were the most accurate and trainer judgments quite inaccurate.

Kraut's 2-year period is in itself not very long for career prediction. Dodd et al. (1970) showed that career success, measured in terms of salary, could be predicted from certain personality test scores, but that it took as many as 8 years for some test scores to become valid predictors. On the other hand, training grades obtained in initial training became less valid predictors as time proceeded. The results obtained by Dodd et al. show that for predicting career success it may be desirable to distinguish between short-term and long-term predictive validity.

## A Windfall Study

This chapter will report on the predictive validity of staff and peer ratings for leadership success in a setting not unlike the one studied by Kraut (1973). It will compare validities of staff ratings over periods varying in length from 1 to 8 years; for peer ratings it uses a period of 3.5 years.

An additional element in this chapter, distinguishing it from previous research, is the influence on staff and peer ratings of language and cultural differences between staff and peers and among peers. The study was carried out in an international setting in which both participants and staff came from several different countries. Most had to communicate in a language other than their own. The careers to be predicted would take place in a cultural environment mostly unknown to the raters. We would expect that in this case the predictive validities of both staff and peer ratings would be lower than those reported in the literature for culturally homogenous groups.

Staff ratings of participants' career potential were made by the staff of a middle-management development program run by the international training center of a multinational corporation between 1960 and 1968. During this period about 800 managers participated; all courses lasted 4 weeks. Although ratings were collected to be available on request to top management as an aid in career decisions, in fact they were rarely used. Rating information was only asked by superiors for approximately 10% of participants and even then, according to the director of the center, often neglected in actual career decisions. In spite of this there may have been a slight contamination of the criterion (career moves) by the ratings. Staff ratings of overall career potential were made by three staff members for each participant on a 5-point forced-distribution scale.[3] The three ratings were averaged into one overall score. Data on career movements since attendance at the program until December 31, 1968, were collected for all participants from five large countries, France, Germany, Italy, Great Britain, and the United States, a total of 322 persons. Career movements were measured on a position level code scale. The position level code is a 2-digit number universally used in this corporation, determined by job analysis and related to the salary level.

Peer ratings were collected in this same center during an experiment in one particular middle-management course in early 1968. Peer ratings and staff ratings were kept separate; peer-rating information was exchanged between participants and made available to the researcher, but not filed by the staff or fed back to any superior. The ratings themselves, therefore, could not affect careers. In mid-1971, after 3.5 years, a reading was done on the career status of the participants and their level increase since the course was determined.

## Results

The correlations between staff ratings and position level increase between the course and December 31, 1968, are shown in Table 15.1. The

**TABLE 15.1** Product-Moment Correlations Between Staff Ratings and Subsequent Position Level Increase

| | | | Correlation Staff Ratings vs. Level Increase | |
|---|---|---|---|---|
| Course Number | Number of Participants in Sample | Average Years to Measurement Date | Uncorrected | Corrected for Level During Course |
| 1–9 | 60 | 8 | .24* | .33* |
| 10–19 | 59 | 6 | .43** | .46** |
| 20–29 | 64 | 4½ | .15 | .28* |
| 30–39 | 83 | 2½ | .11 | .17 |
| 40–46 | 56 | 1 | −.04 | .00 |
| All | 322 | 4 | .23** | .30** |

*Significant at .05 level.
**Significant at .01 level.

bottom line in Table 15.1 shows that across all participants there was a significant, but low correlation (.23**) between staff ratings and subsequent level increase. However, the overall figure is misleading. Careers take time to develop (the average participant in our sample increased .33 levels per year, that is one level increase every 3 years), so we would expect correlations to grow stronger over time. Therefore the data in Table 15.1 have been divided into blocks of courses covering a certain period. In fact, correlations did become stronger over time. The strongest correlation is obtained for Courses 10-19, which took place between 1961 and 1963. Staff ratings during these courses show a .43** correlation with level increase to December 31, 1968. For still earlier courses we do not find a further increase in correlation: for Courses 1-9 (1960-1961) the correlation is only .24*.

Further analysis of the data showed that the correlations were partly suppressed by a particular systematic error of the raters. The source of this error was the position level of the participant when attending the course. Course participants were not all at the same level in the hierarchy—they came from a range of levels. Raters attributed to higher level participants a higher career potential (the correlation coefficient between staff ratings and the participants' level during the course was .20**). But in reality the correlation between the level during the course and subsequent level increases was *negative*: −.27**. This is because people who are already in relatively high positions have less chance of further promotions than those still relatively low in the hierarchy. If we correct for the influence of the position level during the course, our correlations

**TABLE 15.2** Distribution of Staff Ratings and Actual Promotions by Language/Culture Area of Participants

| Country Group | Number of Participants in Sample | Percentage Rated by Staff | | | Percentage Promoted 3 or More Levels[a] |
|---|---|---|---|---|---|
| | | Below Average | Average to Good | Outstanding | |
| USA/Great Britain | 99 | 14 | 71 | 16 | 22 |
| Germany | 86 | 26 | 62 | 12 | 18 |
| France/Italy | 137 | 38 | 52 | 10 | 25 |
| All | 322 | 27 | 61 | 12 | 23 |

a. Corrected for shifts in country quota over time (countries with higher participant quotas in early courses have a higher expected proportion of promotions, but this effect has been eliminated). Chi-square for differences in staff ratings by country group = 18.8*** with 4 $df$.

increase (last column of Table 15.1). Significant correlations of staff ratings with level increase are now found starting about 4.5 years after the course.

The data allow us also to test for other systematic rater errors or biases. Kraut (1973) found that staff tended to give higher ratings to younger participants ($r = -.27$**). The same is true in our case: staff ratings correlated $-.22$** with participants' age. In reality, however, younger participants did *not* move significantly faster in their careers.[4]

The international setting of the training center created a particularly interesting issue in the degree to which language and culture might bias raters' judgments. In Table 15.2 career versus ratings correlations have been compared by participants' home countries.

Table 15.2 shows that English-speaking participants (English was the course language) tended to receive higher staff ratings, Latin participants (French and Italian) lower ones. The last column in Table 15.2 reveals that the actual percentage of fast promotions (three or more position levels) did not follow this rating trend: It was even higher in the Latin countries.

Another source of systematic rater error might be the participants' functional area. As this company was thoroughly marketing oriented, marketing participants might have received higher ratings. Table 15.3 shows this to be the case.

Marketing participants did tend to receive higher ratings, technical (product development, manufacturing, customer service) and staff (finance, personnel, and other), lower ratings. The differences are less pronounced than those by country group. Actual fast promotions (last column in Table 15.3) did not follow the ratings pattern.

**TABLE 15.3** Distribution of Staff Ratings and Actual Promotions by
Functional Area of Participants

| Functional Area | Number of Participants in Sample | Percentage Rated by Staff | | | Percentage Promoted 3 or More Levels |
| | | Below Average | Average to Good | Outstanding | |
|---|---|---|---|---|---|
| Marketing | 150 | 24 | 59 | 17 | 24 |
| Technical (product development, manufacturing, customer service) | 89 | 31 | 58 | 11 | 25 |
| Staff (finance, personnel, other) | 83 | 29 | 66 | 5 | 20 |
| All | 322 | 27 | 61 | 12 | 23 |

NOTE: Chi-square for differences in staff ratings by functional area = 9.4* with 4 $df$.

The results of the peer-rating experiment are shown in Table 15.4. Peers were rated on five characteristics,[5] using in each case a semiforced-distribution 5-point scale (all 5 points had to be used at least once; participants rated all 20 peers and also themselves). The average number of position level increases in the 3.5-year period following the ratings was 1.4, corresponding to .40 levels per year, somewhat faster than for the large sample in Table 15.1 (.33).

The data in Table 15.4 indicate that the best predictor of position level increase after 3.5 years was the peer rating of "potential for growth." The staff rating of "overall potential" had no significant predictive validity. Its value of .06 after 3.5 years was even somewhat lower than (but not significantly different from) the values of .11 after 2.5 years and .15 after 4.5 years in Table 15.1. It is remarkable that in spite of the superior predictive validity of peer ratings over staff ratings in Table 15.4, the intercorrelation of the two was quite high: .76***. The very high correlations of staff ratings for "overall potential" with peer ratings of "involvement in the course" (.90***) and "problem solving" (.82***) show that this is what the staff based their judgment on. The characteristic showing the second-highest correlation (.41) with position level increase was the peer rating for "communication," which was less correlated with staff ratings of overall potential (.58**). It seems that the crucial difference between the two types of ratings concerns the communication skills of the participants, which are perceived much more accurately by peers than by staff and seem to play a key role in the participants' later position level increase.

**TABLE 15.4** Product-Moment Correlation Coefficients Between Peer Ratings, Staff Ratings, and Subsequent Position Level Increase

| | Correlation With | |
|---|---|---|
| Rated Characteristics | Staff Rating of Overall Potential | Position Level Increase |
| Staff rating: Overall potential | (1.00) | .06 |
| Peer ratings: Involvement in the course | .90*** | .23 |
| Problem solving | .82*** | .36 |
| Communication | .58** | .41 |
| Maturity | .41 | .33 |
| Potential for growth | .76*** | .46* |

*Significant at .05 level.
**Significant at .01 level.
***Significant at .001 level.

## A Further Analysis of the Results

It is evident from the data that even in an international setting, staff and peer ratings have a certain predictive validity for management success. Staff ratings take time to become valid predictors, in our case, about 6 years.

Over the 3.5-year period used in the peer-rating experiment, predictive validity was found for ratings by peers (.46*), but not by staff (.06). This in spite of an intercorrelation of .76*** between staff and peer ratings of overall potential. It means that in this case, although staff and peers show considerable consensus in their ratings, it was precisely the part of the variance where peers and staff did *not* agree that made the difference in prediction—and it is the peers who were right.

We also saw that this difference relates mostly to the participants' communication skills. Statistically the staff ratings act as a "suppressor variable" for the validity of the peer ratings. The multiple correlation coefficient for staff and peer ratings combined is as high as $R = .63$. The multiple regression equation is:

$$I = -.74 + 1.45\,P - .71\,S$$

in which I = position level increase after 3.5 years, P = peer ratings, S = staff ratings. The negative sign of the staff ratings coefficient indicates the suppressor effect.

The process of interpersonal perception that takes place in a training program can be conceptualized by a matrix or "window" (Figure 15.1).[6]

| | Visible to Staff | Not Visible to Staff |
|---|---|---|
| Visible to Peers | a | b |
| Not Visible to Peers | c | d |

**Figure 15.1.** Personality Characteristics Visible to Training Staff and Training Peers

I postulate that some personality characteristics are visible to peers and some not, some are visible to the staff and some not, and what is visible to peers is not necessarily the same as what is visible to staff.

As characteristics visible to staff and visible to peers overlap only partly, we get four areas: Area *a* contains those characteristics visible to both staff and peers, Area *b* contains those characteristics visible to peers but not to staff, Area *c* is visible to staff and not to peers, and Area *d* is invisible to both.

The results of the peer-rating experiment can be interpreted as follows: those characteristics predicting career success after 3.5 years were almost exclusively in Area *b*. The increasing validity of staff ratings over a longer time span (Table 15.1) suggests that as time proceeds, characteristics of Area *a* become more important. As long as peer ratings are more valid predictors than staff ratings, the characteristics that determine success are at least partly in Area *b*. In Kraut's (1973) study adding staff ratings to peer ratings did *not* improve the multiple correlation coefficient with career success, which suggests that there were no characteristics in Area *c* (visible to staff but not to peers) that counted. As yet I know of no studies that show staff ratings to be better predictors than peer ratings and therefore would indicate Area *c* to be important. It is possible that this would be the case in the long term. We know that staff ratings correlated .43** with the criterion after 6 years, but we do not know what peer ratings would have done over this term.

If we stay within the shorter term of 3.5 years, we can explain the higher validity of the peer ratings first of all by the greater number of raters, which led to higher reliability. Second, it appears that staff ratings were influenced almost solely by participants' involvement in the course and included irrelevant criteria like participants' age (both in Kraut's study and in mine), position level, and functional area. In our international setting we have shown that language and culture of the participants also influenced staff ratings, in the sense that those using their mother language were rated more favorably. This probably explains why my staff ratings were less effective predictors ($r = .06$) than Kraut's ($r = .23*$), which were collected in a national environment. It appears that peers were less sensitive to such biases; in the same situation I found $r = .46*$ for peers against Kraut's $r = .44**$.[7] It is a well-known phenomenon in international courses that foreign-language participants who never speak up in plenary class sessions do communicate more freely in small peer groups.

The peer-rating experiment was only done for one small sample of participants, so that the outcome may have been strongly influenced by chance.[8] However, the findings were in line with earlier studies using considerably larger samples.

A third reason why peer ratings predicted leadership success better may be that an authority relationship, however benevolent (as between training staff and participants) influences both the behavior of the participants and the staff's ability to perceive clearly. Peers who are not in an authority relationship toward each other will both behave more naturally and observe more accurately.

What is true for a temporary system like a training class may even be more valid for an on-the-job situation, affecting the judgment of superiors and colleagues. If we read in the window of Figure 15.1 "superiors" instead of "staff" and interpret "peers" as "colleagues," we can try to apply it more generally to the promotion process in organizations.

In general, leaders are selected on the basis of Areas $a$ and $c$ with probably an implicit belief that Area $c$ (visible to superiors but not to colleagues) is what counts most. The research data collected by others and by me suggest that the crucial areas may be $a$ and especially $b$ (visible to peers but not to superiors). As a practical consequence, promotion based on the *election* of leaders by their colleagues may yield a higher percentage of successful leaders than the usual *selection* by superiors, although this would also introduce an element of competition between peers not present in the peer ratings described in this chapter.

## Discussion Questions

1. What were the various biases found in staff ratings?

2. What is a "suppressor effect"?

3. Why do correlations between ratings of career potential and actual career moves grow stronger over time? Will there be an upper limit to the period for which this applies? What happens afterward?

4. Give examples of behaviors in Areas *b* and *c* of Figure 15.1.

## Notes

1. The product-moment correlation coefficient was .44**. As in earlier chapters, the notation used here is: *** significant at .001 level, ** significant at .01 level, * significant at .05 level.

2. The correlation coefficient between staff ratings and peer ratings was .60***; between staff ratings and career moves, .23*.

3. From 1960-1961, 4-point scales were used; from 1961-1963, 3-point scales. Other factors being equal, these shorter scales could have suppressed some information and led to lower validities of the ratings. We will see, however, that the earlier ratings showed *higher* validities. This therefore cannot have been because of the different rating scales.

4. The correlation coefficient between age and level increase was −.09, not significant.

5. A factor analysis of the five items showed two factors, one with high loadings for "involvement," "problem solving," and "potential for growth" and one with high loadings for "communication" and "maturity." These correspond to the factors found among 13 items by Kraut (1973) and which he calls "impact" and "tactfulness."

6. This is a variant of the "Johari window" developed at National Training Laboratories in the United States by Jo(seph) Luft and Harri(ngton V.) Ingham (Pfeiffer & Jones, 1969, pp. 66ff). The Johari window deals with the two dimensions of characteristics known to self and characteristics known to others.

7. Kraut's measurement period was 2 years against my 3.5 years; his managers moved faster in their careers, however, so that they showed about the same mobility in 2 years (average increase 1.7 levels) as mine did in 3.5 years (average increase 1.4 levels).

8. For $n = 21$, the 95% confidence interval of $r = .46$ is from .02 to .73; for $r = .06$, from −.37 to .46.

# 16

# Business Managers
# and Business School Faculty

## A Comparison of Value Systems

Seventeen faculty members at a European business school scored two values tests, L. V. Gordon's SPV and SIV. Their scores are compared to those of 372 executive course participants in general, to those of 16 U.S. participants in particular, and to those of participants who were rated by the faculty as top performers in class. Results show faculty differ significantly from participants in the direction of more academic values and less will to manage and that this is a role rather than a nationality difference. Results also show that faculty members evaluate participants most highly who have value profiles largely similar to theirs, but higher in "leadership" and relatively low in "independence." These data are considered as a demonstration of the type of organizational socialization business managers undergo during a campus course.

## Values Transfer in Business Schools

What happens to business managers when they return temporarily to a university environment for postexperience development? Such escapes to academia, following the U.S. example, have become more and more

This chapter was originally published in *Journal of Management Studies*, 15(1), 1978, pp. 77-87. Copyright © 1978 by the *Journal of Management Studies*. Reprinted with permission.

common in many European countries. Usually managers are sent by their employing organizations, and it is expected that this investment of time and money will protect those sent from managerial obsolescence and prepare them for higher responsibilities. The actual effects on the sending organizations of these and other management training efforts are, however, notoriously difficult to evaluate, and results of evaluation studies are almost invariably ambiguous.[1] Also, it is doubtful whether the question of the overall effectiveness of management development for organizations is a relevant one. It is a naive assumption that decision makers in organizations will look at the result of evaluation studies to determine whether they should send managers to courses or not. Such decisions, like most policy decisions, are much more likely to be based on personal beliefs and social norms rather than on figures or reports. Another way of saying the same thing is that for the sending organizations, management development is as much a ritual as a rational activity.

If evaluation studies have been generally unsuccessful in showing conclusive effects of management development on sending organizations, they have been much more productive in showing effects on participants as individuals, and to some extent, in contributing to course design. A general conclusion is that the crucial effect of a course seems to be on managers' attitudes and values rather than on their level of knowledge. The effects on the participants depend not only on what happens on the course, but to an even larger extent on factors in their work situation (Handy, 1970). This applies to all kinds of management development courses, including those not in a university setting, but in this chapter I will deal in particular with campus courses.

Schein (1971) has drawn attention to the *organizational socialization* in a school environment, which he defines as "the process by which a new member learns the value system, the norms, and the required behavior pattern of the society, the organization or the group which he is entering" (p. 3). For the organizational socialization process in his own U.S. business school, Schein found that "student attitudes . . . change away from business attitudes toward the faculty position" (p. 3). The large-scale administration of a set of values tests to participants and faculty of one European business school offered an opportunity to study this process of organizational socialization in another setting, with experienced business managers as students.

As Schein suggested, an important role in the socialization process is played by the values of the professors and the way in which they differ from student values. Values of business school faculty have both explicit and implicit components. The explicit ones are already a mixed bag of often more or less conflicting elements: rationality and economic optimization along with social responsibility, participative leadership, and openness in communication. In addition, each professor will have implicit values, which may or may not run parallel with the explicit ones.

As far as the differences between faculty values and business managers' values go we can formulate some a priori hypotheses. First, the professors chose a teaching rather than a managing career for themselves. George Bernard Shaw, in *Man and Superman*, has one of his characters say, "He, who can, does. He, who cannot, teaches." This rather uncomplimentary quotation points to the undeniable fact that the talents of the average professor and the average businessman differ. We can therefore assume in the professor a lower "will to manage" (Miner, 1973), reinforced by the fact that within the university system managing is an activity with a lower status than in business. The academic frame of reference is likely to make values like creativity and independence of thinking more salient to professors than to business managers, although business school professors may be closer to business managers than non-business school professors. At least, this would be in line with U.S. research that showed business school *students* to behave more like young people in business than like, for example, liberal arts students. Among other things, the business school students rarely participated in critical movements and demonstrations (Miner, 1971).

A specific feature of business schools in Europe is their association with U.S. ideas and values. Because of the lack of a business training tradition in Europe, many European business school professors are actually graduates from U.S. universities. Teaching methods and material are often borrowed from across the Atlantic. We can test, therefore, whether business school professors adhere to value patterns that are specifically American. I have demonstrated the existence of value patterns particular to specific national groups elsewhere (Hofstede, 1976a, 1980, 1991).

We could try to test Schein's finding that values of students move toward the faculty position by administering the same values test to participants before and after the course. However, in such a situation the test scores at the end of the course could be simply attributed to a desire to please the faculty without reflecting any deeper values shift. In this study I use another method, which is to look at the evaluation of participants by professors, showing the values profile of students whom the professors rate as top performers. This will show us what values the faculty, by a process of approval and disapproval, implicitly or explicitly encourage in participants. Evidently this will also affect the evaluation of professors by the participants. Schuh and Crivelli (1973) have shown that professors' evaluations of students and students' evaluations of professors are correlated.

## The Research Setting

Data on value systems, based on self-descriptions, were collected among participants in executive development programs at IMEDE,[2] an international business school located in Lausanne, Switzerland, between 1970 and 1973. In the particular programs studied, the teaching language was English, but both participants and faculty came from all over the world (about 40 nationalities were represented). Only about 15% of participants had English as a mother tongue. Their ages ranked from 25 to 45; their business experience from 1 or 2 years to over 20. Most had considerable experience in practicing management jobs. All in all, they formed a highly positive selection of managerial talent. About 99% were male.

At the beginning of each course participants filled out two paper-and-pencil questionnaires designed for measuring value systems: L. V. Gordon's Survey of Personal Values (SPV) and Survey of Interpersonal Values (SIV) (Gordon, 1967, 1976). The results were used in class as an illustration of differences in value systems between persons and groups, but also analyzed for research purposes (Hofstede, 1976a). After four classes of participants had supplied SPV and SIV scores, faculty members were also asked to fill out the questionnaires. In March-April 1972, all but one of the members of the school's faculty supplied SPV and SIV scores, a total of 17 persons, 12 professors and 5 research assistants. Nine of them were U.S. citizens and eight from other countries; all 17 were male.

L. V. Gordon's SPV and SIV were selected as an instrument pair to measure values from among several possible tests because, although they were entirely developed in the United States, experience in the program indicated that they did not contain words or issues unintelligible or ambiguous to non-Americans. The SPV tries to measure value orientation toward work, the SIV toward fellows. The SPV distinguishes six scales, defined here by what high-scoring individuals claim to value:

P—*Practical-Mindedness.* To always get one's money's worth, to take good care of one's property, to get full use out of one's possessions, to do things that will pay off, to be very careful with one's money

A—*Achievement.* To work on difficult problems, to have a challenging job to tackle, to strive to accomplish something significant, to set the highest standards of accomplishment for oneself, to do an outstanding job in anything one tries

V—*Variety.* To do things that are new and different, to have a variety of experiences, to be able to travel a great deal, to go to strange or unusual places, to experience an element of danger

D—*Decisiveness.* To have strong and firm convictions, to make decisions quickly, to always come directly to the point, to make one's position on matters very clear, to come to a decision and stick to it

O—*Orderliness.* To have well-organized work habits, to keep things in their proper place, to be a very orderly person, to follow a systematic approach in doing things, to do things according to a schedule

G—*Goal Orientation.* To have a definite goal toward which to work, to stick to a problem until it is solved, to direct one's effort toward clear-cut objectives, to know precisely where one is headed, to keep one's goals clearly in mind

The SIV also distinguishes six scales:

S—*Support.* Being treated with understanding, receiving encouragement from other people, being treated with kindness and consideration

C—*Conformity.* Doing what is socially correct, following regulations closely, doing what is accepted and proper, being a conformist

R—*Recognition.* Being looked up to and admired, being considered important, attracting favorable notice, achieving recognition

I—*Independence.* Having the right to do whatever one wants to do, being free to make one's own decisions, being able to do things in one's own way

B—*Benevolence.* Doing things for other people, sharing with others, helping the unfortunate, being generous

L—*Leadership.* Being in charge of other people, having authority over others, being in a position of leadership or power

The total number of points for each of the six scales for either instrument should always add up to 90, so that on the average each scale may receive 15 points. The minimum score for any scale is zero points, the maximum varies from 26 to 32 points.

It should be kept in mind that both questionnaires are based on self-description by respondents and thus yield scores of *espoused values*, which may or may not be identical to the values *in use* in different circumstances (Argyris & Schön, 1974). However, for the SIV, which was developed first (in 1960) a considerable body of validation data is available. Some validation is supplied by the identification of categories of people who show specific answer patterns. Gordon (1969) subjected SIV scores of 59 U.S. respondent categories to a Q-analysis and found five clusters of categories, which he calls Q-types:

1. *Institutional restraint,* e.g., prison guards, prisoners, registered nurses— high on Conformity, low on Leadership.

2. *Control of others*, e.g., managers, officers—high on Leadership, low on Support, Benevolence, and Independence.

3. *Service to others*, e.g., teachers, Peace Corps volunteers—high on Benevolence, low on Conformity.

4. *Self-determination*, e.g., male students, engineers—high on Independence, low on Conformity and Benevolence.

5. *Reciprocal support*, e.g., female students—high on Support, low on Leadership, moderately high on Benevolence.

These clusters show that people in the same occupation or life situation do show value patterns that we would logically assume to correspond with these occupations. I will refer back to them later on.

## Results

Mean scores on SPV and SIV for business managers (course participants) and faculty are compared in Table 16.1. The t-test (two-tailed) used for the significance of the differences in scores between the two groups contains an approximation, because the surveys are scored ipsatively; therefore the six scores on either survey are not completely independent. The average expected correlation between each pair of scores on the same survey is $-.20$ (Hicks, 1970) so that $.20^2 = 4\%$ of the variance in one score can be explained by variation in another score. This effect has been neglected. The alternative would have been a comparison of the entire profiles, which would not have allowed a test of differences on individual value dimensions.

Table 16.1 shows that in spite of its small sample size the faculty group scores significantly differently from the business manager-participants on 10 of the 12 value dimensions. Faculty members tend to score higher on Achievement, Variety, Support, Recognition, and Benevolence and lower on Practical-Mindedness, Orderliness, Goal Orientation, Conformity, and Leadership. On Independence, where we do *not* find a significant difference between faculty and participants' mean scores, we find a large faculty standard deviation (8.3). The 95% confidence interval for the standard deviation of a sample of $n = 17$ of the participant population is from 4.5 to 8.0. The faculty standard deviation is outside this limit, so we can conclude that faculty members differ more among themselves on the Independence score than do participants (some of them score very high, others very low on Independence).

The lower Leadership score of faculty can be interpreted as a less pronounced "will to manage," as expected; their higher score on Variety

**TABLE 16.1** Mean Scores on 12 Value Dimensions for Business Managers and Faculty

| | All Business Managers $n = 372$ | U.S. Business Managers Only $n = 16$ | Faculty $n = 17$ |
|---|---|---|---|
| Survey of Personal Values | | | |
| P —Practical-mindedness | 10.9 | 10.6 | 7.9*** |
| A—Achievement | 18.9 | 20.8* | 23.9*** |
| V —Variety | 10.9 | 12.4 | 18.2*** |
| D—Decisiveness | 15.1 | 15.7 | 15.5 |
| O—Orderliness | 14.5 | 13.3 | 10.3*** |
| G—Goal orientation | 19.6 | 17.2 | 14.2*** |
| Survey of Interpersonal Values | | | |
| S —Support | 12.8 | 13.3 | 16.0*** |
| C —Conformity | 11.1 | 8.1* | 5.5** |
| R —Recognition | 8.4 | 12.2** | 11.2* |
| I —Independence | 20.1 | 17.5 | 21.1 |
| B —Benevolence | 14.1 | 15.2 | 17.1* |
| L —Leadership | 23.3 | 23.6 | 19.2*** |

NOTE: Differences between the first and second and between the first and third columns have been tested with the *t* test, two-tailed.

as more of an interest in new things and more creativity; their lower score on Conformity as a need for intellectual freedom. We do *not* find that professors score consistently higher on Independence, however, which would have been in line with our expectations. Professors score low on typical business values like Practical-Mindedness, Orderliness, and Goal Orientation. They are also ambitious, which is shown by high scores on Achievement and Recognition, and they are socially oriented, which is shown by high scores on both Support and Benevolence.

Comparing both participants and faculty to Gordon's Q-types as described above can be done by calculating the average of the score differences.[3] Participants correspond more than faculty to Type 2 (Control of Others), but faculty more than participants to Type 4 (Self-Determination) and to Type 3 (Service to Others);[4] both groups are very unlike Types 1 and 5. We see that our business managers score more like U.S. managers and our faculty more like students and teachers. Therefore, the differences we found between business managers and faculty are in the same direction as those in similar U.S. data.

As more than half of our faculty was American and most others were trained in the United States, whereas participants were overwhelmingly

**TABLE 16.2** Number of U.S. and Non-U.S. Faculty Members Showing One or
More Deviant Value Scores

| Nationality of Faculty | Showing One or More Deviant Value Scores | Showing No Deviant Value Scores | Total |
|---|---|---|---|
| U.S. | 2 | 7 | 9 |
| Non-U.S. | 6 | 2 | 8 |
| Total | 8 | 9 | 17 |

NOTE: Difference between U.S. and non-U.S. faculty, tested by Fisher's exact test, significant at
.007 level.

non-American, we may wonder to what extent the value differences
between faculty and participants were due to nationality rather than to
role (the latter meaning, being either a professor or a business manager).
Role and nationality effects can be separated by looking at the scores of
the minority of participants who were U.S. nationals ($n = 16$). These
scores are shown in the second column of Table 16.1. We see that U.S.
participants score significantly differently from other participants on
three dimensions only. It is remarkable that for 10 of the 12 dimensions
(all but Independence and Leadership) the U.S. participants score on the
same side of the total participants' mean as the faculty. We conclude that
we cannot explain the score differences between faculty and participants
away by the faculty being American; that the role difference prevails, but
that some nationality effect *is* present.

This nationality trend is also visible in Table 16.2, in which faculty
scores are presented separately for U.S. nationals and non-U.S. nationals.
For the 10 value dimensions for which there is a significant difference
between business managers and faculty (all but Decisiveness and Independence), Table 16.2 lists the number of faculty with "deviant" scores,
that is, scores on the other side of the participants' mean than the majority
of the faculty. We see that most of the "deviant" scores are from the
non-U.S. faculty. Their scores are less "typical," which implies that the
"typical" faculty scores do show a U.S. nationality pattern.

## Faculty Values in Action:
## The Evaluation of Participants

If the faculty values shown by the test scores are not only espoused on
paper but also operational, they will play a role in the socialization of
participants, if not explicitly then at least implicitly. Professors influence

participants, among other things, by showing approval or disapproval. By looking at the values of participants rated most favorably by their professors we can find out which values professors try to transfer. In one class of 64 participants, we collected at the end of the course *evaluations* of all participants by the 7 faculty members mainly involved in teaching this course. These 7 faculty members could, as far as their own value scores were concerned, be considered a random sample of the total group of 17. Participants' value scores had been collected during the first week of the course, 4 months before the evaluations. The faculty members who evaluated had no access to these value scores. Each faculty member evaluated each participant's performance in his subject. These evaluations were subjective, based on the participant's participation in classroom discussions during the 4 months of the course and on one written piece of work. The seven ratings for each participant were combined in order to divide participants into top, middle, and lower third. In Table 16.3, we compare faculty mean scores to those of the 22 top-performing participants and of the remaining 42.

In Table 16.3 we see that in 10 of the 12 value dimensions those participants receiving top-third evaluations scored their own values in the expected direction, that is, more similar to the faculty's values than the other participants, but only in three cases (Achievement, Orderliness, and Recognition) was this trend statistically significant. For Variety and Independence the difference was just over the .05 significance level. For Independence and Leadership, participants receiving top ratings did *not* score more like the faculty than participants receiving lower ratings. Comparing Tables 16.1 and 16.3, we notice that for all 12 dimensions, top performers scored to the same side of the total participants' mean as U.S. participants did. We can therefore also expect that the U.S. participants had a high probability of being rated top performers. Of the 5 U.S. participants in our class of 64, 4 were rated top performers.

## Discussion

In IMEDE in 1971-1973, faculty members espoused values that differed from those of the average business managers who attended their courses. Professors' values were more academic and to some extent also more "American," but the role difference was considerably more important than the nationality difference.

This faculty, in evaluating participants, favored those with value patterns more like their own. Evaluation contains an element of "playing God"—like God, in evaluating we try to create people in our own image,

**TABLE 16.3** Mean Scores on 12 Value Dimensions for Faculty, Top Third, and Remainder of Class

|  | *Faculty* <br> *n = 17* | *Top Third* <br> *of Class* <br> *n = 22* | *Remainder* <br> *of Class* <br> *n = 42* |
|---|---|---|---|
| Survey of Personal Values |  |  |  |
| P —Practical-Mindedness | 7.9 | 9.9 | 11.4 |
| A—Achievement | 23.9 | 21.0* | 18.1 |
| V—Variety | 18.2 | 14.5 | 11.4 |
| D—Decisiveness | 15.5 | 15.4 | 14.6 |
| O—Orderliness | 10.3 | 12.4* | 15.4 |
| G—Goal Orientation | 14.2 | 17.0 | 18.4 |
| Survey of Interpersonal Values |  |  |  |
| S —Support | 16.0 | 13.7 | 12.5 |
| C—Conformity | 5.5 | 8.7 | 11.0 |
| R—Recognition | 11.2 | 11.3* | 7.6 |
| I —Independence | 21.1 | 16.9 | 19.9 |
| B —Benevolence | 17.1 | 15.8 | 15.6 |
| L —Leadership | 19.2 | 23.6 | 22.7 |

NOTE: Difference between top third and total class, tested by $t$ test, significant with *$p < .05$, one-tailed.

although this will often be an unconscious process, as it must have been in the case described.

It is interesting to analyze the exceptions to the general trends found. Both in testing for the "American" component in the faculty values (Table 16.1) and in testing for the similarity of the values of professors and top class performers (Table 16.3), the scores on Leadership and on Independence did not go in the expected direction. Professors score relatively low on Leadership. They have a lower "will to manage," whereas the "American" profile is characterized by a relatively strong will to manage. However, professors do reward a strong will to manage in their course participants: In this respect, they do not expect them to be like themselves. The differences in role dominate over the similarity in values.

For the dimension of Independence, we have seen that faculty members' scores spread widely; the group contains both very high and very low scores (in this case, it can be shown that the faculty's position on the scale has nothing to do with their nationality). Whatever the professors' own value system, the participants who get rewarded tend to be more on the low Independence side than on the high one, and this again corresponds to the "American" pattern. The wide spread on Independence suggests that among business school professors we will meet solo players and team players. But even solo players do not try to encourage their students to be solo players like themselves. As a professor, I can do my thing only if others are willing also, to some extent, to do *my* thing, and not theirs.

Thus the values that these professors consciously or unconsciously try to transfer would, according to our data, be more Achievement and more need for Recognition, less than average Orderliness, more need for Variety, but not too much Independence. These are elements of the organizational socialization process taking place at the business school studied. We have to speculate on whether they would also apply to other business schools in Europe, or whether this is a special case. My guess is that it is *not* a special case and that this set of values to be transferred is fairly typical for business schools in general.

The pragmatic business manager will ask, But are these school values functional in business? Do they contribute to the success of the organizations that sent these participants? In the introduction to this chapter I raised doubts as to whether such a question can ever be answered, and even whether it is relevant in spite of its apparent logic. What we can safely assume is that a business school course will be more functional for managers in organizations in which achievement, recognition, and variety are already at a premium. To the extent that the business school value system differs from the work organization value system, our managers will be quickly resocialized to work values on return. In this case the course is not very likely to have benefited the sending organization. To the individual who was sent, the temporary exposure to a different value system may have been either an enriching or a frustrating experience. In fact, every business school has its anecdotes of participants who became so frustrated on return to their work situation that they quit, and encouraged by the course experience, took a new job more in line with their own values.

## Discussion Questions

1. Can the difference in value scores between course participants and faculty be mainly explained by their jobs or by their nationality?

2. On what values did the faculty most differ from the participants, in what way, and how do you explain this?

3. What do you conclude from the fact that participants rated in the top third of the class scored more like the faculty than the others?

4. Can a 5-month management course change a manager's basic values?

# Notes

1. See for example Hamblin (1974), Hesseling (1966), Kile (1969), Sainsaulieu (1974), and Van der Vegt (1973).

2. Now merged with IMI (formerly CEI) of Geneva into IMD, Lausanne.

3. If the differences are called $\Delta$, the average $\Delta = \sqrt{\Sigma \Delta^2 / 6}$ .

4. For Control of Others: $D_{part} = 3.6$, $D_{fac} = 6.0$; for Self-Determination: $D_{part} = 3.5$, $D_{fac} = 2.6$; for Service to Others: $D_{part} = 4.0$, $D_{fac} = 3.5$.

# 17

# Frustrations of Personnel Managers

The results of two exercises completed in the management training center of a large multinational corporation are used to analyze the role of the personnel function in this corporation. The first exercise, held among 19 nonpersonnel managers, collected descriptive statements about different functions, including personnel. The statements about personnel described it as good at dealing with people, but weak at dealing with other parts of the organization, and as static and low status. The second exercise, among 17 personnel managers, collected descriptions of their department's objectives and about their personal job objectives. They saw their departments as mostly succeeding in their operational objectives but failing in their creative objectives, whereas personally they found their successes in creative contributions rather than in operational ones. This is interpreted as a situation of frustration caused by the ambiguity in the role that the organization allows its personnel departments to play.

## The Ambiguous Role
## of the Personnel Department

The role of the personnel department varies considerably from one organization to another. There is much less consensus between organizations on what the personnel function should do than on the roles of other functions, such as manufacturing, marketing, finance, or research and development. On one side of the scale one finds low-status person-

This chapter was originally published in *Management International Review*, 13(4-5), 1973, pp. 127-143. Copyright © 1973 by the *Management International Review*. Reprinted with permission.

nel departments doing little more than wage and salary administration, and on the other side high-status groups carrying the same name but deeply involved in the organization's long-term objective setting and in the development of its management structure, with all kinds of varieties in between. This same lack of consensus is reflected in the hierarchical position of the top personnel officer, who may be anything from a member of the top-management team, reporting to the chief executive, down to a simple clerk.

Equally striking are the differences in education and experience among personnel managers. It is far from clear what it takes to be a good personnel officer. In Europe, most personnel officers and managers have one of the following backgrounds: (a) an academic degree in law; (b) an academic degree in business administration; (c) an academic or subacademic degree in one of the social sciences; (d) a career as a regular officer in the military services; (e) an administrative career in the company as an accountant or salary administrator; or (f) a technical career in the company, for example, as a production manager, sales manager, or engineer.

Qualifications differ from country to country: For example, in a survey held in 1966, lawyers in personnel functions appeared to be particularly popular in France, Spain, Austria, and Germany; business administration graduates predominated in Italy, social scientists in the Netherlands and Switzerland (Rubenowitz, 1968). One frequently hears about former military officers in personnel jobs in Great Britain and Sweden. There is a relationship between the qualifications of the top personnel manager and those in lower ranks: Lawyers tend to hire lawyers, psychologists hire psychologists, army officers hire other military personnel. Also, the qualifications of the top personnel manager tend to give an indication of the department's priorities. For a lawyer, these may be the implementation of collective contracts and labor laws, and the settling of grievances; for someone with an administrative background, the stress may be on salary and benefits administration, and for a psychologist, on personnel selection and management development.

The ambiguity about the role of the personnel department does not only exist from one organization to another. Even within organizations different people have different expectations on what the personnel department should do. An important question is whether there are any specific interests for which the personnel function should fight. Other departments have their interests, which everybody in the organization expects them to defend. In a manufacturing company, for example, the Production departments can be expected to fight for a minimum of product changes. The Sales departments fight for maximum flexibility in scheduling according to customers' demands. The Controller's department fights for cost reduction. But what does the personnel department fight for? Often, managers of other departments do not expect it to fight for anything at all, but just to implement the other departments' decisions with a minimum of trouble on the part of individual employees or labor unions. In this conception, a "good" personnel department is one that avoids risks and does not "rock the boat." It is still relatively rare to find an organization where a personnel director can successfully defend a line of action against other departments' resistance in the interest of, for example, long-term employee quality or morale.

W. French and Henning (1966) reported on the role ambiguity of U.S. personnel managers as far back as 1966. Odiorne, writing in 1971, distinguished a "high road" and a "low road" in U.S. personnel management: The high road meant involvement in setting objectives and policies, the low road only in setting procedures and rules. From contacts with personnel officers in different organizations and parts of the world, I believe this distinction is as valid in 1993 as it was when Odiorne's book appeared.

The lack of role clarity from which many personnel departments suffer impacts their status and image in the organization as well as the job satisfaction of the personnel officers. The image spread by personnel departments in one particular large company and the kinds of frustrations experienced by their members will be described below.

## The Image of the Personnel Function

The material for this chapter was collected in two exercises used during management courses. Both were carried out in the international management training and development center of a large multinational corporation known for its progressive personnel policies.

The first exercise dealt with the image of the personnel function held by others in this organization. Members of a general management course, a mixed group of 19 middle-level managers from various countries and various functions in the company (but not from personnel), were asked to fill out a questionnaire. This questionnaire dealt with what they thought were typical characteristics of managers in six different functional areas of the company. One of the six was personnel. They were asked to describe these typical characteristics in short statements, in their own words.

The 19 managers produced an average of about 4 statements per functional area per person—a total of 72 statements on the personnel function alone. Fifty-one (71%) of these statements could be classified as favorable, and 21 (29%) as unfavorable. A similar distribution of favorable versus unfavorable statements was found for three of the other five functional areas. Only the sales function received a significantly higher percentage of favorable statements, and sales administration, a separate group in this organization, a significantly higher percentage of unfavorable statements.

Both the positive and the negative statements could be classified into eight categories:

1. Communication (17 positive statements, 1 negative)
2. Concern for people (16 positive, 2 negative)
3. Maturity (6 positive, 1 negative)
4. Problem-solving skill (1 positive)
5. Concern for company policy (5 positive, 3 negative)
6. Helpfulness to others (3 positive, 5 negative)
7. Dynamism (3 positive, 6 negative)
8. Status (3 negative)

Categories 1 to 5 received predominantly positive answers and 6 to 8 predominantly negative. Typical positive comments were "good communicators" (Category 1) and "people oriented" (Category 2). Typical negative comments were "inflexible" (Category 5), "always seem tired" (Category 6), "administrative, not creative," "unimaginative" and "safety minded" (Category 7) and "not glamorous" (Category 8). The statements can be summarized as follows: The personnel function in this company is perceived to be good at dealing with people, but less good at dealing with other parts of the organization, at helping the organization as a whole to change, and at carrying out anything more than a static role, hence its lower status.

## Creative Versus Operational Contributions

The second exercise was carried out among an international group of 17 male personnel managers of the same multinational corporation. They were going to participate in a special seminar, and to help in planning the program, they were asked to complete a "problem identification questionnaire," which had to be mailed to the seminar staff a few weeks before the seminar date. This questionnaire asked two kinds of questions:

1. About their views on their department's objectives in general
2. About their views on their own personal job objectives

Both types of objectives (the department's and the personal) could when analyzed by the seminar staff be divided into *creative* contributions to the organization on the one side, and *operational* contributions on the other side. Creative contributions dealt with building the organizational system, policy making, and setting and changing the rules. Operational contributions dealt with fulfilling one's role in the organizational system and operating according to the rules that had been set.

The *creative contributions* mentioned by the personnel managers could be divided into 15 categories:

1. Planning the personnel structure
2. Planning the job structure
3. Developing new training methods—planning employee development
4. Planning careers
5. Selecting future managers
6. Planning the management structure
7. Developing employment conditions that will keep good employees within the company
8. Developing improved ways of personnel administration
9. Developing personnel policies that contribute to motivation
10. Personnel research
11. Developing internal communication channels
12. Developing worker representative and union relationships
13. Building the company's image on the labor market and to the outside world
14. Contributing to the company's strategic and operating plans
15. Developing their own department, subordinates, etc.

The first 10 of these objectives were both mentioned as objectives for the *department* and as *personal* objectives; the last 5 only as personal objectives.

The *operational contributions* mentioned by the personnel managers could also be divided into 15 categories, related to the 15 creative categories described above:

1. Recruiting quantity and quality
2. Fitting people to jobs

3. Training and developing people
4. Transferring, promoting, and terminating
5. Training and developing managers
6. Helping managers in dealing with people
7. Administering salary and benefits programs
8. Maintaining a personnel administration
9. Implementing the company's personnel policies and practices
10. Signaling morale problems
11. Providing information to and communicating with employees and managers
12. Maintaining the company's industrial relations policies
13. Maintaining outside contacts, e.g., with universities
14. Operating within budgetary limits
15. Managing their own department

Again, the first 10 were both mentioned as objectives for the department and as personal objectives, the last 5 only as personal objectives. Together the two lists cover about all imaginable objectives of a personnel function and show that these personnel managers had a quite sophisticated view of the potential roles of their departments.

In the "problem identification questionnaire" the personnel managers were also asked, after they had stated their department's and personal job objectives, to describe for every objective some examples of successes and failures in achieving them, in their own job experience over the past 2 years.

Table 17.1 lists the number of times the various objectives were mentioned as successes, neutral cases, or failures. For *successes*, the description showed that the objective was satisfactorily achieved. For *neutral cases*, no comments were given that allowed a determination whether the objective had really been met. For *failures*, it was mentioned that the objective had not satisfactorily been realized.

Table 17.1 shows a difference between the degree of successful completion of objectives for the personnel departments in general and for the personnel managers personally. The objectives dealing with *creative* contributions to the organization are described predominantly as successes in so far as they were personal objectives of the personnel manager, but as failures in so far as they were objectives of the personnel department. The reverse is true for the objectives dealing with *operational* contributions.

**TABLE 17.1**  A Classification of the Answers by 17 Personnel Managers on a Problem Identification Questionnaire

| Number of Times Mentioned | For the Personnel Department in General | For the Personnel Manager Personally |
|---|---|---|
| Creative Contributions | | |
| Successes | 6 | 18 |
| Neutral cases | 7 | 19 |
| Failures | 21 | 6 |
| | | |
| Total | 34 | 43 |
| | | |
| Operational Contributions | | |
| | | |
| Successes | 31 | 19 |
| Neutral cases | 13 | 27 |
| Failures | 13 | 25 |
| | | |
| Total | 57 | 71 |

NOTE: Differences between columns are statistically significant: chi-square with 2 $df$ = 19.2*** for creative contributions, 10.1** for operational contributions.

## Conclusions

The interpretation of this result is that these personnel managers see themselves as operating in departments that usually succeed in their operational contributions to the organization (keeping the organizational machine running, operating according to the rules that were set). The departments, however, mostly fail in their creative contributions to the organization. This much is the picture for the personnel departments. The personnel managers themselves experience more personal failures than successes in their operational contributions, and more personal successes than failures in their creative contributions.

This is a picture of frustration. It confirms the image of the personnel function found among other managers in the corporation, that of the function carrying out a predominantly static role. It is not in this role, however, that the personnel managers experience their own successes. It is in the creative contributions to the organization, where they feel their department mostly fails, that they find their personal success experiences. This means a mismatch between personal ambitions and organizational opportunities that we can interpret as an outcome of the lack of role clarity described earlier. This situation cannot just be blamed on the personnel department. It is at least as much determined by the role those who set the organization's rules allow the personnel department to play.

The results of the second exercise can also be explained in another way: When a personnel department fails, the personnel manager sees it as the organization's fault. Where the department succeeds, he sees it as his own personal success. This illustrates the general human characteristic of taking credit for our successes and blaming our failures on others, as emphasized by the attribution theory in psychology. But for the personnel manager this phenomenon occurs only for his or her creative, not for his or her operational contributions. This alternative explanation therefore does not detract from the conclusion that the personnel managers in our sample, who work for a progressive company, still see their departments as predominantly operational and not creative, and that they are personally frustrated by this state of affairs.

The exercises on which this chapter has been based were completed by two small groups of people in one particular organization. The literature cited at the beginning of this chapter reported that the role ambiguity of the personnel department, which seems to be at the root of the problem, was also found in broad surveys of personnel managers. Our data therefore illustrate a phenomenon that is probably fairly general and that readers may recognize in their own organization. Only strong support for the personnel department's creative role by the central decision makers in the organization can change this situation. Of course this presupposes that the key people in personnel be selected from among persons whose abilities and personalities enable them to fight successfully for the fulfillment of their department's creative objectives. Organizations get the personnel managers they deserve.

## Discussion Questions

1. Was the image of the personnel function in the image study worse than that of most other functions?

2. What criterion was used to label an objective as a *creative* or as an *operational* contribution?

3. What forces in an organization prevent the personnel function from being creative?

4. What kind of persons, in your experience, feel attracted to a personnel job?

# References

Aldridge, J. F. L. (1970). Emotional illness and the working environment. *Ergonomics, 13,* 613-621.

Anthony, R. N., Dearden, J., & Vancil, R. F. (1972). *Management control systems: Text, cases and readings* (rev. ed.). Homewood, IL: R. D. Irwin.

Anthony, R. N., & Herzlinger, R. (1975). *Management control in nonprofit organizations.* Homewood, IL: R. D. Irwin.

Argyris, C. (1952). *The impact of budgets on people.* Ithaca, NY: School of Business and Public Administration, Cornell University.

Argyris, C. (1953). Human problems with budgets. *Harvard Business Review, 1,* 97-110.

Argyris, C. (1972). Do personal growth laboratories represent an alternative culture? *Journal of Applied Behavioral Science, 8,* 7-28.

Argyris, C., & Schön, D. A. (1974). *Theory in practice: Increasing professional effectiveness.* San Francisco: Jossey-Bass.

Bairstow, F. (1974). Professionalism and unionism: Are they compatible? *Industrial Engineering, 6*(4), 40-42.

Barnowe, J. T., Mangione, T. W., & Quinn, R. P. (1973). The relative importance of job facets as indicated by an empirically derived model of work satisfaction. In R. P. Quinn & T. W. Mangione (Eds.), *The 1969-1970 survey of working conditions* (pp. 263-320). Ann Arbor, MI: Institute for Social Research.

Bartell, T. (1976). The human relations ideology: An analysis of the social origins of a belief system. *Human Relations, 29*(8), 737-749.

Bartölke, K., & Gohl, J. (1976). *A critical perspective on humanization actions and ongoing experiments in Germany* (Arbeitspapiere des Fachbereichs Wirtschaftswissenschaft der Gesamthochschule Wuppertal, No. 16). Wuppertal, Germany: Gesamthochschule Wuppertal.

Bishop, C. H. (1950). *All things common.* New York: Harper & Bros.

Blauner, R. (1964). *Alienation and freedom.* Chicago: University of Chicago Press.

Bonini, C. P. (1964). Simulation of organizational behavior. In C. P. Bonini, R. K. Jaedicke, & H. M. Wagner (Eds.), *Management controls* (pp. 91-101). New York: McGraw-Hill.

Bovenkerk, F., & Brunt, L. (1976). *Binnenstebuiten en ondersteboven: De anthropologie van de industriële samenleving.* Assen, Netherlands: Van Gorcum.

Bovenkerk, F., & Brunt, L. (1977). *De rafelrand van Amsterdam: Jordaners, pinda-chinezen, ateliermeisjes en venters in de jaren dertig.* Meppel, Netherlands: Boom.

Bowers, D. G. (1973). OD techniques and their results in 23 organizations: The Michigan ICL study. *Journal of Applied Behavioral Science, 9,* 21-43.

Bradford, L. P., Gibb, J. R., & Benne, K. D. (Eds.). (1964). *T-group theory and laboratory method: Innovation in re-education.* New York: John Wiley.

Bray, D. W., & Grant, D. L. (1966). The assessment center in the measurement of potential for business management. *Psychological Monographs, 80*(17), whole no. 625.

Bruns, W. J., Jr., & De Coster, D. T. (Eds.). (1969). *Accounting and its behavioral implications.* New York: McGraw-Hill.

Burnham, J. (1962). *The managerial revolution.* London: Penguin. (Original work published 1941)

Caplan, E. H. (1966 & 1968). Behavioral assumptions of management accounting. *Accounting Review, 41,* 496-509, and *43,* 342-362.

Caplan, R. D., Cobb, S., French, J.R.P., Harrison, R. V., & Pinneau, R. (1975). *Job demands and worker health: Main effects and occupational differences.* Ann Arbor, MI: Institute for Social Research.

Cohen, M. D., March, J. G., & Olsen, J. P. (1972). A garbage can model of organizational choice. *Administrative Science Quarterly, 17,* 1-25.

Crozier, M. (1964). *The bureaucratic phenomenon.* Chicago: University of Chicago Press.

Crozier, M. (1976). Comparing structures and comparing games. In G. Hofstede & M. S. Kassem (Eds.), *European contributions to organization theory* (pp. 193-207). Assen, Netherlands: Van Gorcum.

Delplanque, B. (1976). Aspects humains de l'amélioration des conditions de travail. *Direction et Gestion, 5,* 31-37.

Desplanques, G. (1973). À 35 ans, les instituteurs ont encore 41 ans a vivre, les manoeuvres 34 ans seulement. *Economie et Statistique, 49,* 3-19.

d'Iribarne, P. (1989). *La logique de l'honneur: Gestion des entreprises et traditions nationales.* Paris: Éditions du Seuil.

Dodd, W. E., Wollowick, H. B., & McNamara, W. J. (1970). Task difficulty as a moderator of long-range prediction. *Journal of Applied Psychology, 54,* 265-270.

Dunn, J. P., & Cobb, S. (1962). Frequency of peptic ulcer among executives, craftsmen and foremen. *Journal of Occupational Medicine, 4,* 373-348.

Du Teil, R. (1949). *Communauté de travail.* Paris: Presses Universitaires de France.

Foy, N., & Gadon, H. (1976). Worker participation: Contrasts in three countries. *Harvard Business Review, 54*(3), 71-83.

French, J.R.P., & Caplan, R. D. (1972). Organizational stress and individual strain. In A. J. Marrow (Ed.), *The failure of success* (pp. 30-66). New York: Amacom.

French, W., & Henning, D. (1966). The authority-influence role of the functional specialist in management. *Academy of Management Journal, 9,* 187-203.

Friedlander, F. (1965). Comparative work value systems. *Personnel Psychology, 18*(1), 1-20.

Friedman, M., & Rosenman, R. H. (1975). *Type A behavior and your heart.* Greenwich, CT: Fawcett Crest.

Friedmann, G. (1954). *Problèmes humains du machinisme industriel.* Paris: Gallimard. (Original work published 1946)

Friedmann, G. (1963). *Où va le travail humain?* Paris: Gallimard. (Original work published 1950)

Friedmann, G. (1964). *Le travail en miettes: spécialisation et loisirs.* Paris: Gallimard. (Original work published 1956)

Gadourek, I. (1965). *Absences and well-being of workers.* Assen, the Netherlands: Van Gorcum.

George, C. S. (1972). *The history of management thought*. Englewood Cliffs, NJ: Prentice-Hall.

Gerth, H. H., & Mills, C. W. (Eds.). (1948). *From Max Weber: Essays in sociology*. London: Routledge & Kegan Paul.

Giglioni, G. B., & Bedeian, A. G. (1974). A conspectus of management control theory: 1900-1972. *Academy of Management Journal, 17*, 292-305.

Gohl, J. (1976). Zu Ansätzen der Humanisierungs-debatte. *Zeitschrift für Arbeitswissenschaft, 30*(1), 1-8.

Goldthorpe, H., Lockwood, D., Bechhofer, F., & Platt, J. (1968). *The affluent worker: Industrial attitudes and behaviour*. Cambridge, UK: Cambridge University Press.

Gordon, L. V. (1967). *Survey of personal values—Manual*. Chicago: Science Research Associates.

Gordon, L. V. (1969). Q-typing: An exploration in personality measurement. *Journal of Social Psychology, 78*, 121-136.

Gordon, L. V. (1976). *Survey of interpersonal values—Revised manual*. Chicago: Science Research Associates.

Gordon, L. V., & Medland, F. F. (1965). The cross-group stability of peer ratings of leadership potential. *Personnel Psychology, 18*, 173-177.

Habermas, J. (1973). *Legitimationsprobleme im Spätkapitalismus*. Frankfurt, Germany: Suhrkamp.

Hackman, J. R., & Lawler, E. E. (1971). Employee reactions to job characteristics. *Journal of Applied Psychology Monograph, 55*(3), 259-286.

Hägg, I. (1974). Reviews of capital investments. In S. Asztely (Ed.), *Budgeting och redovisning som instrument for styrning* (pp. 53-68). Stockholm: P. A. Norstedt.

Hall, D. T., & Mansfield, R. (1971). Organizational and individual responses to external stress. *Administrative Science Quarterly, 16*, 533-547.

Hamblin, A. C. (1974). *Evaluation and control of training*. London: McGraw-Hill.

Handy, C. B. (1970). The problem of attitude change in management education. *Journal of Management Studies, 7*(1), 37-44.

Harrison, R. (1962). Impact of the laboratory on perceptions of others by the experimental group. In C. Argyris, *Interpersonal competence and organizational effectiveness* (pp. 261-285). Homewood, IL: Irwin-Dorsey.

Herrick, N. Q. (1973). The new generation of workers. In R. P. Quinn & T. W. Mangione (Eds.), *The 1969-1970 survey of working conditions* (chap. 17). Ann Arbor, MI: Institute for Social Research.

Herzberg, F. (1966). *Work and the nature of man*. Cleveland, OH: World Publishing.

Herzberg, F., Mausner, B., & Snyderman, B. B. (1959). *The motivation to work*. New York: John Wiley.

Hespe, G., & Wall, T. (1976). The demand for participation among employees. *Human Relations, 29*(5), 411-428.

Hesseling, P. (1966). *Strategy of evaluation research*. Assen, Netherlands: Van Gorcum.

Hicks, L. E. (1970). Some properties of ipsative, normative and forced-choice normative measures. *Psychological Bulletin, 74*(3), 167-184.

Hofstede, G. (1967). *The game of budget control*. Assen, Netherlands: Van Gorcum. (Reprinted in 1968 by Tavistock, London)

Hofstede, G. (1975-1976). The importance of being Dutch: National and occupational differences in work goal importance. *International Studies of Management and Organization, 5*(4), 5-28.

Hofstede, G. (1976a). Nationality and espoused values of managers. *Journal of Applied Psychology, 61*(2), 148-155.

Hofstede, G. (1976b). *The construct validity of attitude survey questions dealing with work goals*. Brussels: European Institute for Advanced Studies in Management.

Hofstede, G. (1980). *Culture's consequences: International differences in work-related values.* Beverly Hills, CA: Sage.

Hofstede, G. (1991). *Cultures and organizations: Software of the mind.* London: McGraw-Hill.

Hofstede, G., & Kranenburg, R. Y. (1974). Work goals of migrant workers. *Human Relations, 27*(1), 83-99.

Hofstede, G., Kraut, A. I., & Simonetti, S. H. (1976). *The development of a core attitude survey questionnaire for international use.* Brussels: European Institute for Advanced Studies in Management.

Hofstede, G., & Van Hoesel, P. (1976). *Within-culture and between-culture component structures of work goals in a heterogeneous population.* Brussels: European Institute for Advanced Studies in Management.

Hollingshead, A. B., & Redlich, F. C. (1958). *Social class and mental illness.* New York: John Wiley.

Hopwood, A. G. (1973). *An accounting system and managerial behaviour.* London: Saxon House/Lexington Books.

Hulin, C. I., & Bloom, M. R. (1968). Job enlargement, individual differences and worker responses. *Psychological Bulletin, 69*(1), 41-55.

Ivancevich, J. M. (1974). Changes in performance in a management by objectives program. *Administrative Science Quarterly, 19,* 563-577.

Jenkins, C. D. (1971). Psychologic and social precursors of coronary disease. *New England Journal of Medicine, 2845,* 244-255, and *2846,* 307-312.

Johnson, R. A., Kast, F. E., & Rosenzweig, J. E. (1963). *The theory and management of systems.* New York: McGraw-Hill.

Jonas, H. (1953). A critique of cybernetics. *Social Research, 20,* 172-192.

Juran, J. M. (1964). *Managerial breakthrough: A new concept of the manager's job.* New York: McGraw-Hill.

Kahn, R. L., & Quinn, R. P. (1970). Role stress: A framework for analysis. In A. McLean (Ed.), *Mental health and work organizations* (pp. 50-115). Chicago: Rand McNally.

Kahn, R. L., Wolfe, D. M., Quinn, R. P., Snoek, J. D., & Rosenthal, R. A. (Eds.). (1964). *Organizational stress: Studies in role conflict and ambiguity.* New York: John Wiley.

Kasl, S. V., & French, J.R.P. (1962). The effects of occupational status on physical and mental health. *Journal of Social Issues, 18,* 67-89.

Kets de Vries, M.F.R., Zaleznik, A., & Howard, J. H. (1975). *Stress reactions and organizations: The minotaur revisited.* Montreal: Faculty of Management, McGill University.

Kile, S. M. (1969). *Evaluation of management training.* Bergen, Norway: Institutet for Arbeidspsykologi og Personalforvaltning, Norges Handelshøyskole.

Kirsch, W. (1973). Auf dem Weg zu einem neuen Taylorismus? *IBM Nachrichten, 23,* 561-566.

Klein, L. (1976). *New forms of work organization.* Cambridge, UK: Cambridge University Press.

Kornhauser, A. (1965). *Mental health of the industrial worker: A Detroit study.* New York: John Wiley.

Kraut, A. I. (1969). Intellectual ability and promotional success among high-level managers. *Personnel Psychology, 22,* 281-290.

Kraut, A. I. (1973, November). *The use of ratings by peers and training staff to predict high level managers' success* (Working paper 194/173). Tel Aviv: Leon Recanati Graduate School of Business Administration, Tel Aviv University.

Kraut, A. I., & Ronen, S. (1975). Validity of job facet importance: A multinational, multi-criterion study. *Journal of Applied Psychology, 60,* 671-677.

Kuylaars, A. M. (1951). *Werk en leven van de industriële loonarbeider, als object van een sociale ondernemingspolitiek.* Leiden, Netherlands: Stenfert Kroese.

Lafargue, P. (1975). *Le droit à la paresse.* Paris: François Maspéro. (Original work published 1880)

Laurent, H. (1961, August). *Summary report of the early identification of management potential research project.* Social Science Research Division of the Employee Relations Department, Standard Oil Co., NJ.

Lawrence, P. R., & Lorsch, J. W. (1967). *Organization and environment: Managing differentiation and integration.* Boston, MA: Harvard Business School.

Levinson, H. (1970). Management by whose objectives? *Harvard Business Review, 48*(4), 125-134.

Levinson, H., & Weinbaum, L. (1970). The impact of organization on mental health. In A. McLean (Ed.), *Mental health and work organizations* (pp. 23-49). Chicago: Rand McNally.

Lieberman, M. A., Yalom, I. D., & Miles, M. B. (1972). The impact of encounter groups on participants: Some preliminary findings. *Journal of Applied Behavioral Science, 8,* 29-50.

Likert, R. (1961). *New patterns of management.* New York: McGraw-Hill.

Lindblom, C. E. (1959). The science of muddling through. *Public Administration Review, 191,* 78-88.

March, J. G., & Olsen, J. P. (1976). *Ambiguity and choice in organizations.* Bergen, Norway: Universitetsforlaget.

Marriott, R. (1971). *Incentive payment systems: A review of research and opinion* (4th ed.). London: Staples.

Marx, K. (1966). *Texte zu Methode und Praxis II: Pariser Manuskripte.* Reinbek bei Hamburg, Germany: Rowohlt. (Original work published 1844)

Maslow, A. H. (1970). *Motivation and personality.* New York: Harper & Row.

Mayo, E. (1933). *The human problems of an industrial civilization.* New York: Macmillan.

McGregor, D. (1960). *The human side of enterprise.* New York: McGraw-Hill.

Meister, A. (1958). *Les communauté de travail: Bilan d'une expérience de propriété et de gestion collectives.* Paris: Entente Communautaire.

Mermoz, M. (1978). *L'autogestion c'est pas de la tarte.* Paris: Éditions du Seuil.

Miles, R. E., & Vergin, R. C. (1966). Behavioral properties of variance controls. *California Management Review, 3,* 57-65.

Miles, R. H. (1976). Role requirements as sources of organizational stress. *Journal of Applied Psychology, 61,* 172-179.

Miles, R. H., & Petty, N. M. (1975). Relationships between role clarity, need for clarity and job tension and satisfaction for supervisory and nonsupervisory roles. *Academy of Management Journal, 18,* 877-883.

Miller, E. J. (1976). The open-system approach to organizational analysis, with specific reference to the work of A. K. Rice. In G. Hofstede & M. S. Kassem (Eds.), *European contributions to organization theory* (pp. 43-61). Assen, Netherlands: Van Gorcum.

Miller, S. M., & Mishler, E. G. (1970). Social class, mental illness and American psychiatry: An expository review. In E. O. Laumann, P. M. Siegel, & R. W. Hodge (Eds.), *The logic of social hierarchies* (pp. 644-664). Chicago: Markham.

Miner, J. B. (1971). Changes in student attitudes towards bureaucratic role prescriptions during the 1960s. *Administrative Science Quarterly, 16*(3), 351-364.

Miner, J. B. (1973). The real crunch in managerial manpower. *Harvard Business Review, 51*(6), 146-158.

Morton, R. B. (1965). The organizational training laboratory—Some individual and organization effects. *Advanced Management Journal, 30,* 58-67.

Nisbet, R. A. (1970). *The sociological tradition.* London: Heinemann. (Original work published 1966)

Odiorne, G. S. (1971). *Personnel management by objectives.* Homewood, IL: R. D. Irwin.

OECD. (1975). *Work in a changing industrial society.* Paris: Organization for Economic Co-operation and Development.

Orwell, G. (1945). *Animal farm: A fairy story.* London: Secker & Warburg.

Pennings, J. M. (1970). Work value systems of white-collar workers. *Administrative Science Quarterly, 15,* 397-405.

Perrow, C. (1972). *Complex organizations: A critical essay.* Glenview, IL: Scott, Foresman.

Pfeiffer, J. W., & Jones, J. E. (1969). *A handbook of structured experiences for human relations training* (Vol. 1). Iowa City, IA: University Associates Press.

Quinn, R. P. (1973). What workers want: General descriptive statistics and demographic correlates. In R .P. Quinn & T. W. Mangione (Eds.), *The 1969-1970 survey of working conditions* (pp. 203-262). Ann Arbor, MI: Institute for Social Research.

Richardson, F.L.W., & Walker, C. R. (1948). *Human relations in an expanding company.* New Haven, CT: Labor and Management Center, Yale University.

Roberts, E. B. (1964). Industrial dynamics and the design of management control systems. In C. P. Bonini, R. K. Jaedicke, & H. M. Wagner (Eds.), *Management controls* (pp. 212-223). New York: McGraw-Hill.

Rousselet, J. (1974). *L'allergie au travail* (2nd rev. ed.). Paris: Éditions du Seuil.

Rubenowitz, S. (1968). Personnel management organization in some European societies. *Management International Review, 8,* 4-5.

Sadler, P. J., & Hofstede, G. (1976). Leadership styles: Preferences and perceptions of employees of an international company in different countries. *International Studies of Management and Organization, 6*(3), 87-113.

SAF. (1975). *Job reform in Sweden: Conclusions from 500 shop floor projects.* Stockholm: Swedish Employers' Confederation.

Sainsaulieu, R. (1974, October 6). L'effet de la formation sur l'entreprise. *Esprit,* pp. 407-428.

Saleh, S. D., & Singh, T. (1973). Work values of white-collar employees as a function of sociological background. *Journal of Applied Psychology, 58*(1), 131-133.

Sandkull, B. (1975). *The discontinuity of modern industry: A quest for an alternative principle of organizational control* (Research Report No. 31). Linköping, Sweden: Department of Management and Economics, Linköping University.

Schein, E. H. (1971). Organizational socialization and the profession of management. In D. A. Kolb, I. M. Rubin, & J. M. McIntyre (Eds.), *Organizational psychology* (pp. 1-15). Englewood Cliffs, NJ: Prentice-Hall.

Schuh, A. J., & Crivelli, M. A. (1973). Animadversion error in student evaluations of faculty teaching effectiveness. *Journal of Applied Psychology, 58*(2), 259-260.

Schutz, W. C., & Allen, V. L. (1966). The effects of a T-group laboratory on organizational behavior. *Journal of Applied Behavioral Science, 2,* 265-286.

Seeman, M. (1953). Role conflict and ambivalence in leadership. *American Sociological Review, 18,* 373-380.

Seeman, M. (1959). On the meaning of alienation. *American Sociological Review, 24,* 783-791.

Shepard, J. M. (1971). *Automation and alienation: A study of office and factory workers.* Cambridge, MA: MIT Press.

Shepard, J. M. (1973). Specialization, autonomy, and job satisfaction. *Industrial Relations, 12*(3), 274-281.

Sirota, D., & Greenwood, J. M. (1971). Understand your overseas work force. *Harvard Business Review, 49*(1), 53-60.

Stjernberg, T. (1977). *Organizational change and quality of life.* Stockholm, Sweden: Economic Research Institute, Stockholm School of Economics.

Sudreau, P. (Comité d'Étude). (1975). *La reforme de l'entreprise*. Paris: La Documentation Française.

Sutherland, J. W. (1975). System theoretical limits on the cybernetic paradigm. *Behavioral Science, 20,* 191-200.

Tannenbaum, A. S., Kavcic, B., Rosner, M., Vianello, M., & Wieser, G. (1974). *Hierarchy in organizations*. San Francisco: Jossey-Bass.

Thompson, K., & Tunstall, J. (Eds.). (1971). *Sociological perspectives: Selected readings*. London: Penguin Education.

Thorsrud, E. (1976). Democratization of work as a process of change toward nonbureaucratic types of organizations. In G. Hofstede & M. S. Kassem (Eds.), *European contributions to organization theory* (pp. 244-271). Assen, Netherlands: Van Gorcum.

Trites, D. K. (1960). Adaptability measures as predictors of performance ratings. *Journal of Applied Psychology, 44,* 349-353.

United Nations. (1963). *The universal declaration of human rights: A standard of achievement.* New York: United Nations.

Van Biemen, A. (1950). *De zedelijke waardering van de arbeid in het industrialisme*. Assen, Netherlands: Van Gorcum.

Van der Vegt, R. (1973). *Opleiden en evalueren*. Doctoral dissertation, University of Utrecht, Utrecht, Netherlands.

Vertin, P. G. (1954). *Bedrijfsgeneeskundige aspecten van het ulcus pepticum*. Doctoral dissertation, University of Groningen, Groningen, the Netherlands.

Vickers, G. (1973). *Making institutions work*. London: Associated Business Programmes.

Vilmar, F. (Ed.). (1973). *Menschenwürde im Betrieb: Modelle der Humanisierung und Demokratisierung der industriellen Arbeitswelt*. Reinbek bei Hamburg, Germany: Rowohlt.

Wherry, R. J., & Fryer, D. H. (1949). Buddy ratings: Popularity contest or leadership criteria. *Personnel Psychology, 2,* 147-169.

Whitsett, D. (1976). Obstacles to implementing structural changes in job design in MNCs. *Columbia Journal of World Business, 11*(3), 85-92.

Whyte, W. F. (1955). *Money and motivation: An analysis of incentives in industry*. New York: Harper & Bros.

Wiener, N. (1954). *The human use of human beings: Cybernetics and society* (2nd rev. ed.). New York: Doubleday Anchor.

Wildavsky, A. (1975). *Budgeting: A comparative analysis of the budgetary process*. Boston: Little, Brown.

Williams, S. B., & Leavitt, H. J. (1947). Group opinion as a predictor of military leadership. *Journal of Consulting Psychology, 11,* 283-291.

Wisner, A. (1974). Contenu des tâches et charge de travail. *Sociologie du Travail, 4,* 339-357. (English version in *International Studies of Management and Organization, 1975, 5,* 16-40)

Witte, E. (1973). *Organisation für Innovationsentscheidungen: Das Promotoren-Model*. Göttingen, Germany: Otto Schwartz.

*Work in America*. (1973). Report of a Special Task Force to the Secretary of Health, Education and Welfare. Cambridge, MA: MIT Press.

Yankelovich, D. (1981). *New rules: Searching for self-fulfillment in a world turned upside down.* New York: Random House.

Zaleznik, A., Ondrack, J., & Silver, A. (1970). Social class, occupation and mental illness. In A. McLean (Ed.), *Mental health and work organizations* (pp. 116-142). Chicago: Rand McNally.

Zand, D. E., Steele, F. I., & Zalkind, S. S. (1969). The impact of an organization development program on perceptions of interpersonal, group, and organization functioning. *Journal of Applied Behavioral Science, 5,* 393-410.

# Author Index

# Subject Index

NOTE: Page numbers in italics contain a definition of the concept.

# About the Author

Geert Hofstede is Emeritus Professor of Organizational Anthropology and International Management at the University of Limburg at Maastricht, the Netherlands, and Honorary Professor at the University of Hong Kong. He was the founding director of the Institute for Research on Intercultural Cooperation (IRIC) at the University of Limburg. He is a native of the Netherlands and holds a M.Sc. in mechanical engineering and a Ph.D. in social psychology from Dutch universities. His professional career includes experience as a worker, foreman, plant manager, chief psychologist on the international staff at IBM, and academic researcher. He has lived in Switzerland and Belgium; been a visiting scholar in Austria, Great Britain, France, Hawaii, and Hong Kong; and lectured in some 20 countries. His main books are *The Game of Budget Control* (1967), *Culture's Consequences* (1980), and *Cultures and Organizations: Software of the Mind* (1991). His articles have appeared in professional journals around the world.